The Spider a...

Adrienne Seed

www.hivine.com

www.adrienneseed.com

Copyright ©2009 Adrienne Seed

Adrienne Seed asserts the moral right to be identified as the author of this work.

ISBN 978-1-4452-2244 – 8

This book is dedicated to my mum, Doreen Seed.

Special thanks to my amazing family and friends, in particular my sister Julie and my son Ben, without whose unconditional love and support this book would not have been possible.

Thanks also to my favourite 'Eagle Eyes' - Sue Maxwell Smith and Willo Williams.

P.S. No thanks whatsoever to the Brian Mercer Charitable Trust.

Prologue

Brian's supercilious eyes, the palest of mocking blue, continue to stare at me, long after he's gone. And yet his eyes were not blue at all, they were a sludgy green colour, apart from on the night he died, when they resembled glassy, black marbles: cold, hard and impenetrable, the eyes of a stranger.

"I feel like death, I feel like death," he repeated over and over again, the look in his knowing black marble eyes informing me that he would soon be taking me with him. Or at least, that was the feeling I was left with, as his spirit winged over my shoulder, branding me as it passed with the icy cold finger of death.

His image remains on the wall to haunt me. For some quirk of his eccentric reasoning, Salvador Dali, the surrealist artist and self-confessed genius, painted a rare portrait of 'the crazy inventor' as he saw him, regally enthroned and wrapped in the traditional, surreal white sheet, with golden curls and pale, watery blue eyes. And yet Brian's hair was as black as coal, at least at the time when Dali painted him. Maybe by depicting Brian in this irreverent, sickly sweet manner, Dali was sardonically portraying Brian as he saw himself: angelic, holier than thou, God-like even.

'The Spider and the Fly', my portrait of Brian is very different from that of Dali's as it shows him as he really was and depicts his darker side, his power, his control; his control over me. The two paintings, both copies, are in front of me now and hang side by side on my wall. The original Dali Brian bequeathed to The Royal Society and hangs in a room with his name over the door. My portrait, 'The Spider and the Fly', remains in his house as part of his prestigious art collection, which cannot be removed (according to his last will and testament) for eighty years.

The two copies of the portraits are all I have left now to remind me of him, apart from the other legacy I have been bequeathed, which I will have to live with for the rest of my life.

CHAPTER 1

Snowflakes and Spiders

Once I've told you this story, things will never be the same, because that's what stories can do. Stories can change the way we think and feel about things and everyone's story is different, like fingerprints, like DNA, like snowflakes.

Like a spiralling snowflake, my mind circles back to a moment frozen in time, somewhere in the deep-freeze compartment of my memory. I am once again with Brian, under his roof, under his spell, under his control, as I always was and now, because of what has happened to me, still am.

Underneath the ancient eves of his spooky old house, there is not a sound to be heard. This mausoleum of broken marriages is home only to the surreal works of art and suspended silences - and to me sometimes, when he wants me, when he summons me.

It is so deathly quiet, sitting crouched on the long, white sofa, I can hear the sound of my own breathing. Even though the marble floor is heated from beneath, my feet are as cold as ice and I can feel my sighs warming the skin on my bare arms.

It is the middle of the night, but I am wide awake, sitting here in this long, glass sunroom, shivering in my flimsy Harrods nightdress and feeling exposed, even though there are no lights on and it's dark outside. I clutch a silk cushion to me for warmth, thinking to myself that I must remember to plump it up afterwards. Brian gets very upset if his cushions aren't plumped to perfection. Brian's cushions are not allowed to slouch, have dents, or stray out of their neat, orderly line. And neither am I!

The sky is heavy with cloud and it's snowing out there, even though the daffodils are already in bloom, clustering around the dark silhouettes of the tall trees that Brian planted as young saps many years ago; circling their now mighty trunks in rings of glorious profusion – a veritable host, just for us.

There must be a wind blowing out there because the snowflakes are swirling around in icy spirals and I feel as if I am sitting in one of those glass domes you can shake to make an artificial snowstorm. Not that Brian would allow anything as camp or as tacky as a snow dome in this show house; this museum of works of art and priceless treasures; and me, of course, his very own artist in residence.

I suddenly feel trapped, claustrophobic, closed in; covered over by his glass dome – like a china doll, a stuffed animal. I want to break out, shatter the panes of ice-encrusted glass; let the snowflakes swirl in and fill the room to settle gently on my hair forming a halo of frozen stars that will slowly melt, then drip from my eyelashes like icy tears. I want to run outside and dance in the snow. Twirl around and around within the hypnotic spirals of snowflakes with my arms outstretched like a whirling dervish, until my mind goes completely blank. Become an ice maiden with a frozen heart and jagged icicle curls, the folds of my nightdress carved in ice around my body like white marble, a glittering statue to stand alongside the others in his garden, the ones that watch over us by day and by night with their cold, dead eyes.

Brian is fast asleep, far away upstairs in the pitch-black bedroom with the heavy drapes shut tight and his eyes covered by a silk mask. He can't sleep if there is even the slightest chink of light and I can't sleep without one. Light versus dark, love versus hate, closed windows versus open. But apart from that, the two of us are happy enough in our chosen isolation. Sometimes, we are more than happy and then our fiery love can ignite sparks of pure joy that fill our snow dome and cascade around us, covering us both from head to toe with silver strands of ecstasy. But other times, Brian gets angry with me and shakes the glass dome hard, until I am totally obscured by the cold flakes of his disapproval - like tonight for example. For some reason, I caused a tumultuous snowstorm, an avalanche of anger, a blitz of his scathing disapproval, and I'm not really sure why.

Did the ex-wives ever feel trapped like this I wonder? I suppose they must have done. The three wives sat in this same sunroom, in this glass bubble. The three wives slept in our big bed in the pitch-black room and that's why I can't sleep. I feel like I'm being swallowed up, sinking into the hollow that the wives have made over the years. I can almost feel their presence. Like restless ghosts they lie next to me, tossing with discontent.

It's not the first time I've sat here in this long, glass room in this big old house, waiting for the dark night to end and Brian's dagger-like icicles of anger to dissipate and melt with the morning light. And yet here I am once again, encapsulated in his glass bubble, shivering and flapping my arms like a weak, white moth.

All I need now is a pin.

CHAPTER 2

Ba Ba Black Sheep

In some ways, although I'm ashamed to admit it, I've always resented the fact that I come from the north of England and until now, I've never really felt that I belonged here. Even as a child, I yearned to be something more exotic: Spanish or Greek perhaps, but you can't escape your roots, can you, although it wasn't for the want of trying on my part. I never thought I'd end up right back where I started, but here I am and thereby hangs the tale. I only hope I have enough time left to tell it.

I was born here in the north of England in a town called Blackburn, in a 'prefab' which was situated under a huge, grey square of water called Guide Reservoir. The neat line of white prefabs had been rapidly erected shortly after the Second World War when there had been a housing shortage and flimsily constructed out of sheets of deadly asbestos. In the freezing winters, 'Jack Frost' would swoop down with his icy fingers and etch his frenetic snowflake patterns on the inside of the windows. There was something quite terrifying to me as a child about living under that huge slab of water, and to this day I still shudder when I pass it. I used to imagine that when it rained, (and being the north of England it rained nearly every day), the reservoir would overflow and the tiny box-like houses would float away like paper boats.

My dad had been a navigator during the war on the old Lancaster bombers and when the war was over, he tried living on 'civvy street,' but times were hard so he rejoined the Royal Air Force and whisked us all off to live down south, far away from Blackburn. We still came back to visit the relations, but even as a young girl, I always dreaded coming back up north. There were no such things as motorways then, so those car journeys seemed to go on forever.

"Are we there yet dad?" my brother and I would nag, fighting in the back of the old black Austin, with the curved running boards and temperamental indicators that flicked out like angry, yellow tongues.

"Not yet," my dad would cough from out of the fug of his Senior Service cigarette smoke, "You'll know we're nearly there when the sheep start turning black."

And sure enough, as we crossed over the dark, bleak moors, we would see the timorous sheep, cowering like oily rags by the dry stonewalls, huddled in miserable groups under a low, gunmetal sky, their woolly coats black with soot.

Lancashire and Blackburn, as it was back then, depressed me and filled me with gloom. My young mind was like a magic lantern filled with brightly coloured dreams and pictures of people and places I'd only seen in photographs, mainly derived from the set of encyclopaedias my dad had bought on the 'never never' from a travelling salesman – 'The Hanging Gardens of Babylon,' 'The Seven Wonders of the World,' palm-fringed beaches in exotic locations. I didn't want any part of this dismal looking place called Blackburn, with its line after line of black terraced houses, clinging on to the steep, slimy cobbled streets. The domineering factories and mills with their tall chimneys, belching black smoke into the already polluted atmosphere; their overriding presence surrounded by forbidding iron gates to lock in the workers and high, sooty walls edged with broken glass to deter intruders. Then, all around the basin of what was then the working class town, were the endless, bleak moors, singed with patches of burnt looking heather and littered with dirty, black sheep.

Blackburn - a fitting name for it.

Blackburn was a cotton town in those days and my dad's mother and most of my aunties worked in the mills and had done all their lives. My dad's sister, my Auntie Dora, would sometimes take me with her to the mill.

"It's our Alan's lass," she would mouth over the deafening roar of the looms to the other weavers, bits of cotton flying through the air and sticking to my clothes and hair till I was covered in white floss like a dandelion clock.

I actually saw Brian on one of those visits to the mill, little knowing then, of course, that he was destined to play a major part in my life.

"That's the boss's son," my Auntie Dora told me reverently as he passed by. Brian must have already been in his early twenties then.

As if Blackburn wasn't depressing enough, there were all the tales of gloom and doom to contend with. As soon as we got through the door of my grandma's house, she would tell us who'd just died, and there was always some poor soul – "Mrs. Ramsbottom's popped her clogs or that nice Mr. Legbetter's passed away, it was his heart you know."

Death and ailments, hospitals and doctors were always the main topic of conversation in my grandma's house, in fact everywhere in the north as far as I could see, and still are to this day - especially for me now.

My grandma lived on a council estate in a one bedroomed bungalow, but as they say up here, it was like a little palace inside. A man with a horse and cart would pass by selling sarsaparilla in big, stone bottles and when they were empty my grandma would use them as hot water bottles to air the beds. I had to sleep next to her in her lumpy, eiderdowned double bed and I would peer out from under the covers to watch in fascination as she unhooked her salmon pink corsets and rolled her thick surgical stockings down her bony old legs. Her hair was always tightly permed (the tighter the perm the longer it would last) so the back of her head reminded me of a cauliflower, and she liked to experiment with hair dyes, so every time we came to visit, the 'cauliflower' was a different colour – or sometimes two.

When the other relations came round to visit, by way of escape I would gather all my grandma's ornaments on the drop leaf table and play my 'little games'. The ornaments weren't very interesting; plaster models of girls in crinoline dresses or chipped statues she'd won on the fair. But I was blessed with a lively imagination and could easily transport myself into a world of my own. When I tired of my 'little games', I would force my brother to stand in his cot and dress him up in my grandma's flowered aprons and netted hats, then drag the poor lad screaming by the hand to parade in front of the relatives. It's a wonder he didn't grow up with a complex, but perhaps he did. He doesn't really have much to do with me anymore, so I wouldn't know - and he'd probably have even less to do with me now if he knew what I had!

I much preferred going to visit my Irish granddad who was a painter and decorator by trade and had bunches of sable brushes and books of embossed wallpaper samples to draw on, with slivers of shimmering gold leaf pressed between pieces of fine tissue paper. I would sit on his knee and watch his faded blue eyes grow bright with tears as he sang me his sad Irish songs. I would poke my finger in the bullet hole in his arm. He'd been shot clean through his arm in the First World War and had been presented with the Military Medal for bravery in the field.

On one of my visits he'd set fire to the chimney trying to burn an old wooden clock. I remember staring at the round clock face, licked by the orange tongues of flame as the fire roared like an angry dragon, belching plumes of smoke back into the room. I still have a vision of my granddad, crouched down on his haunches trying to blow the flames back up the chimney, his white flat cap tilted on the back of his head and covered in bits of ash. When the fire finally died down, the metal hands of the clock were still there, bent and shrivelled and pointing to quarter to four. Perhaps that's why I don't like clocks, especially now. Time ticking away. Maybe my granddad also had a fear of time running out and that's why he burnt the clock.

I can't really think of any other reason, unless he'd run out of coal of course.

I have an old faded photograph of my granddad wearing his white flat cap in a little green box I call my 'Irish box,' which I'm very superstitious about. In it I keep my most special mementos, including the rosary he gave me when I was born, still wrapped in the original lace handkerchief. I take it to the clinic with me when I'm going for my latest results and I keep it at the side of my bed with the lid open, so he can watch over me whilst I sleep. Of all the family, I am most like him and I am convinced he is my guardian angel.

CHAPTER 3

The Man in the Mist

They say everyone has a guardian angel. Some have described theirs as an Indian spirit guide or an angelic presence ringed with light, but mine is a little Irish man called Walter Downs with brilliant blue eyes and wearing a white flat cap.

I believe in guardian angels and I also believe in fate. Fate must have been playing its part all those years ago when it deigned to send Brian my way in order to unleash my artistic spirit and reprieve me from the mundanity of my everyday life in Blackburn, or at least, that's how it seemed at the time. That fateful day in question was many years ago now and although I didn't know it then, that first sighting of Brian was to change the course of my life forever, in more ways than one.

I was only nineteen at the time, just about to turn twenty in fact, so I was in my prime where my youth and beauty were concerned, with my hopes and dreams still firmly intact and I was hell bent on becoming a famous artist. With that aim in mind, I'd been slaving away on a huge oil painting in my bedroom-come studio at my parent's pub, named colloquially as "The Clog and Billycock". But it was one of those typically gloomy North of England days and the lack of light had eventually forced me to abandon my efforts and down tools. Frustrated and full of painterly angst, I donned my wide brimmed purple felt hat, put on my long purple coat and went out for a walk. Lost in thought with no particular direction or destination in mind I wandered aimlessly through the fog, letting my boots take me where they wanted to go. Hoisting up my long purple coat, I clambered over the rustic style at the side of the road, then found myself slithering down the grassy hillside, skidding past the huddled groups of ghostly cows munching the soggy grass, the flop of their steaming lips the only sound in the cavernous silence that fog creates.

In my long, purple coat and felt hat, I too must have resembled some strange kind of apparition had anyone happened to chance on me. But apart from the ghostly cows, there wasn't another soul around to witness me and I was happy to let myself be swallowed up by the swirling mist, revelling in the mystery it was giving to my all too familiar surroundings.

I climbed over another style at the bottom of the hill and found myself quite by chance on the road where all the rich people lived and outside the gates to his house. Of course, I didn't know it was 'His' house then, but I had heard of him. Everyone had. Millionaires were few and far between in that small, industrial northern town.

Lost in a world of my own, the sound of my boots echoing along the foggy tunnel of the road which appeared to have no end, I gradually became aware of another sound. A curious, muffled, throbbing noise, resonating from somewhere in the distance, which was gradually getting louder. Disturbed from my reveries, I peered through the mist from under the brim of my purple hat to see what appeared to be an apparition slowly looming towards me, which, as it drew ever closer, revealed itself to be the long, low bonnet of a silver car. I stopped dead in my tracks to watch as the phantom like car lazily nosed the fog to one side and magically approached me as though it was floating on a bank of mist. Mesmerised, I stood as still as a statue at the side of the road as it purred slowly to a halt at my feet. Strangely enough, I didn't feel at all frightened, although these days I suppose I would have been. I just stood there waiting patiently, curious to see what would happen next. I waited for what seemed like an eternity; then the black glass of the electric window slithered down and disappeared inside the car door, revealing a face I was never to forget.

We both stared at each other long and hard. Long enough to glimpse the dark, untouched places in each other's souls and hard enough to engrain that memory in our separate hearts forever - and if that sounds a bit corny, I'm sorry but that's how it was! Then a long, white finger reached over and pressed a button causing the black tinted window to shoot back up, chopping off our tortured gaze like a guillotine. The phantom car and its mysterious driver slid away and disappeared back into the fog, leaving me to wonder if it had all been a dream. So silent it had been.

It would be over a year before fate would bring us together again.

CHAPTER 4

Sofa so Good

I drag myself out of bed and draw back the curtains. These days, I often have a real job just to motivate myself to get out of bed, although, I think part of that is down to the stultifying effects of the ant-retroviral medication. "Here we go," I thought gloomily, "Another day in paradise – I don't think!" It was bloody teeming down again.

"What the hell am I doing here?" I ask myself despondently. How had I ended up back in Blackburn, the very place I'd been trying to escape from all my life?

Well, the answer to that was quite simple. It had been thanks to Brian of course. In fact, when I came to think about it, everything, past future and present, had been and was still being down to him. But he wasn't here anymore - or was he? It sometimes felt like he was, but maybe that was just wishful thinking on my part. The absence of his physical presence was a constant aching void, yet I felt he was still out there somewhere, even though I knew it was impossible because I'd been with him when he died and I swear I'd felt his spirit flying over my shoulder. There were times though, when I had no doubt whatsoever that his ghostly presence was still hanging around and although I should have been glad that we still had some connection, be it only in spirit form, it felt more like he was spying on me rather than watching over me.

Why wouldn't he leave me alone?

Those first terrible months after Brian had died, I'd often sensed his presence and even caught a fleeting shadow of him lurking on my stairs, wearing the red devil mask with the curved gold horns he'd bought when we were in Barcelona and used to like to terrify me with. Well, he was terrifying me now that was for sure. If he was so intent on hanging around in spirit form, then why not present himself as the Brian I had loved for most of my life and not the powerful, schizophrenic Brian, others (myself included) had had good reason to fear. He was obviously out to control me, as they say, from beyond the grave. But I didn't want to be controlled by him anymore, or anyone for that matter and least of all a ghost.

It was always after midnight when he appeared and always in the same place. He never appeared during the day.

"What do you want now?" I'd ask him impatiently, before quickly scurrying into my bedroom. I'd started locking my bedroom door, as if that would keep him out. His tortured spirit could obviously not rest in peace. That's what they say, isn't it, about certain ghosts? But what were you supposed to do with the pesky things? Waft some rosemary in the air, wear a cross; light a candle to send them on their way.

On their way where?

The great beyond; whatever and wherever that may be?

Talking of the great beyond, I'd driven all the way to Liverpool to see this woman, a psychotherapist or something, who claimed in her brochure that she could help recently bereaved people like me who were suffering from the affects of grief.

The first thing she told me to do was to imagine Brian very big, towering over me like a huge shadow, which given the continued circumstances of his presence on my stairs was not hard to do, then shrink him in my mind and send him off to stand in the corner of the room.

"Like a naughty boy?" I asked her.

"If you like," she said.

"There he goes, he's over there in the corner," I tell her. I was enjoying this, affording me as it was an unaccustomed feeling of power over him for a change, "But he looks like a MacDougall's flour man with a round smiling face - a tiny Brian in a big bowler hat!"

"Excellent," she praised me. "I can see you're going to be very good at this."

"So what do I do about the blue then?" was my next question.

"The blue?" she repeated raising an intellectual eyebrow, which I noticed was in desperate need of plucking and about to join forces with her other one. My mum had always warned me to beware of people whose eyebrows met in the middle, a sure sign of the devil she said.

"The blue," I sighed, "I can't look at anything blue without thinking of him."

"Colour association," she scribbled on her pad, "Well, um, in that case you must get rid of everything blue," she ordered, as if that were obvious and the easiest thing in the world to do.

"How on earth do I do that?" I wanted to know, "How do I get rid of the blue sky, the blue sea; my own blue eyes staring back at me when I look in the mirror, lost and lonely and missing him still."

"You just have to move on," she told me briskly.

"Where to?" I demanded, thinking she meant move away and leave Blackburn. "I can't leave Blackburn now. Brian's family and the Executors of his Estate are not adhering to his wishes, especially in relation to me and I have to make sure they carry them out, both for his sake and mine. Anyway, I promised him, I promised him on his death bed," my voice choked with emotion.

"I meant move on mentally," she scowled, "But a change of habitat is always helpful in order to leave the past behind. However," she sniffed dryly, "if you can't move location, then make changes to your habitat, move your furniture around, change your room, buy some new curtains, but obviously not blue."

If only it were that simple. Anyway, who did she think she was, Carol bloody smiley Smillie? Linda buy this sofa Barker, Laurence Llewellyn bloody Bowen?

But nevertheless, I took her advice. Out went the green sofas Brian and I had bought together and off down to the salerooms. I bought some new ones, some blue ones. Bloody hell, why did I do that? What was the matter with me?

All right, I thought, I'll get the decorators in to paint the walls and then move everything around, like she said - disrupt the energy; a bit of feng shui might do the trick.

It didn't.

I know, I had another idea, I'll try painting the bedroom, but I'll do it myself this time, a nice restful pink and move the bed to the other side of the room, then maybe I can get some sleep.

There, that felt better already. But I go to bed that night and from over the cover of my new colour coordinated duvet, I cast my gaze approvingly around the room and then my eyes hit upon a tiny scrap of paper, lying in the middle of the floor.

"That won't do," I tut scoldingly, reluctantly getting out of bed. I bend down to throw it away then stop dead in my tracks. It was Brian's note to me, the one he'd written in his spidery handwriting, just before he died.

"I've always loved you Adrienne."

How the hell had it got there? It was in the study locked away with all my special papers. I'd nearly thrown it away.

He was still hanging around then.

Right, I asked the space at the top of the stairs where he usually stands, what do you want me to do? Carry on fighting your family and the Executors to insist that your wishes are carried out? That's what I'm doing isn't it? Don't stop painting, don't stop sculpting? OK, OK, but I'm getting weak. For some reason my legs had started to ache, especially when I tried to climb the stairs. Try as I might, they didn't want to work anymore. Push, push and up we go. And I kept losing my voice. Where was it going?

Then I got thrush in my mouth. I thought you only got that on your privates.

"Babies often get it in their mouths," the doctor informed me, "It's quite common, take this," he handed me a magic potion.

Swallowed it every few hours, as directed and away it went. Then back it came again.

"It's back again doctor."

"Try these antibiotics," he scribbled a prescription.

But my voice kept coming and going. I never knew if it was going to work or not. Must be something seriously wrong with me I thought, so back to the doctor for some tests and off goes the swab to the lab, but they find nothing untoward.

I was working on a plaster model entitled *'The Couple'*, trying to keep up the momentum and honour my promise to Brian that I would carry on sculpting, regardless of the fact that he was no longer with me to wield the artistic whip. Must be the plaster dust, I decide, getting on my chest. I know what to do, I'll wear a mask. I should really wear one anyway, health and safety and all that. But I keep pulling it off. It hangs under my chin, strung around my neck like a huge goitre. Then one day, I try to move the plaster off the modelling stand and it fell out of my hands and broke in two – just like that!

Bugger! Stuck it back together again with some Araldite, but it was chipped and jagged with parts missing. A bit like me!

What was missing?

Brian was.

Alright, enough is enough I thought. I know what I'll do; I'll go back to Ibiza for a while, get right away from him and his pesky ghost. See Ben, my son – I still felt guilty that I'd been too preoccupied with Brian over the last few years to notice what was going on with him. I could see that now, although I couldn't at the time. For me it had always been hard to see beyond Brian, he was that kind of man.

Anyway, I thought, or rather Brian had thought that Ben was old enough to manage without his 'over protective mother'. But in truth it was because he'd wanted me all to himself, without the added complication of a teenage son tagging along.

Decision made, I book a ticket, pack my suitcase and feel better immediately.

Ibiza. It felt great to be back and to see my only son who seemed to be in good form and I got time to spend time with all my old friends without Brian's jealousy to intervene - sun, sea, no stairs, no ghosts.

"What's happened to your lovely hair?" everyone kept asking me. "It's gone a bit thin hasn't it, why did you have it cut?"

"I didn't," I tell them. "It must be the menopause. It keeps falling out. I must be short of hormones or something."

I go to see a Spanish doctor - the bloody thrush is back, must think it's migration time. "Chew raw garlic," he prescribes, "And eat live yoghurt." "At the same time?" I ask horrified. "Drink this tea made from tree bark, it has ant-fungal properties," he advises. It tastes foul. "And buy a tongue scraper," he recommends as I scuttle out of the door.

Yuk!

The Spanish think garlic is the cure for everything, but it wasn't enough to cure what was ailing me and neither for that matter, was the live yoghurt, the foul tree bark nor the bloody tongue scraper. My voice continued to keep coming and going, but I put it down to the weather. It was winter after all and unaccustomedly cold for Ibiza.

I was starting to act a bit odd, even for me. People begin to notice; then for some reason I decide I have to buy some new sofas for the flat.

"Why?" my friend Anne asks me, "What's wrong with the ones you've got?"

"Wrong colour," I tell her, "They have to be yellow."

I drive miles in the dark on my own to a huge warehouse, somewhere near the airport, stacked full of sofas covered in sheets of heavy plastic. I search and search until I find them. Not really the yellow I had in mind, more of a custard colour really, but I have to have them regardless. Two for the price of one – great! Will they fit in the flat?

Don't care.

They arrive the next day on the back of a lorry. Not enough room for them of course, so I change the rest of the furniture this way and that, but I'm feeling weak, no one there to help me. Ben has gone out. He doesn't like change.

I start to sweat with the effort, use my knees to push things around the room, which instantly brings back painful memories of the time Brian and I had been staying in that hotel in the Lake District, the one we'd escaped to when we'd found out he only had a few months left to live. He'd suffered a bad reaction to the radio iodine they'd pumped into him for the tests and had been burning up with fever. He'd wanted the bed to be nearer the window, so I'd pushed it with him lying on it across the room with my knees. Then I suddenly remembered; Brian had suffered from constant Thrush. Funny, I'd never thought of that before.

I finally manage to squeeze the new sofas in. They are a horrible colour, hideous in fact and I hate them, so I cover them with white cotton bed sheets. There, that's better. I light the fire with some rolled up newspaper, then run a hot bath. I soak there till the water starts to turn cold, then I go to bed. I start shivering sometime in the night, teeth chattering away by themselves, talking to myself, calling out for my mum, my dad, Brian.

In the morning Ben comes in to my bedroom, demands some money, then goes out. I hear the telephone ringing in the living room, but I'm too weak to get up and answer it. Ben comes back at some point and disappears inside his room. I hear the doorbell ring again and again over the repetitive thumps and beats of his Techno music. I know he won't answer the door or let anyone in. But I'm too ill to care.

I toss and turn all that night, burning with fever, throwing up into a plastic bowl, my head hurting like hell as though someone was hitting it repeatedly with a hammer.

My friend Anne finally manages to force her way through the door, past Ben, to find me curled up in a shivering heap, talking rubbish.

"That paranoid son of yours wouldn't let me in," she told me crossly, "I've been ringing and ringing. I knew something was wrong. Let me get you a clean nightie and here, I've made you some chicken soup."

"Get your bony hands off me," I push her away.

"Right, I'm calling for the doctor," she sniffs bossily.

"I'm not going to any bloody Spanish hospital," I swear from inside the plastic bowl.

"You'll do as you're told," she marches to the phone.

An ambulance arrives with a wail of sirens and whisks me off to the noisy Spanish hospital, where I am subjected to countless indignities then they attempt to put me in one of those long tube-like machines to be x-rayed.

"I've got claustrophobia," I try to tell them as they strap me in. "I can't go in tunnels."

"Put these headphones on," a bossy Spanish nurse plonks them over my head.

It sounded like Ben's horrible Techno music thumping in my ears.

I eventually come out the other end of the tube, then I'm whizzed in a wheelchair through a maze of endless brightly lit corridors then left on a high bed in a room all by myself. Someone in a scruffy white coat eventually comes along and wires me up to a cow udder drip dangling from a pole, then shoves a mask over my face.

"What's up with me?" I mumble through the mask in Spanish, but he obviously didn't understand my muffled attempt at the lingo and with a bad tempered grunt and an uncomprehending shrug of the shoulders, he disappears.

Pneumonia, the doctor declares the next morning on his rounds. Funny kind of pneumonia, I think. Different from the kind I had before. I could still breathe, even fancied a cigarette.

More X-rays, blood tests every two minutes, my arms were black and blue. Spanish nurses are not known for their delicacy. Then to my horror I was wheeled off down to theatre where a tube was thrust up my nose and down my throat with some kind of camera attached to it, to see what was going on down there. Nothing it turned out, at least nothing that shouldn't be going on. The specialist couldn't understand it.

After a few days, I start to feel a bit better, but I'm lonely in the room on my own forced to talk to myself, the cleaners, the walls - and my mum of course, every day on the phone.

"Come home," she nags.

"As soon as the doctors will let me," I sniff pitifully.

It was nearly Christmas. Ben didn't come to visit me. He doesn't like hospitals. Most of the other patients had been allowed to go home. Their rooms were empty. I pace the deserted corridors in my dressing gown and ride up and down in the lift to pass the time. I make endless trips to the vending machine. I go to see the Christmas tree and the Nativity in reception six times a day. The surly receptionist is sick of the sight of me. I am sick of the sight of her.

The doctor finally tells me I can go back to England and I am wheeled to the plane in a wheelchair, clutching my laptop on my knees. I can't even lift it to put it in the overhead lockers.

Back in Blackburn my mum nurses me back to health and once I've recovered, we decide to go back to Ibiza. It's spring by this time and all the wild flowers are out. Poppies everywhere; wild orchids, butterflies fluttering around; it was beautiful and everything was going just fine, then would you believe it, the bloody thrush comes back. Off I go again to see another homeopathic doctor, this time in Ibiza town, and my friend Anne comes with me. The doctor chats about this and that and then questions me about my sex life, which to me seemed totally irrelevant. I tell him about Brian dying from sudden liver cancer and he shakes his head in sympathy, but doesn't examine me. Bit strange I think. I try to show him the rash that has appeared all over my body and the strange bullet hole-like spots, exactly the same as Brian's, which itch like hell, but he doesn't seem particularly interested.

"Would you like to have some tests?" he asks brightly.

"Of course," I agree, anything, although I'd already had every test known to man, or at least I'd thought I had, in the hospital. He sends me off for a blood test with a long list of things to test me for. A lot of the things I don't recognize because they are written in Spanish, but some I do, and HIV is one of them. But of course I didn't need to worry about that, did I? After all, I'd just come out of hospital. Surely they would have tested me for HIV wouldn't they?

He makes another appointment for me in three weeks time, but several days later I get a message on my answer machine from his secretary to come to his office urgently. And that's when I found out.

I then had to go back and tell my mum. She was sitting waiting for me at the café on the seafront we always used to frequent. It was a beautiful day I recall and the beach was already filling up with tourists laying their brightly coloured towels on the sand and putting up striped umbrellas. Children were excitedly splashing in the turquoise waves and the air was filled with the scents and the sounds of a bright summer morning. There was a whiff of suntan oil mixed with the gentle, salty breeze and the delicate fragrance emitting from the colour clash of flowers lining the café walls: fluorescent pink, buttercup yellow, blood red petals, turning their vivid heads to the ever warming sun. Every detail of that morning remains etched in my memory and is crystal clear to me as though I was taking part in some kind of Technicolor dream. The early morning bustle of the café echoing around me, the waiters in immaculate white cotton shirts wielding silver trays of orange juice and newly baked croissants, the tantalising aroma of freshly ground coffee.

But it felt all wrong, the sun being out, the happy faces, the bright colours. This wasn't the right scenario to break such shocking news to my poor old mum. I sat down on the wicker chair opposite her and looked at her across the pink tablecloth – how the hell was I going to do this? My mum's eyes were as turquoise as the sparkling sea, the kind of eyes that could see straight through you, so it was pointless trying to hide anything from her. Not that I wanted to. Now was the time when I needed her more than ever and I knew that she would stand by me, whatever it was I was about to tell her, because that's what mothers did – well, at least that's what my mother did and I could stake my life on it. My life? Did I still have one, and if I did, it would be very different from now on - and so would hers after I'd told her.

The waiter came up to our table beaming, pleased as ever to see me and I ordered my usual café con leche in a glass. After he'd gone I looked straight in my mum's piercing blue eyes and told her.

"Mum, I'm HIV positive," I said it out loud for the first time.

I will always remember the look of horror on her face, which she quickly tried to disguise.

"Don't worry love," she reached over the table and squeezed my shaking hand, "At least it's not cancer. We can cope with this."

We get on the first plane back to England.

CHAPTER 5

The Clog and Billycock

I was eighteen when my dad decided to leave the air force and drag us back up north to run a public house. The first pub we had was called 'The Brunswick Hotel' and it was on a cobbled street, next to a canal in the heart of a working class district called Audley Range, which doesn't exist anymore. Well it does, but it's all mosques and Indian restaurants now. I remember my poor old dad had driven us round and round the block before finally daring to tell us that the graffiti covered building, with its dingy peeling walls and faded red sign declaring 'The Brunswick Hotel' hanging over the door was about to become our new home.

My dad who'd been in the RAF for most of his working days was more used to frequenting the likes of the NAAFI or the Sergeant's Mess and as for my mother, she had never been in a pub in her life, let alone run one. As far as pubs go, the Brunswick was very basic to say the least. There was a flag stoned vault that only the flat-capped, domino playing men were allowed to frequent; a ladies room where the downtrodden wives wearing knotted headscarves over their curling pins or tightly permed hair, would sit and gossip while supping their glasses of stout or halves of mild. A long piano room with round formica-covered tables, each circled by a ring of wooden stools with a faded plush bench running the length of the walls, and an ancient upright piano, with worn nicotine yellow ivory keys. In pride of place over the tiled fireplace hung the dartboard, where the men and sometimes the women played their highly competitive games of "arrows". There was also a tiny room called the snug, which was seldom used apart from the odd occasion when the local factory owner deigned to honour us with his presence, accompanied perhaps by a fellow business associate to down a few malt whiskies and puff on fat cigars.

All in all, it was a very different way of life to the one we'd been accustomed to and one which my brother and I found very hard to adjust to. As did my mum who had to quickly learn the landlady's esteemed art of pulling the perfect pint, along with my poor old dad who had to rapidly master the complicated act of changing a barrel when the beer ran out. The customers were an impatient lot who took exception to having to wait for their pints and would mutter comments like, "They think tut beer comes from out oft th' air or from't bloody sea."

It was all a bit of a culture shock really, especially for me as I was not accustomed to having to work for a living. But suddenly there was no choice and I was immediately set to work as a waitress, my tin tray advertising 'Thwaites finest Ales', laden (pumps permitting) with pints of their best bitter and mild. We tended to call the customers by what they drank. For instance there was *'Bad tempered pint of bitter'*, *'Old Dan'*, *'Green top' 'Big Ben'* and *'Pint of mixed in a straight glass.'*

These were typical working class northern males accustomed to being waited on hand and foot by their subservient wives and mothers and after a hard working day, a customary ten or twelve pints of Thwaites best bitter or mild was their reward. Always reluctant to interrupt their game of 'arrows' with a trip to the bar to get the next round in they would delight in constantly ringing the bell to summon me to 'wait on' them. After taking their orders, I would stagger back down the corridor to the piano room, weighted down by my tin tray, where *'Bad tempered pint of bitter'* would invariably wait until I got all the way back to the bar before pressing the bell to summon me back again. "Oh," he would smirk, his unlit pipe clenched between his teeth, "I forgot luv - and a box of Swan Vestas."

On Friday nights someone would come in to play the piano and the place would be packed. If I got the chance, in between running up and down with my tin tray, I would sit with them and join in with the sing-a-longs. That's how I got to know the words to so many old songs. We would sing to the discordant strains of the out of tune piano, sitting shoulder to shoulder on the tatty red velvet bench seats, the round tables covered in dirty glasses and empty beer bottles.

This was in the days before karaoke machines of course with only the accompaniment of an out of tune piano and not even the luxury of a microphone, which in the case of some of the more inebriated or vocally challenged soloists was probably a blessing. But this did nothing to deter the Friday night revellers from putting their hearts and souls into it and they all had their own particular party pieces. One old man called Ernie always sang the same sad tearjerker to Maude his wife of over forty years, about his lovely rose losing her crimson gown.

There were moving moments such as these and rousing nights where tales were told and jokes were cracked, which helped somewhat to alleviate the extreme culture shock of my new and unwanted, it has to be said, northern lifestyle.

I enrolled at Blackburn Art College and on cold, dark winter mornings I would carefully make my way down Cicely Street, slipping on the black ice with my huge art folder tucked under my arm, past the old mills and Tommy Ball's famous shoe factory where the shoes were tied together with pieces of string. From the greenhouse studio at the top of the old college building, we would draw the rooftops of the lines of terraced houses, black and shiny with rain, or cut out designs on bits of lino and make prints on the ancient machines and old printing presses.

Our living quarters in the pub were situated upstairs and I made myself a makeshift studio in one of the disused rooms called the 'concert room' which had bare floorboards and a row of long, dusty windows looking out at the factory across the road and over the slimy green canal. Whenever I could I would hide myself away up there and paint or write poetry in an attempt to elevate myself from the dreariness of my dingy surroundings. At the weekends, to escape from all this doom and gloom, I would go off on my own for long walks in the countryside, which in comparison to the area in which we lived was surprisingly beautiful. I would take Honey with me, our Labrador cross, who was equally grateful for the chance to escape the confines of the pub and it was on one of our excursions that I found what was to be our next home; 'The Clog and Billycock'.

By chance, it was up for new tenancy and I persuaded my dad to take it on. It was a completely different kettle of fish to the scruffy old Brunswick with an allegedly 'better' class of clientele, and in no time at all, we'd turned the place around, doubled the takings and made it into one of the most popular and busiest pubs in Blackburn. The 'Clog and Billycock' was the starting point for many a budding teenage romance and still holds to this day a special place in some people's hearts, mine included, as it turned out to be the setting for my own particular love story and where it all really began, but of course I wasn't to know that at the time.

In our reign the 'Clog and Billycock' was very busy, especially on Friday nights. In fact, it had been busy every night since we'd taken it on. I had to help out most nights, partly because we were so busy and also to finance my way through my foundation course at art school. I stood there pulling pint after frothy pint for the rows of impatient northern men who stood six deep at the bar, waving their empty glasses at me. I don't know what the customers made of me really. I know that some of them thought I was aloof because I was an artist and for that reason considered myself to be on a higher plane. But it wasn't like that at all. I just had nothing in common with them and anyway, I had great plans to escape. I had no intention of staying behind a bar for the rest of my life, pulling pints. I was full of youthful dreams of going to London and becoming a great artist.

The 'Clog and Billycock' was a quaint little pub, nestling at the foot of Billinge woods where in late spring and early summer, the bluebells grew thick and juicy stalked. Behind the pub and beyond, lay the "Yellow Hills" so named because in a certain light, they emitted a curious golden glow. Not often I might add, because most of the time it was raining, that grey, dismal rain you only find in the north of

England. A path led up behind the pub and over the hills, to what felt to me like the top of the world, and there I would sit for hours, back to back with Honey, staring out over the tall chimneys of the now redundant cotton mills, and along the sludgy green lines of the canals far below. On a clear day, I could count the tiny crosses that marked the graves of Pleasington cemetery and watch the smoke rising up from the crematorium. In the far distance, Darwen Tower stood Victorian, austere and alone on the bleak moors. There was an old saying in the pub that if you could see Darwen Tower it was going to rain. If you couldn't, it was already raining!

Sometimes I would linger up on 'Yellow Hills' until dusk fell and walking back I would see the lights of the pub below twinkling a merry welcome. My mum was obsessed with twinkly lights. She had them everywhere, and much to my dad's dismay, she loved fairy lights best of all.

"Bloody hell," he'd often be heard to curse from the top of a ladder, yards of green plastic wire and coloured glass bells entwined around his neck. "Most people only have to suffer this once a year at Christmas."

But for all my dad's moaning and groaning, the lights made the pub look cosy and welcoming: too cosy, in fact and almost too welcoming, because more often than not, the customers refused to go home.

We did a lot of after hours drinking in those days. On Saturday and Sunday afternoons, my dad would lock the doors and we would carry straight on through to the evening session. Most of the customers were down to earth, self-made men, who worked hard all week and liked to let go at the weekends. In those days there was no Breathalyser so they knocked back pint after pint with reckless abandon, sang their hearts out, chatted up my glamorous mother and listened to the long-winded stories of my dad, who was a natural raconteur. They slowly grew to accept me, even though they thought I was a bit peculiar and not your 'typical' barmaid. But I was used to being considered strange. Even my own family thought I was odd. My mum had been known to hide my paintings behind the settee saying they were too 'way out' for the likes of her and my dad was just as bad. "Why can't you paint something normal?" he'd complain, "Nobody is going to buy those weird bloody things you do."

I think my surreal artistic renderings caused me to be a bit of an embarrassment to them both, although eventually my mum came to be my greatest fan. However, it took time.

I had a boyfriend, although he wasn't really my type and it was more to please my mum and dad really, and to stop the other young men chatting me up. He was called Carysforth and I met him on one of the afternoon drinking sessions. He came swaggering in with John Duggan 'The Coin Man.'

"He's driving a bloody great Bentley," my dad quickly pointed out, giving me a hefty nudge. He always noticed people's cars and watches and, like any dad I suppose, lived in hope of marrying me off to a rich man. That way I would maybe give up 'this silly art business' once and for all and become a respectable married lady. A rich one preferably!

"Same again old chap?" he asked Carysforth, "It's on me."

So when Carysforth finally plucked up courage to ask me out for dinner, after several large gin and tonics, compliments of the Landlord, I said yes - mainly to please my dad, but also because I'd never been taken out to dinner before. I sat next to him in the Bentley feeling vaguely ridiculous, hoping that I wouldn't be spotted by any of my art school cronies which would have totally ruined my 'street cred.' From then on, we slipped into a relationship of habit, which held no surprises but was easy and uncomplicated. Twice a week, on Tuesdays and Thursdays, he would take me out for a pub-crawl in the Bentley and on Saturday afternoons, I would serve drinks in the bar and watch him get drunk with his mates.

I'd managed to persuade my dad, against his better judgement naturally, to let me and my fellow art students stage an exhibition in the pub. He wasn't a bit happy about seeing his walls, which were usually adorned with hunting scenes or big bellied monks sitting around tables clutching tankards, suddenly draped with huge canvases of starving Biafrans, a topical subject at the time. Not to mention his daughter's surreal and often erotic fantasies. But the ring of the cash register as the word got round and the art-loving throngs flocked in, cheered him up no end. Some of the locals however, who were creatures of habit and despised change in any shape or form, took exception. "Bloody hell Landlord, I thought you were running a pub, not tut'Tate bloody gallery. I've got no time for this modern art malarkey but I know what I like." etc.

Carysforth was equally unimpressed, especially with my artwork. He was an antique dealer and dealt in old masters, or young mistresses, as he liked to joke. His lack of appreciation of my artistic talent did nothing to endear him to me and we had our first serious argument. My dad of course, immediately joined forces with him, saying it was about time I stopped messing around with art and found myself a decent job. The post office was mentioned.

I immediately retreated into my artistic shell in high dudgeon and ignored them both. Little did I know that day, that fate was about to step in and rescue me.

It was Saturday afternoon and all the hardened drinkers were out in full force and propping up the bar, including the butcher and the 'Egg Bird' who were having an illicit affair and always came in after their rounds to canoodle in the corner. John Duggan 'The Coin Man,' had already bought his usual dozen eggs from the 'Egg Bird' and a scraggy looking chicken from the butcher, to take home to appease 'the wife.' That's if he ever made it back home in time for dinner, as he was usually the last to leave!

As the afternoon wore on and the punters became more inebriated and out of control, the poor chicken found itself being tossed around the pub in some sort of bizarre rugby match, until the self-appointed referee declared "Half Time" and "Get 'em in Landlord. Same again all round."

Glasses replenished, they then started on the eggs, setting out to prove who could and who couldn't eat an egg in its shell. Finally, tiring of that, they resorted to simply hurling the remaining eggs around the room at random. Eggs finished, they moved on to the ever-popular Jacob's Cream Cracker Challenge - i.e. how many dry crackers it was possible to stuff in the human mouth without taking a drink. This, more often than not, involved money changing hands, so it was a very serious business. A respectful hush fell over the bar as I passed a brand new packet of Jacob's Cream Crackers to Jack, the up to now, undisputed champion. He slowly stuffed them in his mouth one by one, until cheeks puffed out like a hamster and on the verge of retaining his title, someone patted him on the back in premature congratulation. A veritable snowstorm of cream cracker flakes gusted out of his mouth and slowly settled on the top of everyone's pints. At that precise moment, the front door opened and everyone froze.

"I thought you'd locked the door," Jack spat at my dad, brushing cracker flakes off his moustache.

"So did I," my dad replied, then turning to the intruders, "Can I help you gentlemen?" Three very tall, distinguished men in dark suits and long black overcoats stood in the vestibule. I recognised one of them immediately. It was the man in the mist. I could never forget that face.

"You know who that IS?" my dad whispered excitedly in my ear "It's himself. Brian Mercer. He owns half of bloody Blackburn. What can I do you gentlemen for?" he asked them, rubbing his hands together in glee. But the man in the mist totally ignored him. He was staring fixedly at one of my paintings, his dark eyes boring holes through the thin canvas of one of my erotic dreams. All eyes upon him, he slowly strolled around the room, the punters reverentially standing aside and making way for him as he briefly studied the rest of the paintings. Then he came back and stood directly in front of mine. The room had gone deathly quiet by this time. A stray cracker flake slowly spiralled down and landed on his black overcoat. He flicked it off impatiently with his long fingers.

"Landlord," he boomed in a deep sonorous tone, "I would like to enquire the name of the artist responsible for this particular canvas?"

One of his companions handed him a large glass of whisky on the rocks and I noticed that his hands were shaking as he took a drink.

"Oh, that's just one of my daughter's," my dad apologised, gesturing towards me, "But there are some better ones in the other room if you'd care to take a look."

My dad could be very disloyal at times.

The man in the mist gave my dad a disgusted scowl and making no further comment, led his henchmen off into what we called the 'Juke Box' room and sat down at one of the red Formica tables, the other two sitting protectively each side of him like pair of bookends.

Conversation resumed at the bar but the party games were definitely over for that day. Reluctantly, John Duggan went home to face 'the wife' with no eggs and the decidedly worse for wear chicken tucked limply under his arm. The butcher and the 'Egg bird' had their last, lingering embrace then slunk back to their respective spouses. Carysforth had passed out and was draped over the bar, a fake daisy from one of my mum's flower arrangements nodding sadly behind his ear.

And I was summoned to the Juke Box room for a conference with "Himself."

I sat on the stool opposite him as directed and we all stared at each other in silence. They reminded me of the Three Wise Monkeys 'Hear no evil' 'Speak no evil' and 'See no evil.'

"This is my lawyer, Ted Hodgkinson," the man in the mist stood up and introduced one of his henchmen, an enormous fat man, with a bulbous nose, huge belly and lecherous, watery eyes, "And this is Tony Wilsonholme, my closest friend."

A distinguished looking man with shiny, silver hair, softly curling over his collar, and bright blue eyes offered me his hand. For once, I found myself longing to be back behind the safety of the bar serving pints.

The man in the mist cleared his throat then looked at me intently. "Can I ask you something?" He waited, his eyes burning through me. I nodded.

"What do you need to REALLY paint?"

Really paint? What did he mean? I was a bit offended to tell the truth. Was he inferring that I wasn't 'really' painting now?

"Well, lots of things," I stuttered, "But I suppose money mainly." It just slipped out before I could help myself. But it was true wasn't it? All artists needed money, didn't they?

He stared at me for what seemed like forever then intoned in his deep, sombre baritone, "Would you, in that case young lady, permit me to speak to your father?" Why on earth did he need to speak to my father I wondered. Was he intending to ask for my hand? Wouldn't my dad just love that!

"I believe you have great artistic talent," he proclaimed pompously, "And as you may or may not be aware, (I wasn't) I have successfully sponsored artists in the past. I would therefore like to fund your art materials and expenses for one whole year."

My eyes nearly dropped out of my head and my mouth fell open in surprise.

"If that is amenable to you of course?" he continued.

Amenable? Was he joking? It was a bloody miracle. I smiled. He didn't.

"No strings attached" he looked at me meaningfully, "I only want you to paint." I was subsequently dismissed and after a brief word with my father, the Three Wise Monkeys left.

My dad, it has to be said, was beside him self with joy. A rich and respected art collector expressing an interest in his daughter's art and what's more, offering to subsidise her? Suddenly, art didn't seem such a 'daft bloody business' after all, and when my new patron arrived the next night and solemnly presented me with the cheque, I could hardly believe my eyes. It seemed like a fortune. After thanking him profusely and promising him faithfully that I wouldn't let him down, I went straight to the art shop where I bought two of everything, including easels, and while I was at it, a new dress from the boutique next door, because I was only human after all, dedicated artist or not.

I found that thanks to my wealthy new patron, I suddenly rocketed up in everyone's estimation, especially Carysforth's who took to 'popping' in to see me every night, instead of only Tuesdays and Thursdays on the off chance that Brian would be there and he could try to sell him some of his more expensive antiques. He'd stroll nonchalantly into the bar with the odd Rodin bust tucked under his arm, or let it be known that he just happened to have a rather nice Ming vase in the boot of the Bentley. But Brian, if he deigned to come in at all that is, made it clear that he was interested in one thing and one thing only. Although he'd said there would be no strings attached, it soon became obvious to everyone, everyone but me that is, that the chase was on. He was the 'Spider' and I was the 'Fly' and nothing would stop him until he had got me well and truly ensnared in his web.

I started to paint like a madwoman. My bedroom-come studio was filled with canvases and the stench of turpentine invaded my very being. I felt driven to paint something wonderful to impress my new benefactor and justify the faith (not to mention the cash) that he'd invested in me. True to his word, at the beginning he left me alone most of the time. He knew that all he had to do was wait and in the meantime, unbeknown to me, he was weaving his web tighter and tighter around me. But he could afford to take his time, couldn't he? After all, didn't he always get what he wanted? Why should I be the exception?

Christmas came and went without a visit from him and I started to get a bit worried. Apart from the fact that by this time the funds were getting a bit low, I also realised to my consternation that I was actually missing him.

It was New Year's Eve and Carysforth and I were having a terrible row in the bar. Brian had finally shown his face but had left suddenly without saying goodbye. After he'd gone, Carysforth (who was slightly tiddled) started having a go at me for upsetting him.

"I can't help speaking my mind, can I?" I defended myself, "Anyway, who gives a damn about him," I swore, losing patience, "I'm going upstairs to get on with my work."

At twelve o'clock I could hear everyone downstairs in the pub bringing in the New Year. I was glad I was safely upstairs and not in danger of having to kiss any of the customers under the mistletoe. My feelings of security were short lived however, because suddenly my studio door was flung open and there stood Brian in his long, black overcoat, looking like the Grim Reaper.

"Happy New Year," he droned in his voice of doom, not sounding happy at all. He moved a sheaf of drawings off the bed and slumped down wearily.

"I can't stand other people" he sighed deeply, "Can you?"

He stared at the painting on the easel for a long time, without making any comment then beckoned me with his long white hand to sit on the bed beside him. We sat there in silence, side by side, listening to the sounds of revelry rising up from the bar.

Two big tears slowly rolled down his face and plopped onto the drawing he was holding in his shaky hand.

"How are you?" he asked miserably, "I mean how are you really? Are you happy?"

I was considering how to answer this complicated question and at the same time trying to resist the urge to mop his tearstains off my drawing, when taking me completely by surprise, he suddenly leant over and sank his teeth in my bare arm.

I sat there stunned, immune to the pain as though he was injecting me with some kind of drug. Then without saying a word, he stood up and walked out of the door. After he'd gone, I looked in trepidation at the neat ring of teeth marks on my bare flesh and feared for my New Year.

If not the rest of my life!

CHAPTER 6

Supermarket Sweep

Years later, I now find myself with a very real and totally unexpected reason to fear for my life and wonder if the two things were somehow connected. Who knows, it could be I'd had a kind of premonition. I shudder at the memory as though someone had just walked over my grave - and maybe they had.

With the news of my positive diagnosis still ringing in my ears causing shock waves to my system, although somehow or other, but God only knows how, I was still managing to function, my mum and I pack our bags and get ready to leave for the airport to catch our flight. Ben is still in bed, he has no idea why we have to cut our holiday short and for the time being I want it to stay that way. The taxi speeds off heading towards Ibiza airport. I am wondering at this point whether I will ever return to the island or even see my son again. Who knew what horrors lay ahead or how I would cope. All I knew was I wanted to get back to England as soon a possible, be on home territory, speak to an English doctor, get a second opinion. Maybe they'd made a mistake. It can happen.

We'd been very lucky to get tickets as it was the height of the holiday season and last minute seats were hard to come by. My mum and I sit side by side on the packed charter flight crammed with jolly tourists who were literally glowing with sunburn and post holiday exuberance; their boisterous offspring running up and down the aisles making countless trips to the toilets and being generally annoying. Precocious little girls with peeling pink noses, their beaded sun streaked hair woven into thousands of tiny plaits. Whole families wearing tee shirts emblazoned with Ibiza in fluorescent colours to remind them of their happy holiday on that magical isle.

Maybe, I think sardonically to myself, I should be wearing a tee shirt with my new status emblazoned in fluorescent letters in order to warn people I am now a 'danger' to society. I already feel as if I have the mark of Cain tattooed on my forehead and people can somehow tell I am HIV positive, even though I know that is impossible - at least for the moment. Who knew what future damage the disease would inflict on my body and they say you can always spot a person with AIDS. But I haven't got AIDS I quickly remind myself, I have only been diagnosed with HIV (only?) but that doesn't make me feel any less conspicuous. I still feel as though everyone knows. Once again the whole scenario feels wrong; I shouldn't be sitting here in the midst of normal happy, smiling people and their obvious vitality and well being is really getting on my nerves and making me feel resentful. Why has this terrible thing happened to me?

We fumble with our in-flight meals; the plastic packages, knives, forks, spoons, miniscule blocks of rubbery cheese and those stupid tubs of milk that are impossible to open. I glance at my mum as I help her to open hers. She is terrified of flying, always has been and because she suffers from claustrophobia hates being trapped on a plane. But this time, I know by her set profile that on this particular occasion, fears for her daughter are her main concern. We endure the two and a quarter hour flight in relative silence, both in a complete daze, the uncertain future stretching before us.

When we finally descend through the grey clouds and land at Manchester airport we get a taxi back to Blackburn and go directly to the familiar welcome of my mum's cosy terraced cottage. I don't want to stay in my own house, even though it's only a few doors down from hers. I don't want to be on my own, not that I will ever be on my own again thanks to this unwanted usurper that has invaded my being. There will be me and 'it' forevermore and I will just have to get used to sharing my body with a deadly virus; living alongside a prospective murderer, something that wants to see me off at the first available opportunity, and will do, if it's given half a chance.

My poor mum is trying her level best to keep my spirits up and doing everything she can to take my mind off the horrors that inevitably lay ahead. But it's hard for her, because as she says, she's not as young as she was. Aside from that, she has to somehow try to keep her own spirits up as well as mine. She insists on giving up her bedroom for me and sleeping in the tiny spare room so that I can sleep in her big double bed. At least I try to sleep, but it's impossible. Three, four, five o'clock in the morning and sleep for me has suddenly become a thing of the past. I lie there tossing and turning, kicking the covers off, which feel like a ton weight and look in despair at my thin, bony legs. It's strange, I hadn't really noticed how emaciated I'd become. All of a sudden I feel very weak and ill. I look at the rest of my body which is peppered with bright red spots, resembling tiny neat bullet holes on the stark white background of my once bronzed, and according to Brian, beautiful skin.

"Your skin is so soft and smooth," he used to tell me, "And I love to touch it."

But who would want to touch it now I think to myself? I don't even want to touch it myself, but I can't stop myself from scratching. It feels as though a million centipedes are lined up and performing the River Dance under my skin.

Was this Brian's final legacy to me, did he know I wonder? The night he died there was something dark and desperate in his eyes that I never could quite fathom. Something he wasn't telling me.

I get out of bed and look at myself in the long mirror in my mum's bedroom. I look like a plucked chicken. I seriously think I've had it.

I am going to die.

Don't want to.

Not going to.

I'll try some mind over matter I think to myself resolutely. That nice handsome homeopathic doctor in Ibiza, albeit the harbinger of my bad news, told me to imagine a supermarket trolley and fill it up with all the bad things in my body, then take it to the check out - or was it the good things? I can't remember, so I forget all about 'Supermarket Sweep' and the gorgeous but camp Dale Winton and play some rousing music in my head instead. Battle songs, the good cells are the orchestra, that's the red cells, or hang on a minute, should they be the white ones? I'm not quite sure which way round it should be. Who are the goodies and who are the baddies? So I think I'd better leave it, just in case the wrong battalion wins. Worn out by a battle I have only just begun, I finally drop off to sleep exhausted. I would have been totally useless in the trenches.

The next day I decide I need some allies, someone else to turn to in case of emergencies, which there will surely be. My poor old mum is nearly eighty and I'm not sure she can deal with all this. Then again, what am I saying? My mum has survived far worse than this; the Second World War, losing two babies. She keeps telling me to call on my true British grit, but it seems to have deserted me.

I don't really know who else to tell. I don't really want to tell anyone to be honest, but I finally decide on my neighbours who are both artists like me, although what that's got to do with it I haven't got a clue. Maybe I think they will be more open-minded or less shockable. I knock nervously on their front door and I can see the tall figure of Paul loom behind the glass. He looks the epitome of the typical artist dressed in his customary navy blue jumper and jeans, but his piercing blue eyes and clipped white beard also give him a nautical appearance and he could easily be mistaken for a captain of the high seas. All that's missing is the clay pipe, but he hates smoking and spends his life nagging me to give up. His long time partner Willo peers around his legs and tries to squeeze past him, curious to see who is at the door. She is half the size of him and practically obscured by a voluminous plaster spattered smock, her long multi-coloured hair rolled up in curling pins because they are going out later to an exhibition opening. They ask me in for a cup of tea and I sit primly on the settee clutching my china beaker. Paul has just been awarded yet another prestigious art prize so we talk about painting and forthcoming exhibitions for a while and then I just blurt it out. There's no way of saying it subtly and anyway, I just want to get it over and done with.

By complete coincidence, it turns out that Willo has a girl friend she knew from her time in Africa who has been living with HIV for eight years, so she is well clued up about the disease and also how I must be feeling. They are both very concerned for me and totally sympathetic. In fact they are overly sympathetic and insist on enveloping me in a joint hug.

"Don't come near me," I scream, trying to push them away, "Don't touch me, I'm a leper." They hug me anyway and promise to help me in any way they can and I'm glad I've told them. Willo comes with me to the clinic. She's only recently started to call herself Willo. She was plain Pat before that, although I would hardly describe her as plain. Anything less!

A tea lady passes with a laden trolley as we sit nervously in the waiting room. "Can I get you anything ladies?" she offers.

"Two gin and tonics perhaps?" Willo jokes.

She's dressed very eccentrically for the occasion, a velvet baker boy hat perched on the top of her head with ringlets of different coloured hair curling around her ears and intermingling with her long, silver earrings. Regardless of the bleak and rainy day, she is sporting some tiny pointed embroidered shoes she bought in Hong Kong. Alternatively, I'm dressed very smartly, trying to look like a secretary or something straight. Not an artist and not the kind of person who would have this!

"I bet she thinks we're a pair of hookers," Willo whispers in my ear.

We cover our knees, straighten our shoulders and try to look respectable.

I am assigned a kind lady counsellor called Janet who listens patiently to my story. I only cry a bit as I relate all the sorry details. She has a box of tissues to hand and she makes us all a cup of tea. She keeps patting my arm with her soft white hand. I tell her everything and she is fascinated, or maybe not. She's probably heard it all before. She sends me off for another blood test in the hope that the Spanish one was wrong.

"It can happen," she says optimistically, putting her arm around my shoulder.

But I'm not so sure. I'm a total wimp when it comes to blood tests.

"At least now I have a good excuse not to be a donor," I shudder to Willo, who is at my side, holding my hand.

The 'blood nurse' as she is descriptively known, has a hard time finding a vein.

"Let's sing a song," Willo suggests brightly, trying to take my mind off the gory proceedings. I turn my head to face the wall. There is a poster of a dolphin flapping in the breeze from the noisy fan. The fan is there presumably in case anyone faints and there's a strong possibility that I might do just that.

Willo warbles a choir favourite, and I try to join in, in a weedy little voice. 'Nurse Blood' looks at us as though we were both stark raving mad.

While we are waiting to see the doctor, Willo imparts a few of the awful experiences she'd had to endure when she was battling with cancer. It does the trick and stops me feeling sorry for myself. Willo tells me she still has the tattoos on her body to remind her.

"I didn't know they did that," I exclaim, shocked, "Branded for life like an Auschwitz prisoner."

Paul is waiting outside in the car to drive us home. Apparently, it will take two weeks for the results to come back. Two long weeks, how will I ever survive them? Even though in my heart I know it is futile, I am still hoping that there's been some kind of stupid mistake. I decline a coffee with my arty neighbours and go straight back to my mum's. I am continuing to stay at her house, even though in some ways it would make life much easier to stay at my own, but I simply can't stand to be by myself. To get us over that time, we start watching football, even though I've never been what you would call a football fan, I used to hate it in fact. But it's The World Cup and sheer patriotism aided by the more pressing need to take my mind off the matter in hand, lead me to become involved. The play offs are staged at odd times of the day and night. This is good as far as we're concerned, because it means we have an agenda, other than just waiting for my results. Sometimes we have to get up very early, four or five o'clock in the morning, or stay up all night in order to watch the different matches. We even set the alarm clock so that we won't miss them. Well, it's an objective, a reason to carry on, a reason to get up - a reason to live even. We have to support the team, whichever one – it didn't really matter. England was knocked out early on, so we supported Holland instead. We had it to do - had to do something. Anything else was just too much for me.

Paint? - Impossible.

Sculpt? - Too weak.

Write? - Too painful

Have to keep the secret.

Why me?

Why not?

Why anyone?

Two weeks later the test is confirmed. It's positive of course. My sister Julie has flown over from Holland to support me in my hour of need. Where would we be without our sisters, or our mothers, or even our neighbours for that matter? I for one would have been a total wreck without their unconditional love and support.

Julie's big blue eyes, the same blue as mine, well with tears, as Janet tells me the bad news and Willo reaches for my hand. Janet gives me some booklets in a brown paper bag and I'm sent off to see Dr Gayed who is a specialist in HIV and AIDS and who will look after me from now on.

CHAPTER 7

The Secret Garden

Thinking back to those early days in the 'Clog', I must have been terribly naïve not to have realised Brian had a hidden agenda for me and that by allowing him to become my benefactor and master, I was walking straight into his hands, or his web, as the portrait of him I later painted, 'The Spider and the Fly', so accurately predicted. I'd genuinely believed it was my art, as opposed to my heart, to use a corny play on words that he was so interested in. But now, looking back, I suppose it was obvious to everyone, everyone but me that is, that he was intent on seducing me right from the start. It was just a matter of when. That was the way he worked I was to later find out.

What few people considered, especially me, was the possibility we would fall in love with each other. He was twenty years older than me and we lived in two completely different worlds. Brian's world was all about money and power and was the exact opposite of mine as an impoverished art student and reluctant barmaid. But when it happened, when we did fall head over heels in love with each other, suddenly none of that mattered anymore. We were made for each other he told me and I believed him.

"I don't know anyone remotely like me," he used to say to me, "And I don't know anyone remotely like you."

He had a wife of course, lurking somewhere in the background, but he told me they were separated due to irreconcilable differences and the fact that he didn't love her anymore - if in fact he ever had. Rumours about his failed marriage abounded in the 'Clog'. She was an alcoholic. He'd driven her to it with his strange, eccentric ways and outrageous behaviour. He was mean and cruel; sadistic even according to hearsay. But by this time, I was besotted with him and deaf, dumb and blind to other people's remarks. Some claimed he was a genius, others said he'd stolen the idea for the invention which had made him so much money from someone else; the name of the person he'd allegedly stolen it from, whispered from the sides of mouths and behind hands at the bar. However, this didn't stop Brian from being a figure who commanded a certain respect, albeit the kind of respect that so often walks hand in hand with vast amounts of money. Either way, Brian was a force to be reckoned with and when he walked into a room, everyone took notice.

He added to his air of power and mystery, played upon it some might accuse him, by saying very little. By way of looks, he was tall, dark and imposing, with smouldering eyes and a roguish smile. That's when he condescended to smile, which didn't happen very often. He preferred to adopt the mysterious, tortured look, which he used to great effect, especially on me. I'd never met anyone like him and I was totally fascinated by him. Before he came into my life I'd always been a loner and I was accustomed to living in my own world and being the odd one out. And now suddenly, I'd found someone I felt I could relate too at last, although I suppose in many ways, like everyone else, I was also a bit in awe of him.

Sometimes, at the beginning of our relationship, I often had the feeling that Brian was playing with me. Always the puppet master, he liked to be the one in control and he knew just when and how to pull those strings. The longer he stayed away, the more I longed to see him. At first, I hardly ever saw him during the day. He would appear late at night, when all the customers had gone home and then whisk me down to his house in his Lamborghini.

The first time he took me there, I was petrified; both of being alone in his presence away from the safety of the 'Clog' and also so by the possibility that his estranged wife might suddenly materialise, like a ghost from the past. He'd quickly tried to reassure me, insisting that I had nothing to fear, that she didn't live there anymore and hadn't for quite some time. Nevertheless, I still felt like an intruder as the Lamborghini purred to a halt outside the fortress- like wooden gates, which with a flick of the remote control, slowly opened like a hungry mouth, ingesting the long silver fish of the car as it slithered down the curved throat of the gravel drive like a slippery eel, then snapped shut behind us. Jonah and the whale, I thought with trepidation; this is it - no turning back now - no escape. Not that I wanted to.

The walled gardens and the ivy-covered house were bathed in moonlight, but inside the leather-lined womb of the car, it was pitch black. Brian and I sat side by side in the sudden, silvery silence and I could picture the silhouettes of our two heads, as though I was looking down on the scene from above.

"Allow me to escort you on a tour of the moonlit gardens Miss Seed," he turned to look at me and I could just about make out the dark cardboard cut out of his profile. He slid his long legs out of the car door and I could hear the soft crunch of his shiny black crocodile skin shoes on the glittering gravel as he walked around the low, silver bonnet, tapping his fingers lightly on the gleaming metal as he passed. He opened my door for me and graciously took my hand to help me out. We stood there, suddenly feeling like strangers in this dreamlike scenario, Brian incongruous in his immaculate business suit and tie and me, more in keeping with the ethereal ambience of our surroundings, in my long, floaty, hippy-style dress.

Sitting down on the low stone wall, Brian kicked off his crocodile skin shoes then bade me to do the same. Caught up in the magic of the moment, I untied the straps of my leather sandals and abandoned them side by side, next to his, on the gravel beach of the parking bay.

"I feel like I'm symbolically stepping into dangerous new waters," I smiled feeling reckless, "And leaving my past life behind."

"In years to come," Brian took my hand, "someone will find our shoes and wonder what has happened to us. But they will never find us, because we will have completely disappeared."

Hand in hand, as though we'd made a silent suicide pact, we ventured into the pretend moonlit sea, tiptoeing across the manicured lawns in our bare feet, the silver blades of grass sliding between our toes like silken seaweed.

"Look at us, we can walk on water," Brian laughed exultantly.

From the very start, that's what I loved about this strange, enigmatic man; his ability, at least when he was with me, to let down his guard and throw himself into whatever dream or surreal fantasy that captured our artistic minds.

Having safely reached the other shore, he led me under a rose-covered arch and along a winding path, to what he described as his 'secret gardens', enclosed by their high, stone walls. Like furtive Red Indians we crept alongside the maze of hedges, as tall as he was, imagining we could see faces and peculiar shaped animals in the clipped foliage. We brushed past heavy bushes, laden with blooms, the moon highlighting the tips of the waxen petals, cupped by clusters of black, shiny leaves then weaved our way under sinuous Willow trees, swimming through the shimmering fronds cascading like leafy waterfalls over our heads that caught in our hair and caressed our lips.

Brian personally introduced me to all of his favourite trees and plants. "This is Mr Sakamoti," he announced courteously, as I respectfully bent down to shake hands (or branches) with a small Japanese bush.

"And allow me to introduce Mr. and Mrs. Beech and their young son Harold."

Allowing myself to be captivated by this mystical dream, I could forget everything. Who he was, that by rights he was still a married man, that he was so much older than me. None of it mattered. It felt almost as though we had been transported to another time zone and were floating magically hand in hand around the perimeters of the old house, with its tall chimneys and twinkling leaded windows peeping out from under the tightly knit chain mail coat of silver and bronze ivy that covered its walls. Adventurers, on a voyage of discovery, we followed each twist and turn of the neat gravel paths that criss-crossed the vegetable gardens; Brian, every now and then, stooping down to break off sprigs of mint and fragrant herbs, which he crushed to dust in the palm of his hand, then offered me to breathe.

The magical mystery tour of the secret gardens now complete, Brian reached in his pocket and took out a huge 'Alice in Wonderland' like brass key, then opened the heavy oak door to the house and led me into the entrance hall. The first thing that hit me, taking me instantly back to those bygone days of childhood, was the fragrant scent of lavender polish, followed by the soft tick of a big grandfather clock leaning against the shadowed wall, the golden glint of the pendulum swinging hypnotically from side to side. In the centre of the hall, on the polished Maplewood table was a gleaming brass bowl of carefully arranged flowers and a neat line of unopened letters addressed to Mr and Mrs Mercer.

Branching off from the entrance hall, I could make out two shadowy rooms; one filled with dark furniture, old leather sofas, big wooden desks and fringed standard lamps and in the other a huge dining table surrounded by matching chairs. In both rooms there was a fireplace with neatly arranged logs, all ready to light. A dark intimidating corridor led off to other rooms, the first of which appeared to be a cloakroom filled with coats on hangers and which reminded me of a painting by Magritte. The house felt vaguely spooky and gave off the feeling that nobody really lived there anymore. It was cold and old fashioned and not at all how I expected it to be. Brian told me that it was still exactly the same as when his parents had lived there. The only additions he had made were his collection of surreal and impressionist paintings adorning the walls, which when he turned on the special overhead lighting, suddenly sprang to life, making splashes of vivid, vibrant colour like static tropical aquariums in the otherwise dead rooms.

I followed Brian's long shadow into the darkened lounge then the atmosphere suddenly lifted as we passed through to a huge sunroom, a glass extension, which Brian had designed himself and stretched the entire length of the house. In the ceiling were curved domes of glass through which the midnight blue sky twinkled with a thousand stars. In the half light cast by the moon, two long, white sofas faced each other, separated by the mirrored lake of a glass coffee table, covered with scattered water lily leaves of magazines and art books. The room was filled with plants and exotic flowers, and in every corner standing on plinths, were bronze and marble sculptures.

After the first time Brian took me to his house which was called 'Kenolbri', an abbreviation of the names of the siblings who had grown up there, it became an almost nightly occurrence. The customers at the 'Clog' became accustomed to seeing his Lamborghini parked outside at closing time, waiting to whisk me off. At other times, when he wanted to be more discreet, he'd sneak up in his mini cooper and hide it on the pub car park. Then we'd creep out of the back door without anyone noticing and speed off down to 'Kenolbri', maintaining a conspiratorial silence; always waiting until we were safely behind closed doors before we spoke.

Free from prying eyes at last, we would cuddle up close together on one of the white sofas in the long, glass sunroom, holding hands and talking about art, while listening to the eerie music of Bartok until dawn. And then he'd take me home

I loved being with Brian in that long, glass room, with the moonlight shining on the sculptures casting their stretched shadows across the heated marble floor; or when it was dark and rainy, with the wind beating against the glass panes and whistling through the bare branches of the tall trees in the surreal, misty garden outside. Sometimes it was foggy and then it felt as though we were floating somewhere in space and not really on this planet at all. It often seemed to be foggy on the nights we were together. Brian said it was so that we couldn't be seen by the private detectives hiding outside in the bushes that his estranged wife had sent to spy on us. I think he was only teasing me, but then again, maybe he wasn't.

On the nights he didn't come for me, I would sit in my room pretending I wasn't waiting for him.

But I was.

CHAPTER 8

My Little Soldiers

Now here I was waiting for something else, my latest test results or my viral load and CD4 count as they're officially called, to find out if the good guys were winning the war or whether the bad guys, the enemy, the dreaded virus was taking control. I remembered the first time I'd sat here in this clinic, waiting for the Spanish test to be confirmed, which it had been of course, thus making me yet another statistic, an innocent victim in the ever increasing numbers of men, women and children infected with this deadly disease.

"This is a lifetime commitment," Dr Gayed had told me as he'd prescribed the medication.

"How long is a lifetime?" I'd asked him.

How long is a piece of string he could have answered, but he didn't.

"We have good results nowadays," he'd said, "But I have to tell you that there is still no cure."

I hate taking pills, I always have. A sachet of Lemsip is enough to knock me out for the count, so what upshot this lucky bag of toxic treats would have on my delicate constitution didn't bear thinking about. Well, I wouldn't think about it I told myself, the maraca bag of pills rattling an unconvincing calypso in my hand. I'd just do as the doctor ordered and swallow them down, simple as that. Only, it wasn't that simple at all.

I reluctantly shake the boxes of pills out on the kitchen table and line them up in a neat, orderly row, ready to commence battle. 'My little soldiers' somebody told me to call them, so I try to imagine them as my allies as opposed to my enemies. I call on my granddad with his Military medal for bravery in the field to come down from heaven to help me and my dad, who'd also been a wartime hero, flying off in the dead of night as little more than a young lad to drop bombs over Germany. I call on him too and anyone else who cares to listen – The Dam Busters, the SAS, the squadrons and battalions that would hopefully help me win the war raging inside my body.

I look down at the line of toxic pills in despair and select the chosen three to the forefront, the bright yellow ones. These will be the leaders, the front line; the first soldiers into battle.

They are enormous; there is no way I will ever be able to swallow them. My throat constricts at the mere thought. With their torpedo-like shape, not to mention their size and fluorescent orange lettering marking their sides, they look more like bombs than soldiers. The arsenal of war: my very own nuclear armaments, my cruise missiles, my chemical warfare. I shake my head ruefully - to think I once went on CND marches to ban the bomb.

Dr Gayed had warned me, that when I started taking the medication I would feel ill for a few weeks, but tactfully, he failed to mention exactly how ill. In order to mark the time I cut up an antique necklace Brian had given me for my birthday and filled a jam jar with enough coloured beads to get me over the next thirty days. I then placed an empty jam jar beside it. When the second jar was full, hopefully, the worst would be over.

My mum and I had performed a similar ritual when I was a little girl, when my dad had been sent away for training purposes by the RAF to frightening sounding places, where he'd be forced to take part in jungle survival courses and would come back as thin as a stick and covered in Leech bites. I'd hated my dad going away, so on those traumatic occasions we'd used the coloured pegs from a game of Chinese chequers to count the days till he came home. On my way upstairs to bed I'd put another peg in the jar and every night there would be one less peg, till at last he came safely home again.

The only consolation about these leaves of absence was that he always brought me unusual presents back from the exotic places he'd visited, which would be the envy of all my friends. An embroidered grey velvet elephant, which when I wound the tiny brass key in its side would slowly judder across the shiny lino floor, swinging its creased trunk. Strange looking animals carved out of wood that I could add to my 'little games'; long-necked giraffes, a gazelle, the three wise monkeys and a squat-legged, square-nosed hippopotamus. For the house he brought brightly coloured wall hangings and embroidered cushion covers of the Taj Mahal, sparkling with sequins and embossed with gold and silver thread. And one time, my favourite present of all, a plastic bath for my doll you could actually put water in with a plug hole so you could let the water out.

How I wished my dad was still alive and with me right now as I considered the daunting task before me. But at least I had my mum here at my side, although I'd banished her to the living room where she was prohibited from talking to me in case she caught me mid swallow. Although chance would be a fine thing as at the rate I was going I was never going to pluck up enough courage to get these dreaded pills down my neck.

I paced the kitchen floor. I determinedly approached the line of yellow soldiers lying belly up on the kitchen table; then backed off, making a cowardly retreat.

Yellow bellies - mustn't be a yellow belly. I sang to myself like an American G.I.

'If you want to win the war..... this is what these pills are for'.

I tried to metamorphose into Goldie Hawn in her role as a reluctant female soldier in 'Private Benjamin'; people sometimes used to say that I looked a bit like her. But it was all prevarication and I would be standing here forever if I didn't make a move; it had to be done at some point. I had to literally bite the bullet and get on with it.

I picked them up in my trembling hand. Here goes, I thought as I reluctantly swallowed the three huge 'soldiers' in their bright yellow uniforms with great difficulty, the words of the doctor ringing through my head.

"You want to live don't you?"

"Yes, I do doctor."

"I do," I thought sadly - a lifetime commitment, for better for worse, for richer for poorer, in sickness and in health. Suddenly, for richer or poorer didn't matter anymore. Only health matters in the end. It seemed I'd had my priorities wrong all along.

I was living back in my own house by this time, but my mum had come to stay with me in case I suffered a bad reaction to the medication - and it was a good job she had as it turned out. The scene was all set; the house was warm and cosy, the fire was lit and we had something planned to watch on telly. I'd bought a knitting pattern and some needles and balls of wool so I could knit myself something, while taking my mind off the proceedings at the same time. The last time I'd resorted to knitting was when I'd been pregnant with Ben, but the lacy matinee jackets and tiny bootees I'd stitched so painstakingly had turned out to be way too small for him as he'd weighed in at a thumping ten pounds and eleven ounces. Later, as a carrot topped toddler with hair the colour of a belisha beacon, I'd knitted him ethnic styled jumpers with brightly coloured designs I'd made up myself as I went along. But he'd always complained they were way too itchy and had refused point blank to wear them. Anyway, by that time, I'd already come to the conclusion that life was far too short to knit. But right now, I needed something to do with my hands apart from biting my nails and scratching my spots, not to mention tearing my hair out in sheer panic. So I got out my needles and started to knit and waited for the effects of the drugs to kick in. I'd deliberately chosen a complicated pattern, which would take me months, if not years to complete. I laughed wryly to myself. Comedians often make jokes about this kind of thing, don't they?

Doctor - "I'm afraid it's bad news."

Patient – "Oh dear, how long have I got doc?"

Doctor – "Well, it's hard to say, but don't go buying any long playing records or start reading War and Peace!"

I was up to row six, or thereabouts, when suddenly all hell was let loose and I was forced to toss my needles to one side, causing the stitches to slip off and start to unravel. What was happening to me? My body was going mad. My ears had started to burn as if they were on fire and not because someone was talking about me, although I supposed everyone would be once the news of my new found 'status' had got out. In fact, my ears had become so hot I was forced to take my earrings out for fear that they would melt.

I felt like a nuclear Power station. I was Sellafield, Chernobyl and Pearl Harbour, all rolled into one. My head started to spin and my blood felt as though it was about to boil over like a pan of bubbly red milk. That vision was enough to make me want to throw up, but I tried my best not to in case I regurgitated the yellow soldiers.

"Are you alright?" my mum asked concerned.

"No, I don't know what on earth's happening to me," I jumped up out of my seat and made my way to the stairs, needing the safety of my bed in case I fainted. Clinging onto the banister rail, I hoisted myself up the stairs and threw myself on the bed. The room was spinning round and round as though I was suffering from the whirly pits after drinking too much alcohol. But this was far worse than being drunk. Strange visions had started to flash through my mind; reeling cartwheels and kaleidoscopes of colour – psychedelic patterns with jagged edges of light. It was how I would imagine a bad trip on acid would be, not that I've ever taken it. I never needed to open my own particular doors of perception through the taking of drugs. My surreal visions and dreams had always been enough. Anyway, I'd always been very anti- drugs of any kind as I'd seen first hand the detrimental effects that they could cause to people's minds, especially acid. But I had no choice now. Take them or die. There was no other option.

My hands tightly gripping the side of the bed, I lay there hallucinating, the flashing lights and strange visions fighting to present themselves behind my eyes, one after the other in rapid succession like some kind of bizarre film strip. Then the next thing I knew, I was a paddle steamer, paddling backwards down the Mississippi, with long arms and huge hands in boxing gloves.

"I'm a paddle steamer," I told my mum, who had followed me up as fast as her sciatica would allow.

"Yes dear," she soothed consolingly, "Shall I make you a nice cup of tea?"

That poor woman, I thought. The things she's had to go through one way and another with me. But she says she doesn't mind. She would gladly take it off me if she could.

I was so worried about taking the medication the next night, Willo came to lay on the bed with me. I suppose I was fortunate to have the kind of girlfriend and neighbour I could ask to come to bed with me. We lay side-by-side in our nighties and talked about silly mundane things, reading household hints and boring articles in one of my mum's 'Chat' magazines, until the drugs kicked in and I started to hallucinate again.

"My feet are silver forks," I told Willo, "With very long prongs."

"Now's probably not the right time to be thinking about long prongs," Willo advised sagely, "After all, it was a long prong that got you into this mess in the first place."

"Don't you mean a long dong?" I replied, fuzzily.

My mum struggled up with two 'nice' cups of tea.

"My feet are silver forks," I informed her.

"Oh well, never mind dear," she said briskly, "Drink your tea."

I'd always had the feeling that Brian wanted to take me with him when he died. He couldn't bear the thought that I would go on living without him. I'd seen him through the difficult time before his death and it hadn't been easy when a man as rich as Brian was, had been suddenly told out of the blue that he only had three months left to live. He'd thought he'd live till his nineties at least and was busy working on his latest invention to solve the world's energy crisis. Death was definitely not on his agenda. He didn't consider himself to be a normal human being and I supposed he wasn't, that's why I'd loved him. But I hadn't always liked him.

Willo comes back with me to the clinic so the doctor can check how I'm faring with the medication. It's becoming a regular outing for her. We even dress up for the occasion. While we wait to see the doctor, I think about Brian. I never stop thinking of him now. He certainly made sure that I wouldn't forget him.

I twiddle nervously with my thin, straggly hair (another clump falls out) and wait for the latest results. I don't think I can cope with any more bad news. Luckily, this time it was only that my potassium level is very high and I have to give up bananas.

"No problem doc!" I laugh, "I can handle that."

And I'm out of there like a speeding bullet.

Willo suggests that I come round to her house to look through her collection of wigs. She was as bald as a coot apparently after her chemotherapy.

"I have a lovely Egyptian one with lots of little plaits," she remembers fondly.

"I can't really see myself as Cleopatra," I shake my straggly locks sadly, "Lady Godiva perhaps!"

My sister has flown over again from Holland for the weekend, thanks to Stellios and good old easyJet, so I go to bed that night surrounded by female support, my mum and my sister in the next bedroom and Willo lying next to me.

"It's like the bloody Waltons," I joke as I turn out the light, "Night John boy, night Betty Lou. On second thoughts," I add, "forget John boy! I'm not too keen on men at the moment."

Every night now strange happenings and visions are taking place inside my head. I see my dad's profile on shiny new coins with edges like jigsaws, turning in different directions then finally joining together; a line of birds, two red ones, two blue ones, ad infinitum, frantically pecking first one way then the other. Tap, tap, tap – tap, tap, tap. Little men with ice picks (the seven dwarfs possibly) hacking away behind my breastbone. Then of course, there's the dreaded itching. But they said I had a very high viral load of two million or so. That's a lot for any hackers or peckers to contend with, not to mention the seven dwarfs. High ho, high ho!

I try to stay bright and optimistic, although it's hard. I buy a sequinned bag to keep my pills in to make them seem less threatening and a new duvet cover sprinkled with pink rosebuds to make me feel clean. Yet every morning I wake up crying. I wake up with tears rolling down my cheeks and a huge lump in my throat and there are times when I can't stop crying all day. My mum tries to comfort me and put her arms around me, but I shoo her away.

"I'm crying because I don't feel like 'ME' anymore," I sob. "My body and my mind are being controlled by these strange drugs, which I'll have to take for the rest of my life – however long, or however short that might be."

Before Brian went to sleep on the night he died, he'd stared at me with that strange, desperate look, the one that haunts me to this day. I remembered the ugly sore, the one that he'd had at the corner of his mouth that simply wouldn't heal, suddenly disappeared when he'd died. And so had he.

Or so I thought.

His ghost was lurking constantly at the top of my stairs. Strange things would happen. Photos of him would disappear and then reappear in odd places.

I kept telling people that I was turning into him.

"Look," I told them "I've got those funny spots on my body, just like his."

But no one would listen to me, not until now that is.

CHAPTER 9

Bread and Butter Pudding

My mum has always been my best friend, well apart from a few errant years when I was a rebellious teenager, but even then we were still close. Some people can't understand how your mum can also be your best friend and I've often been accused, especially by Brian, who was jealous of anyone I was close to (even my own son), that I was still attached to her apron strings. But it wasn't like that at all. My mum had always there for me, no matter what and during those dark, horrific days, when I first started to take the medication, she was my best support and somehow, as mothers do, she'd known just what to do to get me through.

Those were the blackest of times and now when I think back, I don't know how we survived them. The worst thing of all was not being able to tell anyone what I was going through, or what we were going through to be exact. But what I didn't realise at the time was the huge burden it was for both my mum and my sister to keep the shocking news of my status to themselves. They also had to keep up the pretence, live a lie; and for a close family such as ours, it can't have been easy for them. But we somehow had to keep the secret of this terrible thing that had happened to me, that had turned our lives upside down, to ourselves.

Why me? I often asked myself.

Why not?

Why anyone?

"You want to live don't you?" the doctor had said.

I do – or do I?

What will it be like living with this?

"Try not to cry," my mum did her best to console me, "There's worse things happening at sea."

But are there?

I could have this, that, or the other – but I've got this.

Or has this got me?

Keep knitting, busy hands, stitch after stitch to see something grow, instead of disintegrate and fall apart at the seams - like me. Click clacking needles – stick it in, wrap it round, pull it through, knock it off, then repeat over and over and over again.

My mum, steadfast and calm, pretending to be strong for my sake. She told me later she'd prayed to my Irish Granddad. "Please help my daughter, your special granddaughter, who takes so much after you and make her eyes, the same Irish eyes as yours, smile again," she'd begged him, and a huge bee had flown in the room, buzzed around her head a few times then curled up and died on the windowsill. Then I apparently came downstairs and said, it was really weird, but the sore on my lip, just like the one that Brian had had, the one that wouldn't go away, was buzzing as if there was a bee inside it – buzz – buzz – buzz – and the day after, it had gone.

My mum was convinced that the bee had been my granddad, so she was reluctant to dispose of its furry corpse. It's probably still there on her windowsill, covered in dust.

Something had to be done without further ado to kick my ailing body back into shape, so I make myself an action plan. With kicking directly in mind, the first thing I decide to do is to take up the ancient art of Tai Chi, which according to those who practice it is supposed to be one of the best forms of exercise to build up your immune system. I definitely need all the help I can get in that particular department so I sign on for classes which are being held once a week at the local community centre as part of a council funded rejuvenation plan for the 'over fifties'. But when I get there, to my dismay, most of the participants looked more like they were over ninety - me included probably on a bad day! In fact, some of them were so old and infirm and in the process (or not) of recovering from strokes and hip replacements etc. that they had to do it sitting down.

As I watched one poor old soul lopsidedly punching the air as he sat slumped in his chair, I thought to myself someone should come up with one of those stickers with the slogan – *'old men do it sitting down'* - to put on the fridge or the back window of your car. You could say, I suppose, in view of our twenty year age difference that in relation to me Brian had been an old man, but he could do it sitting down, standing up, or on his head probably - well, at least back in the good old days. Sometimes, when I watched the old men struggling behind me performing their Ninja turtle poses in the mirror, I would think about Brian, although he would have been horrified to be considered as an old man, or a Ninja turtle for that matter. He always thought he was immortal and so did I; anyway, he would never have attended a class like that. He didn't like to mix with Joe public.

Over the course of time I'd grown rather fond of some of the old men in the group, who have christened me 'pink stocking' because of my florescent pink socks and slavishly follow my every move, even though as a relatively new student to the ancient art, I tend to toss in a bit of flamenco every now and then and sometimes imagine while carried away by the tweeting bird sounds mixed with the mystical clangs of Chinese music, that I'm performing with the Cirque Soleil.

I always pop round to my mum's for a coffee before I go.

"Are you going to Typhoo after coffee?" my mum asks? She suffers from a Mrs Malaprop tendency and has trouble with certain words, especially foreign ones. I'd stopped bothering to correct her long ago and had even adopted a few of her more colourful verbal adaptations into my own vocabulary, which if you don't know us, can be very confusing when you hear us talk.

"I'm going straight after this coffee," I told her, grabbing my trainers, "Then after Typhoo I'll come back and get you and we can go for a drive in the country to get some fresh air."

We'd taken to going for regular jaunts to the countryside as part of my get fit routine, but the fresh air aspect was a bit of a myth as it was usually pissing it down with rain, so the only fresh air we got was when we rolled the car window down to have a fag. Another of our favourite rituals, although not the healthiest of options it has to be said, was to drive through the drive in at Mcdonald's, order two girl's 'happy meals' and two cups of tea, then park up outside Aldi and sadistically watch the bedraggled shoppers unloading their trolleys in the rain from the cosy comfort of the car.

Sometimes we'd forget about the 'happy meals' and just order two cups of tea. My mum swore it was the best tea in town because it was always piping hot; dangerously hot in regard to health and safety issues and my mum's arthritic hands, but she had an iron tongue as far as tea was concerned. However, these days her famous iron constitution of yore was beginning to let her down, which under the circumstances, considering what was going on with me, was not surprising. In that respect we were two of a kind, in the same boat so to speak, only here's hoping it wasn't the Titanic.

My mum has always loved the theatre, especially musicals, and I must admit so do I, so I decide to take her to Blackpool to see "Carmen on Ice." Maybe not the lavish theatrical extravaganza she would have chosen of her own accord, but what can you do? We were living in the north of England after all and there wasn't that much choice, a fact of which my mum was constantly complaining. Anything of any interest, according to my mum, only happened down South and that when it came to culture, they completely forgot about us up here in the North - and in many ways she was right, hence, "Carmen on Ice."

Nevertheless, it was something to look forward to in an otherwise bleak and mentally, as well as physically challenged world, so I call up the box office to book the tickets and find out that pensioner discount applies for the matinee on Wednesday afternoon, so I suggest we take my dear friend Erik along with us. Aside from being a bona fide pensioner, Erik is also gay, so 'Carmen' in any shape or form, even on ice, I felt would be right up his street. And I was right.

"I simply can't wait Darling," he enthused over the phone. "I haven't been invited anywhere for ages, especially to the theatre," he pronounced theatre, *theee – ar – tar*, in his deep, Vincent Price horror movie type voice, "But are you sure you can cope with us two old crocks?" he intoned, "You know me and your dear mother, bless her cotton socks, can't get around like we used to."

I didn't think my mum would take too kindly to being called an old crock, or having her cotton socks blessed (not that she would ever wear socks of any description) but I assured him that I could manage and it was true. Thanks to the Tai Chi I was slowly beginning to regain the strength in my arms and legs and could just about handle pushing my mum around in her wheelchair. Mind you, she was as light as a feather these days and seemed to be wasting away before my very eyes. Erik, on the other hand was a different matter entirely. He was getting decidedly obese since he'd given up smoking. But he had his stroller to help him get along and his rather elegant walking stick.

The great day arrived and I manage to fit the two of them and their various mobility aids in the car and off we set for our trip to the seaside. My mum has made the usual selection of sandwiches of course, which she gets out as soon as we set off, even though I'd promised to take them for fish and chips after the performance.

Erik is one of my closest friends and I have known him for years, but there was no way I was intending to let on to him what had happened to me. For one thing HIV was previously known as the gay plague, so would therefore, I presumed, hold a morbid fascination for him and sadly, he'd already lost two people he'd loved to the disease. The other thing was, I didn't want to shock him and cause him to have yet another heart attack. But aside from all that, Erik, although renowned for his astrological and psychic powers, was definitely not to be relied upon for his powers of discretion and therefore could not be trusted to keep his notoriously big mouth shut. The word would be out on Blackburn's gay scene before you could say Jack Robinson, whoever he was, so I'd decided to keep to the pretence that everything was normal as far as my health was concerned, something I was getting accustomed to doing by now. Let's just hope, I prayed, that Erik's powers of foresight and divination would not enable him to see right through me and give the game away. I would be forced to remain constantly on my guard, not an easy thing to do with such a familiar and close, not to mention extremely nosy friend.

"How are we dear hearts?" Erik enquires as we drive along, "How's the sciatica darling?" he shouts over his shoulder to my mum. He's going a bit deaf and thinks everyone else is too

"It's no fun getting old Erik, is it?" she yells back; which is their cue to start rabbiting on about their water pills, the main topic of conversation it seems for anyone over sixty. I keep my eyes firmly fixed on the road ahead and deliberately refrain from mentioning my own daily cocktail of pills. Fortunately, neither of them had taken theirs today on purpose, so thankfully we don't have to keep stopping for the toilet. Although on saying that, they'd probably both end up with swollen ankles and wheezing like a pair of bagpipes and I'd never get them back in the car.

When we eventually hit the coast it's a typical March day and a lively wind is causing havoc on the sea front. I find a disabled parking spot close to the tower and the main pier and manage to lift the ungainly wheelchair with its spinning wheels out of the boot without trapping my fingers.'

"This will blow all the cobwebs away," my mum mouths breathlessly, trying to protect her carefully coiffed hair with her handbag as I wrap her up in a brightly striped Mexican style throw from Matalan (she refuses to be seen dead in the more appropriate tartan rug I got free at the petrol station) and plonk a furry hat, which she also hates from M&S on her head. Meanwhile, Erik is having a bit of a job hanging on to his theatrical black cape, his coat of a thousand camels as he calls it, that he bought in Algeria, which is flapping around his shoulders like something out of Phantom of the Opera.

We visit the tower ballroom first, where my mum gets all dreamy-eyed and nostalgic, remembering the days when the dance floor was packed with servicemen in their various uniforms during the war and thinking about my dad, or maybe even Harry Stones, her very first love, who she unceremoniously dumped to marry my dad. My mum was an absolute stunner in her day, a bit like Ginger Rogers everyone said and could allegedly dance like her too. She was still the receiver of admiring glances, even in her wheelchair, but obviously she couldn't dance anymore. Although, if there had been the slightest possibility, I'm sure she would have been up there on the dance floor. And so would Erik, who was ruefully tapping his stick to the music, wistfully reliving the days when he could still do the tango, when he'd been a beautiful but outrageously camp young man, back in the times when that sort of thing was still illegal and you could be sent to prison for being gay. It's incomprehensible to imagine that kind of thing happening now. I start to feel a bit emotional myself watching the two of them, lost in memories of days gone by, the 'good old days' as they called them and wondered what I would consider to be my 'good old days' when the time came. A memory suddenly springs to mind of a warm summer night, over twenty years ago it must be now and I am standing in my white high heel stilettos by the ropes of a circus like marquee on the scuffed grass, the silk of my long evening dress caressing my bare leg as I impatiently tap the tent peg with the pointed toe of my shoe. The marquee is lit from within like a huge Chinese lantern and I am watching the dancers moving like shadow puppets to the sultry music of the jazz band through the tarpaulin.

It is the annual summer dance at the golf club and I have gone along with my mum and dad, knowing that Brian will surely be there. Our clandestine love affair is still a closely guarded secret, one which has to be kept hidden from the public gaze, at least until his divorce is finalised. So I stay outside the marquee, too nervous to go in for fear of being unable to hide my true emotions should we meet face to face.

He is somewhere inside that magic lantern, probably dancing with someone, maybe even his ex-wife, although in reality I know in view of the acrimonious circumstances surrounding their impending divorce that that is highly unlikely. I want to be inside that tent dancing with him, but I am forced to stay outside, a jealous voyeur. I feel like cutting the ropes of the marquee and watching it slowly fold over the dancing couples; see them lie flat and still, black blobs through the transparency of luminous skin like frogspawn. Instead, I stay hiding behind the tent flap. A mistress in hiding; always hiding, but that was what it was like in those days, and probably still is if you are having an affair with a married man, whether they're about to be divorced or not.

I wanted to be inside that marquee, a part of that crowd and for Brian to gaze at me from afar with his smouldering eyes from over the shoulders of the tight posse of associates and hangers on that constantly surrounded him. I watch the silhouette of a couple swaying past, locked together in a close embrace and I imagine it is him and reach out to trace his shadow on the backdrop of the lit tarpaulin. I follow the shadow dancers around the tent, then as if by magic they suddenly part and his single shadow looms towards me and materialises through the tent flap, as though I had summoned him - and perhaps I had.

He takes my hand and we escape, running across the grass over the golf course. Sitting down on a circular stone wall to catch our breath, I stare at Brian's familiar crocodile skin shoes glistening with dew as he tells me that he loves me and how he hates other people. Then he abruptly stands up, pulling me with him and informs me regretfully that he'd better go back before he is missed. He disappears back inside the tent and once again I am outside looking in, a lonely wallflower, an outsider and that's exactly how I felt, that I could never truly be a part of his world, nor he of mine.

Now he was no longer part of any world, he was gone and I had to accept the fact. A huge lump comes to my throat and I am forced to hold back the tears, but I don't know whether this surge of emotion has been brought about by the pain of recalling that far-distant memory or by watching the old lady who has suddenly decided to take to the dance floor unaccompanied and is now meandering under the spotlight, dancing the anniversary waltz all by herself. I wonder if she is picturing herself dancing with her dear departed husband, or then again, I think less romantically, she may just be plain nuts and on day release from the local asylum.

Talking of asylums and loony bins, the mood is lightened somewhat by the appearance on the dance floor of a very odd-looking couple, who definitely look like they've escaped from an institution for the mentally challenged. Without preamble and with little regard for the rhythm of the music, they enthusiastically embark on their very own rendition of the rumba, which involves charging across the floor, bull versus bullfighter style and stopping now and then (usually by our table) for the woman to seductively reveal her surgical stockings.

My mum and Erik of course are both doubled up with laughter, whereas I am trying to be more discreet for fear of hurting the dancer's feelings.

"That's nowt," declares the waitress, noticing our obvious merriment as she sets our glasses before us, "You've not seen nothing yet. Just wait till they do 'tut pasadoble."

I'd always harboured a secret hankering to 'master' the undoubted challenges of the pasadoble myself. In fact, not long after Brian had died, in an effort to raise myself from my spiralling despondency, I'd signed up for ballroom dancing lessons. But because I no longer had a partner, I'd had to go privately. Not that Brian would have been seen dead doing the pasadoble, or in Blackpool Tower for that matter. But either with or without a partner, the ballroom dancing lessons hadn't been a great success, mainly because of the badly disguised reluctance and sheer determination of the instructor not to teach me the pasadoble.

"Now ducks, tut thing is," he'd sighed, attempting to light his pipe with a Swan Vesta, "I could 'appen teach you tut pasadoble, but chances are," he puffed his cheeks in and out, experiencing some incendiary difficulty in getting his pipe going, "No one," *puff... suck... puff...* "I say, no one, would ever ask you to dance it."

So I'd learnt the cha cha instead.

But chances were no one would ever ask me to dance that either, so I'd given up ballroom dancing as a bad job.

I used to love dancing, especially ballet classes when I was a little girl and taking part in all the shows and performances. The thrill of dressing up, the nerves and excitement of being backstage, the frenetic bustle mixed with the smell of powder and paint and the rows of net tutus hanging on pegs, their upturned snow white underbellies like swan's feathers; the tiny silver tiaras and coral pink satin shoes with wood in the toes. The pillar box red tap shoes and soft black leather ballet slippers with laces that crossed up your legs. Then later when I was much older and moved to Spain, the more passionate art of flamenco with the swirling skirts and whirling shawls, the heavy dresses which weighed a ton with frilly sleeves like lampshades, the shoes with nails hammered in the toes. But it looked like my dancing, not to mention my passionate days were over, as were my mum's and Erik's.

"I could take it in turns to push you both around in the wheelchair?" I suggest wryly, but they decline my generous offer.

As for 'Carmen on ice', that turned out to be a great disappointment to us all. Not only were the cast Russian, Carmen herself, or himself, was a man in drag, at least according to Erik who should know about these things. Aside from that, the music was not even from Carmen and the choreographer had obviously never set foot in Spain as the routines featured boisterous Cossack dancing with much whooping, combined with joint-defying leg kicks; quite dangerous I would imagine with skates on.

After the performance to make up for the immense cultural let down, I took them directly to Harry Ramsden's, supposedly the best venue in the north of England, if not the whole world (I do believe Harry's recently gone global) for fish and chip suppers. After queuing up for half an hour outside the hallowed doors on the wind-lashed seafront (Lancashire people do so love to queue - my mum says it goes back to the war, when you felt obliged to automatically join any queue even if you didn't know what you were queuing for) they allowed us in, two at a time. As honoured and respected pensioners, who had done their bit for King and country and survived to tell the tale, my mum and Erik were overjoyed to find they could dine at a reduced price. But when it came time to order dessert, their faces fell to their arthritic knees when, instead of sherry trifle, they were only entitled to order bread and butter pudding.

"I've never eaten bread and pudding in my entire life," my mum announced sulkily, "And I'm too old to start eating it now."

"*Hare rams dens, hare rams dens,*" I sang George Harrison style as I pushed her back to the car in the wheelchair. Erik, who is definitely going a bit deaf and thinks that he may need a horn, joined in with a rousing chorus of tiddly om pom pom, which didn't really apply, but I suppose he got the 'om' bit right.

We carried on with our sing-along all the way home. I think my mum must know the words to every old song in the world and Erik is a close contender. There was no shutting them up and then, as is often the case when they are in each other's company, they regressed to their distant childhood days and started reciting their old school poems and seeing who could remember the most lines. This, I feel, was mainly to prove to me, as well as to themselves, that they were not suffering from the early onset of Alzheimer's, although in Erik's case this is debatable.

"It's a shame they don't teach poetry in schools anymore," my mum complained. "You know, that's where they're going wrong with the youth of today."

If only it were that simple. Obviously there wasn't any trouble with teenage yobs, asbos or drugs in her day, because everyone was much too busy reciting poetry.

CHAPTER 10

Over The Moon

Brian and I went to Blackpool once; but only once mind. Blackpool wasn't exactly what you could call his cup of tea; in other words, it was a bit too common for the likes of him. It was round about the time when our relationship was starting to mysteriously transform from patron and artist into something else, something much more meaningful; magical, momentous, at least for me, but also somehow disturbing, menacing - sinister even.

Of course, we hadn't gone on a bright, sunny day in the summer like normal folk, to sit in deckchairs or paddle in the waves; it had been in the dead of a November night, with the wind howling off the sea and not a deckchair or a tourist in sight.

I remember, it had been unusually quiet in the 'Clog' that particular evening and the few customers we'd had, had already gone home and I'd been just about to lock up early when Brian had suddenly appeared at my side making me jump out of my skin. He must have snuck in through the back door like he sometimes did if he was trying to keep a low profile, although why he'd bothered on this particular occasion I don't know, because it turned out he'd parked his car, the distinctive Lamborghini, right at the front entrance.

He seemed particularly twitchy and unable to relax that night and when I'd asked him what was wrong, he'd said that he was feeling restless and wanted to do something out of the ordinary; to escape, to get away from Blackburn and the too many prying eyes. Although it was getting late by this time, he suggested that we go out for a drive somewhere in his car. Excited by the prospect of doing something totally off the wall and impulsive, I grabbed my coat and we crept out of the front door like mutinous teenagers.

The silver Lamborghini was parked outside in readiness, looking like something that had just landed from outer space, waiting to whisk me off into the unknown. I knew even then, that once I'd taken that first step and got into the car with him, there would be no turning back. But I didn't care. I was more than ready.

Brian opened the car door for me and I lowered myself into the dark, womblike cocoon of the Lamborghini's cockpit, breathing in the smell of luxury and new leather.

"Where would you like to go my lady?" he asked me jokingly, his long, white hands resting on the steering wheel.

I didn't have a clue where I wanted to go; I hadn't had time to think and anyway, I'd automatically presumed that he would take control, like he always did. But to be honest, it hadn't really mattered to me where we went, as long as I was with him.

"I'd like to go to the edge of the land, or better still, to the end of the earth," the drama of the idea suddenly captivated me, "To see the sea."

"To the end of the earth - so be it madam. Your wish is my command," he put the car into gear and off we sped.

Brian drove very fast and in no time at all we were whizzing along the motorway. I watched the speedometer soar over a hundred, then a hundred and twenty and I wouldn't have been surprised if we had taken off like a supersonic jet, and soared up into the midnight sky. In the distance, to our left, the lights of Blackpool glittered along the flat coastline.

"I've never been to Blackpool," Brian suddenly spoke. "I've been to Las Vegas," he added, almost apologetically, "In fact I've been all around the world. But I've never been to Blackpool. My mother and father thought it too working class."

I had of course, many times. My mum and dad had often taken us there as children, excitedly clutching our buckets and spades to make sandcastles on the wrinkled, muddy beach; the tightly coiled sand worms squelching between our bare white toes. And then later, if we'd been good, there would be the reward of a jog up and down the sands on the mangy, straw-hatted donkeys with daft names like 'Betty' and 'Mabel.'

"Well, you don't know what you've been missing," I smiled sardonically at Brian's set profile, his eyes glued fixedly on the road ahead. "Anyway," I added meaningfully, "There's a first time for everything."

Brian didn't respond verbally to my challenge, instead he reigned in the speeding car with the gears, veered suddenly to the left and pointed the long, silver bonnet of the Lamborghini towards the coast and we zoomed towards the glow of orange lights in silence. It was a crystal clear moonlit night and as we drew nearer, I could see the tip of Blackpool Tower reaching up on its anorexic frame of charcoal-like sticks to scratch the sky with smudgy graphite clouds. The Lamborghini slid like molten silver under the arch of a paint-peeling rainbow welcoming us to the famous holiday town; but it was bleak and deserted at this time of year. There was hardly a soul to be seen, apart from the occasional drunk staggering home, almost bent double with the force of the wind; empty cartons and fish and chip papers flapping against their legs.

We slowly drove along the wind battered sea front, past the shuttered gates of the pleasure beach with its motionless merry-go-rounds; the big-bellied statue of the laughing policeman standing silently on guard with his permanently frozen grin; the enormous, black metal frame of the big dipper curved menacingly against the sky, like the humped skeleton of some prehistoric beast. We cruised silently along the deserted promenade, passing the endless line of desolate hotels with their peeling facades, the empty bingo halls and penny arcades, the weathered signs for fish and chips and Blackpool rock creaking on their rusty chains. Strutting out into the murky sea, I could just about make out the corroded metal legs of the three piers, strung with tawdry lines of bulbs swinging back and forth on their looping wires. Every now and then an empty tram would cross our path, sparking on its rails.

The lights of the town eventually fizzled out and the coastline turned bleak and empty, pock-marked with sand dunes like the surface of the moon; the whistling sea grass whipped into a silver frenzy by the salty wind. Brian parked the car and we got out, pulling our coat collars up over our ears as we staggered over the windswept dunes. Then crouching down, we sat side by side in a basin of sand, protected somewhat from the wind by the pale rustling grasses.

"The edge of the land, Miss Seed," Brian proclaimed with a dramatic sweep of his hand. It was pitch black and although we could hear the roar of the waves and taste the salt on our lips, we couldn't actually see the sea. But we knew it was out there somewhere and that was all that mattered.

A ghostly looking ship sailed slowly by on the far horizon bedecked with rows of misty, twinkling lights.

"I wish the two of us could just get on that ship and sail away together, far away from everyone," Brian sighed, reaching over to take my young hand in his older, blue-veined one, then putting it inside his shirt to warm against his chest. I could feel the heat of his skin under my frozen fingers and the thud of his heart beating softly against the palm of my hand.

"So do I," I echoed wistfully, although the ghost ship was probably only the Isle of Man ferry. How could I have known then and neither could he of course, that one day, many years later, we would get on a boat and sail away together. Not the Isle of Man ferry, but on Brian's magnificent yacht Corinthian. We would sail away on our very own tempestuous ocean of love – out to sea, off the edge, over the moon and back again.

CHAPTER 11

Red Donkey Dream

For as long as I can remember, I have always wanted to be an artist and I still do. Without painting my life would feel bleak and empty, as it does right now. I keep trying to paint, but the heart seems to have gone out of me somehow, not to mention the inspiration, and yet without that creative outlet I feel bereft. As though one of my vital organs has been savagely torn out, but I can still feel where it used to be; like an amputated leg that still itches even though it's no longer there – a stunted arm on the end of which the absent hand still twitches.

Brian had always understood my need to be creative and had done everything he could in order to encourage me, but at times, especially back in those early days, his patronage had become too much for me and I'd rebelled against it and against him, as well as everything he stood for. The rich benefactor and the 'starving' artist, the old man and the young girl; it was too classic a role and I didn't want to fall into that stereotype. Aside from that, Brian was a hard taskmaster, a total perfectionist and sometimes a downright bully and his intimidating tactics, instead of encouraging me, more often than not had the adverse effect and only made me even more rebellious.

"Where are the canvases?" he would consistently nag, "You have to work harder. You have to be prepared to work night and day, day and night; you have to give yourself one hundred and one percent to your art, as I do when I'm working on my inventions. That's if you want to be a great painter of course, as opposed to an ordinary, run-of-the-mill painter, and above all," he threatened, "if you want me to promote you."

But I didn't want him to promote me, by then I only wanted him to love me, for who I was and not only for my art. Brian despised anything he considered to be mediocre or ordinary, especially people. In that respect we were totally different and his superior, patronising attitude to those he felt were below him drove me mad at times. There were many things about him that drove me mad, drove me to distraction even, but these were all overcome by my growing feelings of love for him. Confused and insecure about the true nature of his feelings towards me, I also started to nag him. "Where are you? Where were you? I need to see you more often."

Brian didn't take kindly to being nagged, or told what to do and neither did I, so we went through entire stages when we didn't speak or see each other. But I was always conscious of him in my innermost thoughts; he was always there lurking at the back of my mind, as he still is to this day. And I'm sure he was always thinking about me.

That unsettled and fiery period when Brian first started to sponsor me, was to be the most creative and productive period of my artistic career and looking back on it now, all that creativity and inspiration was directly down to him. From the moment he walked into my life and took control, everything changed for me and yet in other ways, things remained exactly the same. I continued to live at the pub with my parents and to the undiscerning eye, you would think nothing was going on between Brian and I other than an artistic 'business' arrangement of sorts. At least, that's what I tried to convince myself. The truth of the matter was that everyone probably knew it was so much more than that. But regardless of the fact that in their eyes I'd managed to find myself a rich benefactor and in mine the future love of my life, day to day living had gone on pretty much as normal in the 'Clog and Billycock', apart from one unsavoury aspect. We'd had to summon pest control due to an infestation of mice and rats. In a valiant attempt to exterminate the 'filthy blighters' himself, my dad had taken to bursting into my studio brandishing an air rifle over his head (which wasn't very conducive to producing great masterpieces I have to say) while trying to get a pot shot through my window at the vermin who liked to hang out near the gent's outside loo. Despite these constant and unwelcome interruptions to my work, I'd managed to produce some really interesting paintings; the best I'd ever done, my art tutor told me. He added that I'd finally found the confidence I needed to become a great artist, although he couldn't understand from whence this sudden burst of confidence had come. I knew of course, but I wasn't letting on.

Apart from working on the canvases I already had stacking up in my room, I'd started a new painting in an attempt to express all the mixed up emotions I was feeling about Brian. Artists always tell the story of their lives in one way or another through their work and I was no exception. This new painting was entitled, 'The Spider and the Fly' and I had become totally obsessed with it, taking Brian's words religiously to heart and working on it all day and sometimes through the night. In fact, I was working on it when he appeared unexpectedly one evening at my studio door, taking me completely by surprise, causing the brushes to shoot out of my hand and fly through the air then land at his feet like crossed swords. I could tell immediately by his disapproving stance, that he'd been drinking, and it was obvious that he was in one of his black, sombre moods, because he turned his back on me and just stood there staring at the new painting on the easel without saying a word.

I have to admit it was a disturbing piece of work; it even disturbed me - and it still does to this day. The man in the painting with the coal black hair was obviously Brian, although you couldn't actually see his face, but there was no doubt about whose hand it was squeezing the woman's buttock, the luminous flesh bulging out between his unmistakably long fingers. The headless woman was sitting astride his knee, her sloping back curved in a sensuous arch. Apart from one dark, sinister eye, peering out over her shoulder, Brian's face was hidden behind a horned mask. With one hand he was forcefully pulling the woman to him and with the other he was casually pushing her away with a long, dismissive finger. Snaking around the woman's body was a bright red tie, patterned with white net, the net slowly starting to unravel. The headless woman was me of course, unable or unwilling to acknowledge the disturbing and erotic passions this powerful, controlling man was stirring up in me and yet submitting to the contrariness of his whims nevertheless.

I waited with baited breath, anxious to hear my 'master's' comments. I was sure that he was going to like it, that he was going to tell me it was the best painting I'd ever done; that he would tell me with pride that I was 'really painting' at last. But when he finally turned round to face me, he just looked at me with cold distain before pronouncing in his most pompous voice, "You're not going to put a 'Netlon' tie on that are you?"

"Why not?" against my will my eyes filled with tears. "This painting is about you, about us. It's called 'The Spider and the Fly,' and it depicts our relationship. The tie and the net are symbolic." I quickly bent down to pick my scattered paint brushes off the floor where they lay like a game of casually tossed pick up sticks, so that he wouldn't see my tears.

"Symbolic?" Brian scoffed, tapping his long finger on the edge of the canvas with a dismissive flick, "Symbolic of what may one ask?"

"Your web," I offered weakly, clutching the bouquet of wooden brushes in my trembling hands.

"My web?" he repeated sarcastically, then sneered, "And what web would that be?"

What was he doing? Why was he being like this with me?

"You know, your power over me," I was beginning to lose my confidence.

He gave me another one of his cold, hard, uncomprehending looks and then turned on his heel and walked out of the door, leaving me standing there, staring at my 'great work of art' feeling like a deflated balloon.

I took the canvas off the easel and turned it round to face the wall; then burst into tears.

I didn't see him for days after that, and I was starting to wonder if I'd ever see him again. By this time I was totally besotted with the man and thought about little else. I had strange, tortured dreams about him every night, unsettling dreams that continued to haunt me throughout each following day. In one of these dreams, he had huge, black wings strapped to his arms and was strutting around my bed like a predatory bird. His gleaming white torso was a curve, a half moon, pivoted to the top of his long, shapely legs, and in the dream, I got out of bed and put my arms around his waist and tried to rest my head on his puffed chest. But it was too high, I couldn't reach. So I rocked the half moon of his torso with my little finger. I sat in the curve of his back and wrapped his huge, feathered wings around me. I looked up at his face and he bent over me and sank his teeth into my shoulder, shaking his head like a dog worrying a rat; releasing a blue, moon shaped bruise, which he sealed on my arm with a flick of his tongue.

I woke up with a pounding heart, my body covered with sweat. I lifted the tangled sheet and looked down at my bare arm in trepidation for the brand of the 'blue moon' or any sign of teeth marks, but of course, there was nothing there.

It had only been a dream.

He finally reappeared late one night and came up to my studio armed with a projector and a bottle of wine. We hung a white sheet on the wall, turned out all the lights and lay down on my bed to watch a slide show of an exhibition he'd just been to see in Belgium. It was my first introduction to abstract expressionism and I found it totally inspirational. I realised at that moment as we lay side by side, holding hands, lost in a mystical world of colour and form that I'd fallen in love with him and later, when he'd gone, I wrote in my diary.

"I think I love him, but don't worry," I told myself confidently, "I can handle it." Famous last words!

Brian continued with his Houdini-like pattern of disappearing and then reappearing when I least expected him to, but he knew exactly what he was doing, it was adding to his mystery and increasing my fascination for him. Only each time he disappeared I found myself waiting longer and longer for him and the longer I waited, the more I longed to see him. I waited night after night for his call.

He doesn't call. I keep working on my painting of him, 'The Spider and the Fly' until there's nothing more to do on it, nowhere else to go and exhaustion overcomes me. I throw down my brushes in despair. Where was he damn him? How could he stay away from me like this?

I try to sleep but it's impossible. I walk the floor. I stare as if bewitched at the finished painting lit by a solitary lamp, as Brian's face, hidden behind the horned mask, evolves and recedes before my eyes as I slowly rock to and fro in my white rocking chair. I hug myself.

I feel cold and empty, completely drained, now that it's finally completed. No more brush strokes to smooth out; nothing more to add. Empty tubes of paint, twisted and squashed, litter the floor. I grab my sketchpad and scrawl big, tortured words of love to him, then tear them out, screw them up and toss them in the air like origami snowballs. Screwed up thoughts, I laugh bitterly to myself and kick them around the room in frustration. Maybe we are finished too, I think forlornly, like the painting. Well good, I console myself; at least I will get my life back again. But it's already too late for that I fear. I am bereft without him. I look at my face in the mirror and it stares back at me, mocking, foreign, like a total stranger. I look mad and wild-eyed from too much time spent staring at the canvas. I try to calm myself, but my nerves are on edge. I have worked too hard, too long. I sigh in despair and my hair seems to sigh with me as I brush it away from this stranger's, this madwoman's face and my naïve, gullible, love-struck young heart sighs deep within me as I wait for tomorrow in the hope that he will come.

Is this how it is going to be from now on I ask myself? I am angry with myself for allowing him to take possession of my mind and my spirit, as well as my body.

I cannot allow it. I will not allow it and I promise myself I will escape from him.

With that resolution firmly in mind, I finally manage to rock myself to sleep in the white rocking chair, listening to the spooky, dissonant strains of Bartok and I have a strange but beautiful dream about him. I wake up stiff and aching but I quickly write it down in my best italic, slide it in a parchment envelope, carefully seal the flap and then send it to him before I have chance to change my mind.

Dear Brian,

I am sitting in my studio in the white rocking chair, listening to Bartok. It's just beginning to get light and I am looking at my painting of you, "The Spider and the Fly" and I feel so full of love and longing for you, that I can hardly bear it.

I had a very strange but incredibly beautiful dream about you sometime during the long, lonely night. I was riding on a red donkey, galloping along an endless white beach under a cobalt blue sky. Other red donkeys were racing alongside us, pressing against us, all trying to get somewhere but I do not know where.

The fur of my red donkey was wild and tufted, like a red nylon teddy bear and I was clutching on to it as hard as I could and digging my nails in so I wouldn't fall off

I was trying to hide my naked body in the fur, because chasing after us were some huge yellow and black striped bees and they were trying to sting me.

Every time I managed to cover my body with fur, the galloping motion joggled me out again. I started to frantically search amongst the red tufts, looking for something but I didn't know what. Then all at once, I found a very smooth patch of soft, red silky hair. I tried to brush it away, quickly and then slowly - and it was soft, so soft and warm.

I finally managed to part it aside and I found a body amongst the fur and it was your body. I looked deeper and I saw a face and it was your face, smiling up at me, so I kissed it. I kissed your face and you stopped smiling and pulled me down into the bright red and I could see through the crimson glow, like the sun shining through closed eyelids. Then, you jerked me down into the dark and for a moment, there were two bright red dots behind my eyes, lighting up my mind. Then they gradually faded away and I was left with nothing but the dark black warmth of you.

Adrienne

Brian kept that letter till the day he died. He kept it in the safe along with my other letters that I wrote to him over the years. And as for the painting of the 'Spider and the Fly,' well that it is still down at Brian's house 'Kenolbri' languishing with the rest of his art collection in what has now become his personal mausoleum. It will remain there, in accordance with his last Will and testament, for the next eighty years.

My mum always said that that painting was like the child Brian and I never had, because we fought over it like cat and dog and it was always backwardsing and forwardsing between us, even though Brian had officially bought it from me on more than one occasion.

One time when we'd fallen out, I'd borrowed it back for an exhibition and just for spite, I'd put it up for sale. Brian had sent one of his henchmen to the gallery to buy it back - and no, I'm not proud of the fact, but that's just the way things were between us. We had a volatile relationship to put it mildly and that painting was often used as a pawn between us. It had a history, that's for sure and it's funny how prophetic it was in its way. Apart from the fact that it clearly depicts the power Brian had and continues to have over me, it's got the swirling red ribbon on it, the international symbol for HIV/AIDS. I painted it over thirty years ago, not even knowing then what AIDS was and even if I had, never thinking for one moment in my wildest 'red donkey' dreams, that it would ever apply to me.

CHAPTER 12

The lethal bequests of love

Now here I was living a different kind of dream, only this time it was a nightmare, the nightmare that each and every one of us dreads and prays will never happen to them - the nightmare of HIV. The difference was that this time my nightmare was real. I had to wake up every day to the stark realisation that this wasn't a bad dream, it was reality and it wouldn't fade away and dissipate with the morning light. It would stay with me forever and what's more, it would only get worse. Somehow I had to come to terms with that indisputably harsh fact, as well as trying to cope with the other challenging issues that this cruel and anti-social disease throws at those of us unfortunate enough to be afflicted by it, such as the stigma and discrimination. I needed help aside from the purely physical in order to be able to survive mentally without succumbing to a profound depression, so I decided to enrol on a counselling course at Blackburn College.

My idea was that if I trained to be a counsellor, as well as helping myself, in the future when I was qualified I could also help people like me with HIV, especially through the trauma of their initial diagnosis. I remembered only too well what it felt like to hear those dreaded words, I'm sorry, but I'm afraid that the test has come back positive. In Ibiza there had been no sympathetic counsellor to hand; I'd had to step out of the doctor's surgery with those terrifying, earth shattering words echoing in my head; out of the door and into the bright, glaring sunlight - and yet for me it was dark. The darkest day I had ever known. However, that dreadful day was behind me now and nothing I felt could ever be as bad again as hearing that terrible news. If I could handle that I could handle anything, I told myself, even the nerve racking prospect of going back to college and facing a whole new group of people who didn't know my status. I had no idea how they would react to me if they did. Would these new people, these trainee counsellors, think any differently about me if they knew the truth, that I was HIV positive? Would they judge me, make presumptions about my lifestyle, avoid physical contact with me, or even want to sit next to me? At the time I was still riddled with the same stigma and paranoia about this disease as everyone else.

My mum, of course, had been totally against the idea of me going back to college, thinking that it would all be too much for me and had tried her very best to talk me out of it. I was often sick in those early days as my immune system was still compromised, so I was prone to infections and my mum worried about me coming into contact with germs. But on saying that, I'd been over protected by my mum since the day I was born, although as it turned out there was nothing even she could have done to protect me from this. She'd had her reasons however for being so fiercely protective about me as a new born infant as, tragically, she'd lost two babies before she finally managed to give birth to me. The first, who would have been my older brother Phillip, had been left on the weighing scales in the unheated hospital room for too long by the nurse, and subsequently died of pneumonia. She got pregnant again too quickly, in her grief, and within a year another brother was stillborn. Because of what happened to poor baby Phillip, my mum was paranoid about me catching cold, so she used to hide me away from danger and the public gaze. She would place me, for example, behind the clothes rack so I wouldn't be caught in a draught, therefore most of my formative years were spent in involuntary hiding.

"Don't look at her, she doesn't like it," she would shoo relations away as they cooed into my pram mouthing, 'Eeeh int she bonny,' or, 'I could eat 'er on a butty', as they tend to do up north, but in reality it was so they wouldn't breathe their filthy germs on me. She'd only recently confessed to the fact that when my Irish granddad, who was a coach painter by trade, had done up an old pram for me and decorated it with his own loving hand with my initials AJS inscribed on the side, she'd hidden it in the coal cellar and instead bought a brand new Silver Cross, (which she could hardly afford), just so I would be higher up and therefore out of reach of low flying bacteria.

I was determined however, to run the risk of contamination from my fellow students in order to train as a counsellor, so for once I'd gone against her wishes. I signed myself up, for what was going to be a lengthy process, as it would be three years until I finally qualified. I'd attended my very first session the night before, so the next morning I walked along to my mum's house to tell her all about it.

"Coffee?" she asks as soon as I get through the door, even though the milk is already on the boil about to froth over. Every morning, without fail, we follow this exact same routine. I walk the short distance along the street to her house, a few doors from mine, to check that she is alright and has survived the night (well, you never know at her age) have a coffee and a chat together and put my 'face', as in make-up, on.

"Can you just open this packet for me?" she faffs from the realms of the kitchen, "Honestly, they don't consider old people like me when they're designing these stupid things." As well as having trouble with her hands due to arthritis, not to mention her poor old legs, my mum's eyesight was rapidly starting to deteriorate and I'd had to buy two hideous, brightly striped mugs, just so she could see them to pour the milk in. But even then she sometimes missed. I would have made the coffee myself of course, but she still likes to do things for me, as she has done all her life. She gets cross with herself when, because of her failing health, she can't even perform what she used to consider the simplest task. But all in all, apart from her 'Arthur-itus' as she calls it and severe shortage of breath, caused in the main by her reluctance to give up smoking, I suppose she isn't doing too bad for her eighty odd years. I was getting worried about her eyesight though, as I didn't think she'd be able to cope if she lost her sight.

"How did college go?" she asks me, the brightly striped mug shaking in her hand as she set it on the coffee table in front of me.

"It was great, but I have to admit I was a bit nervous about meeting everyone."

"It was a very brave thing to do, all things considering," she admits, "Although I don't really understand why you're even bothering to put yourself through all that; as if you haven't got enough to contend with. And I still don't think it was a wise move, not in your condition," she chastises me.

"I'm not brave at all," I deny vigorously, ignoring her other comments.

"Yes you are," argues my mum, "And I'm proud of you."

"I'm not brave. I'm a wimp, as well you know, especially where my health is concerned. But there's one thing for sure, I wouldn't be doing it and I couldn't have got through any of this without you," I told her honestly, because I really couldn't have. Then I try to quickly change the subject before we both got too emotional (neither of us being very good at that sort of thing) and busily resorted to applying my eye makeup.

"Anyway, I can see now," I told her, although in actual fact I couldn't because I'd poked myself in the eye with my mascara wand, "how this person-centred counselling stuff can work. In fact, I think I'll try it out on Ben."

"It'll take more than a bit of counselling to sort that son of yours out," my mum frowned sternly, although she loved him to bits really, and for all his faults, he was still her favourite grandson. "Bring back national service I say, that would sort him out. That would sort the lot of them out."

"Well, maybe I'll give it a go anyway," I shrugged in despair. "I've tried everything else, but what we really need is for him to come home by himself, not because I'm telling him to, or his granny's telling him to, that's how person-centred counselling works."

Ben had refused to come back to England with me, insisting that Ibiza was his true home as he'd grown up there, and anyway, he hated

Blackburn. He still didn't know about me of course and why I had every reason to be here.

She shook her head, "You shouldn't have to be doing all this counselling stuff and wasting your time at college, mark my words it will only make you ill. It's too much for you. Anyway, it's ridiculous trying to start a new career and find a job in your condition, not to mention at your age. He should have looked after you properly."

By 'him' she meant Brian. And she had a point there.

She also had a point about it being too much for me, because I wake up the next morning and all hell had seemingly been let loose. Now what, I curse, trying to sit up without success. What the bloody hell was happening to me now? I get out of bed only to find I can't walk. I am doubled up with pain and my legs are refusing to work. I crawl to the telephone and ring my mum who rushes as fast as she can, with the aid of her stroller, down to my house. After she has caught her breath, she gets straight on the phone and calls Paul, my trusty neighbour, to drive me to hospital. By this time, I am in so much pain, I can't even lift my arms to take my nightie off to get dressed, so my mum throws a coat over my shoulders and Paul practically has to carry me to the car. Willo, of course, refusing to be left out has come with him and between them they wheel me to the clinic in a wheelchair.

Dr Gayed seems very concerned about the amount of pain I appear to be in, which seems to have no justifiable cause. He pokes and prods my stomach thinking it might be my appendix, but sends for a specialist for a second opinion. They both now suspect that it could be Shingles, but as yet there is nothing to show apart from a few red patches around my ribcage and midriff and a row of itchy spots, but hey, what's new. Dr Gayed told me later that the pain of Shingles is so intense that it is often misdiagnosed as appendicitis and there have been occasions when patients have had their appendix whipped out unnecessarily, only to find later that it was the dreaded Shingles that was the cause. There is nothing, apparently, that any doctor can do, or any treatment available to alleviate the pain of Shingles. The only thing the doctor can do is send you home with a stack of pills and a bottle of calamine lotion and you just have to sit it out, which is exactly what I did. Paul helped my mum make up a bed for me on the settee and I lay there in agony, watching daytime television and the clock ticking away the seconds on endless episodes of Countdown.

Over the next few days, the medication does its work and unsightly sores begin to sprout on my back and under my bosoms, like the surface of the moon.

Shingles - such a jolly name for such a painful condition!

My poor old mum, dabbing camomile on the weeping scabs with her arthritic hands: trying to pick me up off the floor where I'd fainted in a pool of vomit. Whoops – up come the bloody pills, including my anti-retroviral meds, my little soldiers. That won't do. Try to swallow some more, but they refuse to go down. My mum sends for Willo and she lies next to me on the bed, waking me up at the allotted time, every four hours and forcing me to swallow them. She lies at my side, listening to me talking my feverish nonsense; washing my sick-covered nighties then carefully ironing them, cutting up slivers of orange in neat half moons, mopping my brow. She takes close up photographs of my Shingles with her digital camera – 'Rich man's legacy' she calls them and says she is going to do a sculpture of them: a monument to the lethal bequests of love.

Eventually the pain eases and the scabs fall off, leaving me branded with a ring of criss crossed scars around my ribcage and circling my back you could play noughts and crosses on. But I am still finding it hard to walk, I'm constantly dizzy and I keep banging into things; I can't walk in a straight line, can't bend down without toppling over.

9th of July, six months later and I make a note of the date because I am starting to feel a bit better, the Shingles is long gone and touch wood, nothing else has recently gone amiss. I awake one morning with the dawn and experience a feeling akin to joy. I even whistle a little tune to myself as I get dressed.

Willo comes with me to the clinic for the results of my latest blood tests. Dr Gayed shakes my hand and tells me that I am doing very well and the HIV virus is now undetectable.

"Will you repeat that?" I ask him, afraid that I misheard.

"Undetectable," he smiles. Undetectable, such a lovely word. I went around all day singing to myself – *Undetectable, that's what you are…… undetectable ….. da da da da*

And guess what? A bit of new fringe was starting to grow on my forehead. I could never understand why women over a certain age grew their hair long, but now I do. It's obvious. It's because they can!

Like the age-old joke - why does a dog lick its balls?

Because it can!

Why does a man who loves you, give you Aids?

Because, unfortunately - he can.

CHAPTER 13

On the Rocks

Now I was feeling so much better health-wise, it was easier to be more optimistic and positive about life, although I was still having trouble with the word 'positive' as obviously it had a whole new double meaning for me now. Things were nevertheless starting to look up, even though I knew that thanks to my HIV status, life as I'd known it would never be the same. How could it be?

It felt good to be a student again and to have a definite purpose, a worthy goal in mind, even though I'd always been a bit suspicious of people who either needed or practised therapy and thought it was rather like the Emperor's new clothes – i.e. nothing there unless you really wanted to believe it. My life, it seemed, had turned full circle; I was back at college even though this time it was to study the more academic topic of counselling as opposed to the more frivolous, some might say (my dad for instance), indulgence of Fine Art. But it was uncanny how somehow the circle always seemed to spiral right back to Brian.

By absconding to art college all those years ago I'd managed to briefly escape from my patron 'The Spider's' clutches, although he'd never really forgiven me for choosing to follow my own path and break free from his strategically woven web. Even though I'd known my actions would disrupt his agenda for me as an artist, I'd also had a strategy, a hidden agenda of my own. Without him knowing, I'd been secretly applying to art colleges and I'd trailed up and down the country with my huge art folder tucked under my arm, so far without success. I'd been rejected from all of them. Of course, I never let on to Brian that I'd been rejected, or to anybody for that matter. But not about to give up, I finally decided who wanted a place at one of their second-rate institutions anyway and instead applied to one of the best and most fashionable art schools in England, which at the time was St Martin's in London. To my amazement I got an interview, so off I went down to London on the train, laden with my huge portfolio and a couple of canvases, one of which was 'The Spider and the Fly.' The competition was incredibly fierce and my chances of being accepted seemed extremely slim, but against all the odds and, according to one of the tutors who had interviewed me, it was the painting of 'The Spider and the Fly' that had finally swung it for me. So against his will, Brian had unwittingly secured my passport to freedom. I was offered a place and I was over the moon. I carefully chose my moment to tell him, knowing that he wouldn't be happy about it. And I wasn't wrong.

"Please don't go to London, Adrienne," he begged me, "I couldn't bear it - and anyway, I can do far more for you than any art college."

"But Brian, it's a once in a lifetime opportunity," I tried to reason with him, "I managed to get in against all that competition. Surely you're proud of me? I thought you wanted me to be a great artist."

"You are already a great artist and I can make you an even greater one," he pronounced sulkily. "I can set you up with exhibitions all over Europe, which is more than any art college can do."

"I don't want everything made easy for me and laid on a plate," I told him stubbornly. "I suppose you want to suffer for your art and starve in a garret," he threw back sarcastically. "Yes, I 'suppose' I do," I answered.

In those days I foolishly believed in the myth that great art could only come out of great suffering. I was also, in my way, rebelling against being controlled as an artist and of falling into the age-old trap, that artists over the years have been forced to succumb to in order to survive, which is financial ownership by their patron.

"Stay here with me then and we'll get married," Brian suddenly proposed, offering as I saw it then, yet another form of control.

"Married?" I echoed stupidly. "I don't want to get married. I don't want to be a wife. I want to be an artist."

Wives didn't paint did they? They cooked and cleaned and were social hostesses. Even if, by the grace of Brian's vast wealth, I may have been reprieved from the more mundane domestic obligations, being a wife (especially to a multi-millionaire) would entail looking and acting the part. It would mean endless visits to the beauty parlour and the hairdresser, dealing with servants and the running of a big house. There was no way I could take on that particular role, no matter how much I loved him and that's what he would have expected of me. I remembered what he'd told me about his first wife and how she'd cracked under the pressure of it all.

We'd been sitting on the white sofas in the sunroom at the time, during one of our secret midnight sojourns. Brian had been in a particularly sombre mood that night I recall and his hands had been shaking even more than usual. He'd told me that his divorce had finally come through and that he was now a free man, but he didn't seemed to be celebrating the fact.

"She simply didn't understand me," he'd sighed, using the age-old excuse. "And when she found out we couldn't have children, she started to drink. One night, I remember, I'd invited some very important business associates round for dinner and she appeared at the top of the stairs, blind drunk, screaming and shouting abuse at me. Then she tripped over her evening gown and toppled down the stairs, her gown ending up over her head. I think the pressure of living with me was too much for her and I was away a lot. I tried to help her of course," he shook his head sadly, "I took her on holiday to Switzerland, but she went crazy saying she could see little men in top hats running up and down the hotel corridors. In the end I had to send her to a clinic to dry out, but it was no use; she was an alcoholic by that time." He'd stood up at that untimely point and poured us both another drink, "Anyway, that's all in the past now," he sighed and put his arm around me, "I'd much rather talk about us. You know, I've never felt this way about anyone before. I think about you constantly, day and night, night and day."

With his words the moon suddenly appeared from behind a cloud, filling the long glass room with shimmering reflections and a strange blue light. It was as if someone had filled it up with water, illuminating the sweeping crescent of waxy white orchids on the coffee table, making them appear to be lit from within by ultraviolet light and floating on a sea of crystal glass. In stark contrast, Brian's face was in complete shadow, his solemn features indistinguishable and yet the collar of his shirt and the edges of the starched cuffs encircling his long, white hands were glowing brightly.

I felt him take a deep, shuddering breath, as he pulled me closer to him and then started to caress me with the luminous white glove of his hand. I watched transfixed as the seemingly unattached glove moved over my body and performed its magic. We made love that night for the very first time to the wild accompaniment of Bartok and afterwards, we sat stunned and silent, filled with wonder that we had found each other at last.

He was due to leave in a few hours to fly to Switzerland and his suitcase was packed and ready in the hall. I'd wanted to go with him but he'd said no, not this time, there would be plenty of other times he'd promised, handing me his big, white handkerchief to dry my tears. Then, as the early morning sun tinged the garden with a fluorescent rosy glow, he'd driven me home and kissed me goodbye in the doorway, no longer caring if anyone saw us. I'd gone straight upstairs to my room and lain down on my bed eager to relive the magical events of the night before in my head. Bursting with all the new emotions that were flooding my body, I wanted to share them with him before he left, so I picked up the phone and dialled his number. I didn't usually call his house; in fact, this was the very first time. The phone rang twice and then his deep, shaky voice answered. "Hello, it's me," I'd offered nervously, "I just wanted to tell you...."

Click. He'd slammed the phone down.

"That I think I love you," I told the silent phone. I buried my face in the big white handkerchief he'd given me earlier and cried my heart out. It had that very special aroma of him woven into every fibre and stitched into every seam. I'd breathed it in for all my worth, but it wasn't long before I'd become too accustomed to the familiar scent of him and had to move it away from my face, only to bring it back again a few seconds later to renew the sensation. Love is like that, I'd thought sadly to myself. You become too accustomed to each other and have to move away in order to fall in love all over again when you reunite. And maybe that's what Brian had done, I tried to convince myself, or perhaps the sheer intensity of the depth of our newly discovered feelings for each other had somehow frightened him, causing him to back off. But at that moment, it felt to me as though he'd handed his love to me in that now tear-soaked, creased and crumpled handkerchief, then taken it back, put it in his pocket and probably intended to send it off to the laundry the following day.

Recalling that not too distant memory and being reminded of the way Brian could suddenly push me away and then hook me back with a twist of his little finger, I knew there was no way I could marry him and be subject to his contrary will for the rest of my life. Then there was the disturbing evidence of what had happened to his ex-wife. Perhaps the same thing would happen to me?

No, I couldn't suddenly become the wife (and all that it entailed) of a very rich man. I didn't even like rich people and although I'd fallen in love with Brian, sometimes I didn't even like him. Besides, I was only twenty-one, too young to settle down and become his wife or anyone's wife for that matter. I wanted to be an artist, a brilliant artist. I was eager to learn, to succeed on my own merit, not his money and to make him proud of me. Anyway, the thought of leaving Blackburn and living in London was far too exciting a prospect.

"Going to Art College won't change how I feel about you," I told him honestly, "We can still see each other. You can come down to London and take me out for tea at the Savoy." He was not amused.

"Well, if that's what you want," he stood up angrily and stomped off, "It's your decision."

Whether it was the right decision or the wrong one, I will never know. But a few weeks later, my dad drove me down to London; the car packed to the hilt with all my various bits and pieces and my painting equipment of course, the tip of my easel poking out of a side window offering a wooden finger up to Blackburn as we sped off down the motorway to the great metropolis and my new life. My dad waited until I was safely installed in my new living quarters, a single room in a student hostel on the third floor of a small tower block, just over the Albert Bridge. My room comprised a narrow single bed, a wardrobe with a sliding door which also housed a washbasin, and a wooden desk complete with the scribblings and ink marks of the previous student occupier. The desk was conveniently situated under a large dusty window which looked out across the busy traffic-filled road and over the windswept tree tops of Battersea Park. Later, in the early spring, those same autumnal trees would be resplendent with pink cherry blossoms, but for now they were nothing more than bleak reminders of the approaching winter, silhouetted against the sulphurous glow of the vast and unfamiliar city sky.

After my dad had reluctantly taken his leave, loath to leave his daughter to the mercy of the big city, I sat on the narrow, unmade bed, feeling truly alone for the first time. I suddenly felt very far from home and was beginning to have severe misgivings about what I'd done, taking off like that without even making the effort to at least contact Brian to say goodbye. But then again, he hadn't made any effort to contact me. I looked around my cell-like room despondently. I was missing my dad already and he'd only been gone for five minutes and I felt homesick for the 'Clog.' But most of all I was missing Brian. We hadn't spoken since I'd broken the news to him, and although I'd felt guilty about leaving him, especially after all he'd done for me, I'd been too excited about everything else to truly consider his feelings. He'd come round to my way of thinking eventually, I'd told myself. But I'd forgotten who I was dealing with.

To ease my feelings of excruciating loneliness, I poked my head around the door and wandered along the corridor in the hope of meeting some of the other new students. But they were all busily settling into their rooms. I would catch up with them later in the canteen for dinner, I thought to myself, and decided to pass the time until then by going outside for a walk to familiarise myself with my new surroundings. I descended the three flights of concrete stairs and ventured out of the main entrance, where the noise of the busy traffic hit me like a barrage of artillery, nearly bowling me over with its intensity. Clutching my bag firmly to my side, I tentatively crossed over the Albert Bridge, feeling dwarfed by its sheer enormity, which afforded me the belittling sensation of appearing to be even more insignificant than I already felt. Once on the other side, I set off bravely along the King's Road, all the way to World's End, glancing in the brightly lit windows of the many hippy shops with their range of ethnic wares, and weird and wonderful posters advertising transcendental meditation and Yoga. An all pervading smell of patchouli and incense wafted out onto the street. I meandered along the fashionable road, passing the American hamburger joints and bistros. The pubs were crowded, jam-packed with long haired men dressed in velvet jackets and frilly shirts and sophisticated looking women with haughty faces. The thought suddenly struck me that I didn't know one single soul in this entire city, inducing in me a feeling of total panic. I quickly turned tail, and almost ran back over the Albert Bridge, dodging the cars beeping their horns at me like I was some kind of country bumpkin; back to the unfamiliar safety of the tower block.

But what a great feeling to actually be in London; it was what I had always wanted. And London really was 'swinging' as they said in those days and St Martin's School of Art was 'the' place to be. My arrival on the scene coincided with those most decadent of times; the smoking of pot, the taking of recreational drugs, David Bowie, cross-gender dressing, outrageous fashions and debauched lifestyles and I wanted to be a part of it all. Well, maybe not the debauched lifestyles, but certainly to be there right in the heart of it all and back again with my own generation. Brian was from another era as far as I was concerned and at times it showed.

On my first day at the prestigious as well as notorious St Martin's School of Art, I walked through those famous doors feeling proud and privileged to be there, but also very nervous. Was I really a good enough painter to be here? What would my fellow first year students be like and, more importantly, would they all be better artists than me? Riddled with self doubt, I paced up and down the maze of corridors looking for the Fine Art studios. It was a huge warehouse-like building, which, as well as being home to the Fine Art department, also housed the renowned sculpture and fashion departments. There were students rushing everywhere and the smell of paint and linseed oil filled the air, the familiar stench making me feel slightly more at home. This was where I was meant to be, with young people, with artists, the cream of the creative world. St Martin's had the reputation at the time, of producing the most interesting new artists in all the creative fields: painters, sculptors and fashion designers, and I was now lucky enough to be counted as one of the select few.

I finally managed to locate the first year Fine Art studio, which was a cavernous room framed by enormous dusty windows looking down on the Charing Cross road. The room was partitioned into sections, each cubicle splattered with paint and obscure poetic words that previous students had daubed on the walls and left as their insignia, like prisoners on their cell walls. I wondered which cubicle I would be allocated and hoped it would be by a window so I could benefit from the natural light.

All the other new students were huddled together in a corner of the room looking lost and obviously feeling as insecure as I was. We were an odd looking bunch, it has to be said. We had all been specifically selected for our very different styles of painting, so there were a wide range of characters and (being temperamental artists), egos I supposed.

The tutors, who appeared to be even more eccentric and bizarre than their new students, briefly introduced themselves before allocating us our workspaces. I laid out my oil paints territorially on the work table and commandeered an easel. Then, in order to break the ice, and as a supposed confidence building exercise, we were instructed to stand in a circle while one unfortunate student was singled out and ordered to lay flat on the floor in the centre of the circle. The rest of us then had to lift the poor soul up and down in the air, his dreadlocked hair sweeping the paint stained floor, as though we were giving him the birthday bumps. We were supposed to take it in turns to be on the receiving end of this bizarre ritual, but after a while someone said, 'Sod this for a game of soldiers. I'm off to the pub,' and everyone followed suit. The busy, inner city pub was very different from the 'Clog.' It was packed to the doors with interesting looking people; theatrical types, actors, newspaper reporters and eccentric gay couples.

Loud conversation ricocheted around the nicotine-stained walls competing with the music blasting from the jukebox and the fuggy air was blue with smoke. There, in the noisy, bustling pub, we broke the ice and got to know each other in a more typical art student way, and after a few drinks, I teamed up with a dreamy looking hippy called Kathy and a butch lesbian called Liz. Kathy had long, pre-Raphaelite locks and a flask of Southern Comfort in her bag alongside her watercolours. Although we were an odd threesome, we instantly became firm friends and remained so throughout our entire time there.

I'd still heard nothing from Brian, no goodbyes, no letters; no phone calls to see how I was getting on. I was missing him like mad, but I tried to put him out of my mind and concentrate on my new life at St Martin's. Being the diverse and experimental institution that it was, rather than teaching us the straightforward techniques of painting and drawing, our first work assignment had been to create a 'happening.' Mine involved, for some reason I can't quite remember, a goldfish swimming in a Perspex tank, and I was in the process of carrying a bucketful of slimy green pond water back from the park, trying hard not to spill it, when I bumped into Albert, my tutor.

"Two gentlemen were up in the Fine Art department looking for you," he informed me, obviously impressed. "They said they would come back later."

Brian? My heart leapt. It had to be. I certainly didn't know anyone else around here who could be described as a 'gentleman'.

Later on that same afternoon, I was down on my hands and knees draping the box that held the Perspex tank with black plastic bin liners and just about to launch the goldfish, when I saw Brian's shiny crocodile skin shoes suddenly appear in my line of vision. I looked up and there he was, towering over me.

"I've come to take you out for tea at the Savoy," he smiled down at me.

He was with his best friend, Tony Wilsonholme, and the pair of them looked very out of place in their Savile Row suits and long overcoats, amongst the scruffy, paint splattered students. I grabbed the long blue velvet cape I'd recently bought out of my grant, and threw it over my work clothes; then the three of us boarded the rickety, black metal cage of the lift and precariously descended to street level. Once outside on the Charing Cross road, Tony hailed a taxi and I climbed in the back with Brian, while Tony sat on the folding chair facing us, and we drove through the busy streets of London to the Savoy Hotel.

I'd never been anywhere as luxurious as the Savoy in my life and felt justifiably nervous as the taxi pulled up outside the revolving glass door. A resplendent footman, dressed in a top hat and tails, and who obviously knew Brian well, opened the taxi door with a flourish and heralded us in. Brian and Tony walked protectively either side of me as I swept across the marbled floor in my long, flowing cape, causing a few quizzical looks from the staff on the reception desk. I was then escorted along the thickly carpeted corridor to the mirrored elevator and up to Brian's suite on the fifth floor (I later discovered that this was the one he was always allocated while staying at the Savoy). I felt as though I had been suddenly whisked into another world. The suite was the height of elegance, of course, if rather dated, with mirrored doors, huge white lamps and an enormous window which looked down over the river Thames. There were several other businessmen already in the room, including Ted Hodgkinson, Brian's lawyer, the missing member of the 'Three Wise Monkeys.' The authoritative looking businessmen were all sitting around a polished wooden table with papers and folders spread out in front of them. Brian must have interrupted their meeting to come and get me, and by the icy looks they were giving me, evidently they weren't too pleased about it, especially 'Fat Ted' as I'd christened him for obvious reasons. But they would never dare to complain to Brian of course.

I sat primly on the gold velvet sofa feeling very out of place, pretending to look out of the huge window at the magnificent vista of London's famous river, while surreptitiously trying to scratch the dried up paint off my nails. Brian very courteously asked me what I would like to drink, then after passing me my gin and tonic, casually strolled back to take his place at the head of the conference table. Clinking ice buckets and bottles of scotch came and went, wheeled in on trolleys by seemingly invisible waiters. After a while, feeling as though I was invisible myself, amongst all that business talk and masculinity, the urge to make my escape back to my familiar world of paint and turps ever mounting, I was on the point of excusing myself and taking my leave, when Brian, obviously sensing that I was about to do a runner, suddenly rushed over to my side and took my hand.

"Why don't you come to Paris with me tomorrow?" he suggested out of the blue.

"Paris?" I exclaimed, completely taken off guard, "I can't. What about college and anyway, I don't have my passport with me." I made a mental note never to leave home without it ever again. I'd never been to Paris and would have loved to have gone, especially with Brian. It was every artist's dream and the thought of being there in the city of lovers with him was particularly romantic

On Brian's instructions, Ted made a feeble attempt at ringing round various offices to try to get me a temporary passport, but with no success. Giving up in disgust, he threw his fat belly back in a silken armchair, sneered in my direction then made a derogatory comment about the size of my bosoms. How dare he? I knew the man didn't like me for some reason and disapproved of Brian's relationship with me and maybe that was why he felt justified in insulting me. But nevertheless, I felt his behaviour was totally uncalled for and out of order. I looked meaningfully over at Brian, willing him to stand up for me, but either he hadn't heard Ted's snide comment or had chosen to ignore it, because he was carrying on as if nothing had happened and was busily pouring himself yet another drink. In retrospect, I'd wished I'd been quicker off the mark by retaliating with something equally derogatory about Ted, but I was too intimidated by his apparent worldliness and supposed sophistication, and Brian (who was drunk by this time) hadn't exactly jumped to my defence. So I waited, inwardly seething, until they'd emptied the final whisky bottle and went off to their own rooms and Brian and I were finally left alone.

"Why didn't you say anything?" I demanded sulkily, referring to Ted's rude comment.

"Oh, don't take any notice of Ted," Brian casually smirked, as in boys will be boys, "He's like that with everyone. Just forget it. Come to the bedroom and lie down on the bed and relax," he suggested, opening a mirrored door and disappearing into the dimly lit adjoining room. I followed meekly behind him and sat on the edge of the ornate gilded stool in front of the Elizabeth Taylor-styled dressing table, watching his reflection through the three mirrors as he started to change out of his business suit into a short, black silk kimono I'd never seen before, still wearing his black crocodile skin shoes and silk socks. I don't know if it was the lighting, but his legs looked improbably long and very white and the short black kimono was barely managing to cover his bottom. He looked vaguely ridiculous standing there still wearing his shoes and socks, but at the same time there was something almost threatening about him, as if being who he was, he knew he could get away with anything, even looking silly.

By this time, I was beginning to wonder what I was doing here, as this whole scenario didn't feel right somehow. This wasn't the Brian I knew, the person I'd fallen in love with. This Brian was all about power and money and I was suddenly seeing a very different side to him to the one he presented at home. Here in London, in his plush suite at the Savoy, he was Brian the businessman, Brian the multimillionaire, rich, powerful and manipulative. But nevertheless, I did as I was told and nervously perched on one of the high twin beds and following his example, slowly started to undress. I was hoping that, stripped of the armour of his business suit, and the even more unfamiliar and vaguely threatening martial arts-styled kimono, he would somehow change back into the Brian I knew and loved.

From my elevated position on, what now felt to be more like the sacrificial bed, I watched as this apparent stranger, still swaddled by the unfamiliar oriental kimono, made his way slowly around the room turning off most of the lights, then staggering slightly, made his way unsteadily towards me, the ice bucket rattling in his shaky hands. His long shadow bent across the wall and half way across the ceiling like a Balinese shadow puppet and I imagined I could see (or at least I thought it was my imagination) the shadow of a black horn curving out from the kimono like a bent, black penis. Although it was boiling hot in the room, I suddenly felt a cold shiver of fear run up my spine. But before I had chance to put my clothes back on and make a run for it, he lunged towards me and taking a lump of ice out of the bucket, bent over me and started to rub it over my body, trying to push it inside me. The unexpected shock of the frozen ice against my feverish skin made me reel in horror and I roughly pushed his hand away.

"What on earth are you doing?" I asked totally bewildered.

"Just relax and enjoy it," he slurred, "I won't hurt you."

I tried to get off the bed but he held onto me with a vice-like grip and started to kiss me, gently at first, then as I slowly began to relax in his familiar arms, I felt the old passion for him start to return, so I kissed him back. He tried to make love to me but obviously the ice hadn't had the desired effect (whatever that was supposed to be!) and besides, he was too drunk. He eventually gave up and rolled off me with a grunt, then shuffled off to the bathroom, leaving me lying there between the damp sheets, feeling cold, miserable and abandoned.

After a while, he came back wearing his perfectly pressed pale blue pyjamas and slid into the dry, pristine bed next to me, with the sheet neatly turned down.

"Goodnight Adrienne," he pursed his lips in a kiss, turned over and went straight to sleep. I watched him as he lay there hardly moving, his body, corpse-like beneath the sheet, tinged a dull orange by the eternal London glow.

I didn't know what to do. Should I just sneak off and go back to the Hall of Residence? I had just about enough money for a taxi. I'd felt like I'd been somehow violated by his bizarre ritual with the ice, and worse, I was now forced to acknowledge that there was a kinkier sexual side to this man with whom I was so in love, that I wasn't familiar with - and didn't particularly want to be.

I lay there staring at his hunched back; he'd turned over by this time and was snoring ever so slightly. I wanted to climb in next to him and curl up in the safety of his familiar arms, but somehow those arms didn't feel so safe anymore, or so familiar. So instead, I lay there, damp and shivering on my high bed, until I finally fell into a fitful asleep.

When I awoke the next morning, he'd already gone off to Paris with Ted without even saying goodbye. I leapt out of bed in a panic in case the maids came in and found me. Was the bed still wet I worried and what would those maids in their frilly pink aprons and neat little caps think of me if it was? I was angry with Brian, to put it mildly, for not waking me up before he left, so in an act of vengeance I stuffed the Savoy notepaper and envelopes in my bag, along with the bubble bath, the spare toilet roll and the contents of the fruit basket, but decided against the towel and the bathrobe in case I ever returned. I did, however, when I was halfway through the door, decide to go back and empty the minibar. Liz, Kathy and I would enjoy that later, especially the champagne. Then I beat a hasty retreat along the thickly carpeted corridors and out (by mistake) through the servant's entrance. It must have been my natural homing instincts. Once a peasant, always a peasant, I thought to myself as I sat down at the café under Charing Cross bridge, along with all the down and outs, and breathed a huge sigh of relief. I stirred my cup of tea in its cracked beaker and looked up at the window of his suite, thinking about all the strange goings on that must take place in those hotel rooms by night. I imagined the maids in their immaculate pink aprons busily stripping our high twin beds while chatting away to each other. From the absence of 'freebies' not to mention basic necessities like writing paper and loo rolls, they must have thought that Brian had suddenly turned into a prolific letter writer, not to mention drinker (although they were probably used to that) with a liking for fruit, a bed-wetting problem and an acute case of diarrhoea.

Back at St Martins, there was mild curiosity as to who my well-heeled companions had been. The Scottish socialist who worked in the next cubicle to me, and had already, in his chauvinistic way, marked me down as a 'Sunday afternoon painter', passing time until I got married, growled in my direction: "Och aye, yous'll probably do very well and sell to banks." This was the worst insult he could throw at me; although it sounded quite promising to me.

Liz, Kathy and I went for a Wimpy at lunchtime. Liz had a thing about fast food and all things normal and mundane to try to equalise her weirdness. By that I don't mean she was weird because she was a lesbian. She was just weird full stop and her choice of clothing did nothing to detract from this illusion. For example, that particular day she had chosen to don some baggy, diamond-patterned clown pants with red braces over an old ladies surgical vest, coupled with some vicious looking Doc Marten boots and a knitted bobble hat on her cropped head.

While we were eating our greasy burgers I told them about the ice cubes.

"Maybe he's into having it off with dead bodies," Liz snorted loudly, adjusting her braces in order to accommodate the cheeseburger, as well as her mirth. The people on the next table with their tomato sauce-smeared offspring, turned round to look at us in horror, faces aghast.

"Millionaires are always kinky," Kathy added knowingly, washing her burger down with a slug of Southern Comfort from her flask, "That's how they rise to riches and fame."

We laughed about the ice all the way home, clutching our stomachs and swinging on the leather straps as the underground train roared its way through the claustrophobic black tunnels from Piccadilly Station to Sloane Square.

As soon as Brian got back from Paris, he called me up at college and invited me for lunch at the Savoy. "Bring some of your artist friends," he offered, "And I'll book a private dining room."

I had my reservations after our last rendezvous, but the temptation was just too strong not to see him again, so I did as he asked. There were about twelve of us in total and we arrived at the Savoy, causing a few raised eyebrows with our strange array of fashions and unkempt hairstyles. Being 'starving art students' they all had enormous appetites, but I was far too nervous about seeing Brian again to even think about eating.

"Peeled grapes in champagne," Kathy sighed, licking her lips in anticipation, more for the champagne, it has to be said, rather than the grapes.

"Steak tat arrrrrrrr," the Scottish socialist growled, salivating at the mere thought.

"Are there no beef burgers?" Liz complained.

Brian was in his element, surrounded by artists for a change, instead of boring businessmen and the conversation was animated and lively, developing into lengthy, heated debates about art, as the luncheon party continued well into the cocktail hour. When the other students had eventually staggered home, most of them as drunk as lords and Brian and I were finally left on our own, he suggested that we go up to his suite for a drink.

"Perhaps that's not such a good idea," I declined nervously, remembering the last time and the unfortunate episode with the ice cubes. "Why don't we have a drink in the bar instead?" The only ice I had in mind that night would be floating in my gin and tonic! But Brian didn't take kindly to being turned down or having his plans interfered with.

"I'll order you a taxi then," he said huffily. "Bring madam's cape," he ordered the waiter. He wrapped my velvet cape around my shoulders, then ushered me to the door and after tipping the doorman, pecked me briskly on the cheek as I climbed into the back of a black cab. I turned to wave at him as the taxi pulled away, but the revolving brass door had already spun him back into the Savoy, and his 'other' life.

CHAPTER 14

The Great Oracle

After our last, disastrous rendezvous at the Savoy i.e. the drunken luncheon party with my reprobate art student pals, Brian had seen fit to not contact me and the longer he left it, the more I was determined not to contact him. I was used to his erratic, moody behaviour by now and to be honest, there was so much going on in my life at that time I didn't pay it much mind. Instead, I totally immersed myself in my painting and living my new life as an art student. Time passed and late one evening, I was standing in the corridor of the student's hall of residence, shivering in my old embroidered kaftan which also served as a makeshift nightdress, talking to my dad on the phone.

"Sorry dad, what did you say?" I clutched the phone tightly to my chest and took a deep, steadying breath. "Can you repeat that?" I could have sworn he'd said something about Brian having been sighted driving up and down the road outside the 'Clog and Billycock' on a yellow scooter with a young opera singer on the back. My ears must have been playing tricks on me, I quickly reasoned, because Brian would never be seen dead on a scooter, let alone a yellow one. A Lamborghini was more his style and anyway, wasn't he too old for such youthful antics?

"Yes, a Lambretta," my dad confirmed, trying in his own strange way I suppose to lighten the news. "Anyway love, never mind all that, how are you doing? How's college going?"

"Which opera singer?" I interrupted tartly, as if I knew hundreds of them. Actually, now I came to think about it, I had a pretty good idea who my dad had been referring to. "You mean that Vera, don't you? She's always had her eye on him." Vera had been in the 'Clog' on several occasions with her sister, a glamorous air hostess and the pair of them had made a direct bee line for Brian.

"Well love, according to the Lancashire Evening Telegraph," said my dad, hurrying to get it over with, "They're engaged and about to get married."

As soon as he'd hung up, I immediately scrounged some change from a passing student and dialled Brian's home number.

For once he picked up. "Is it true?" I screamed down the phone.

"Is what true, Adrienne?" he sighed.

"That you've been driving up and down outside the 'Clog' on a yellow scooter with that bloody opera singer." I think the yellow scooter was upsetting me as much as anything else. "And you've gone and got yourself engaged."

"So what if I have?" He demanded defensively, "What would you care?" He sounded a bit drunk, "And yes, it's true." There was silence for a moment as my world fell from under my feet, "Well, what was I supposed to do," he slurred belligerently, "Sit here and wait for you for three years while you were in London studying for your degree?"

"But everyone says she's a gold-digger," I shouted angrily. To be honest, people said that about any woman who was interested in Brian; they'd probably said exactly the same about me and yet here I was about to cast the very same aspersions. "She probably only wants you to further her career; it won't work, you know," I raged hysterically, "You'll have another divorce on your hands before you know where you are and then you'll come crying to me again

Silence.

"Well?"

"Come back to Blackburn then," he bribed, "Before it's too late."

"It's already too late," I announced decisively, "Well, at least until I've finished my degree."

That would have been his opportunity to rectify the situation, by agreeing to wait for me. But no, he chose to let it go. The line went dead. He'd hung up on me.

I read about the wedding in the local paper a few months later. My mum had very kindly sent me a copy. It was waiting for me when I got back from my part time job - washing kipper plates at the old musician's home in Soho. Just what you need! Vera, the opera diva, as Liz and Kathy had aptly christened her, hadn't wasted much time in getting him down the aisle, had she, I fumed. "Apparently," I told them, "He bought her a white grand piano, a Steinway no less, as a wedding present and even took her singing coach on honeymoon with them. Couldn't have been much of a honeymoon then, could it," I looked at Liz and Kathy for confirmation, trying to console myself, "with her practising her scales and tickling the ivories all day."

But that wasn't the end of it. To totally rub salt in the wound, I later discovered he'd only gone and taken his brand new wife with him to meet Salvador Dali, my absolute idol in those days, who was painting his portrait at the time. It should have been me and not her, I inwardly raged, but I had to stop tormenting myself with these jealous visions and try not to think about it in too much detail, otherwise I would have driven myself stark raving mad. The opera diva was welcome to him I decided and the best of British luck to her. Instead, I threw myself wholeheartedly into my work and in trying to survive in London living on a student grant, which wasn't easy. Liz, Kathy and I had rented a flat together in Richmond by this time, and we'd all had to take part time jobs in order to pay the rent. Kathy worked in a 'Help the Aged' shop, Liz was a barmaid in a gay pub and I also became an usherette in a local cinema. As well as that, on Wednesdays and Fridays, I still washed plates in the old musician's home in Soho. Wednesdays it was Welsh Rarebit, which wasn't too bad, but on Fridays, it was kippers. To this day I can't look at a kipper, especially as I now associate them with Brian's marriage to the opera diva.

I decided to go up North for the Easter vacation. My mum had been reporting back to me with regular updates on the, as we liked to think of it 'doomed' marriage, gleaned from local tittle-tattle she'd overheard from the customers, who like us, enjoyed a good gossip and were dying for it to all go wrong. She'd also informed me that Brian had been frequently coming in to the 'Clog' and standing at the bar on his own, looking desolate and repeatedly asking her how I was in his deep, miserable voice.

"But how is she *really,* Doreen?" I could just picture him laying it on thick for my mum.

How was I really? Well, I was fuming with him of course and seething with jealousy, not to mention suffering from a broken heart.

Word must have quickly spread that I was back in Blackburn, because I'd only been home for a day, when a hand-delivered invitation arrived requesting my presence at a garden party at 'Kenolbri.'

"The cheek of the man; how dare he?" I ranted to my mum, "A garden party? I'll bet that was her idea. Who does she think she is, the Queen bloody Mother?"

"Well, at least you'd get to meet her and find out what's really going on," my mum suggested, playing devil's advocate.

"I've already met her," I sniffed, "And I don't particularly want to meet her again. What's he trying to do, rub my nose in it?"

But the temptation was just too great in the end and with more than a bit of motherly encouragement I decided to 'attend', telling everyone that it was only out of curiosity to see how Vera was reacting to her new role as Lady of the Manor. But the real truth of the matter was, I was desperate to see Brian again.

When I arrived at 'Kenolbri' on the allotted day, with a certain amount of trepidation it has to be said, the first thing I noticed was that the entire house had been refurbished. God, that hadn't taken her long, she's a fast worker, I thought to myself; but then I already knew that.

The old-fashioned furnishings Brian had been so fond of, passed down through the generations, had all been done away with and more modern additions now stood in their place. Gone were the slightly faded Persian rugs, the sitting room floor was now carpeted from wall to wall in a rich, rose pink. How had she managed to talk him into that; Brian hated pink.

Talking of Brian, where was he? My heart was turning somersaults as I looked around the room, hoping for a glimpse of him, but I made a staunch effort to compose myself. There were two new sage green settees, I noted with appreciation, with neat rows of brightly coloured silk scatter cushions; actually, I quite liked those, they brightened up the room and were more in line with my taste. But I wasn't keen on the chintzy floral curtains now replacing the familiar heavy velvet drapes that Brian used to ceremoniously draw when twilight fell, to shut out the prying eyes of the world and close us in, like the final curtain on the day's end. The dark, dramatic feel of the house had completely gone and it now felt light and airy, filled with a new energy as though it was a different house, a show house, something out of 'House and Garden' with a decided feminine touch and not somewhere I would have imagined Brian would have chosen to live. I was pleased to see however that his collection of paintings was still hanging on the newly painted walls, including one of mine.

The new 'Lady of the Manor' hadn't yet tampered too much with the long, glass sunroom, the two white sofas where Brian and I had spent so many happy hours were still facing each other across the glass coffee table. But now, standing in pride of position and taking up more than its fair share of floor space, stood the infamous white grand piano; its territorial wooden legs planted firmly on the heated marble tiles with its flap defiantly pointing skywards.

For some reason, the overpowering presence of the grand piano annoyed me even more than the 'grand' presence of Vera herself, who I had yet to clap eyes on, but what did it have to do with me? After all, how or where the newlyweds chose to arrange their furniture, or grand bloody pianos, had little, or in fact nothing to do with me now. I looked frantically around for Brian. He should be here to welcome his guests, but he was nowhere to be seen. Instead my coat had been taken from me at the door by a young man who looked liked an impromptu butler. Where had he sprung from?

I stood nervously in a corner of the sunroom, clutching my drink and feeling like the traditional wallflower, surrounded by people I'd never seen before in my life and by the sound of them, would never want to see ever again. I could hear a lot of pretentious, theatrical-sounding chitter chatter. No wonder Brian was nowhere to be found. He couldn't stand listening to small talk. Moving away, I glanced out of the window and caught my first sight of Vera, who was sitting on the lawn next to the pool, another new addition - the diggers, aside from gold, I thought bitterly, must have been out in full force. She was delicately plucking a guitar with her long, manicured nails and warbling something operatic to her captive audience. I resisted the overwhelming desire to rush outside and quietly strangle the woman, but I was pleased to hear that she was already doing quite a good job of that herself on some of the higher notes. I quickly pulled myself together. I must behave with dignity. Where was Brian? He had to be around somewhere, but where?

I sat myself down next to a very odd looking couple who were huddled up together on one of the white sofas. The distinguished looking man, sporting a huge black fedora over his curly silver hair and a jewelled collar around his neck, was swathed in a long, black cape, draped dramatically over his right shoulder and adorned with a diamond pin. The woman who was clinging to his side, bore an uncanny resemblance to Morticia, the wife from out of the Adams family. She was also clothed from head to toe in black, her voluptuous form obscured by a long flowing kaftan, apart from her protuberant white cleavage over which her deathly pale face waned like a rising moon. Two curtains of shiny raven's wing hair theatrically framed her ghostly countenance, accentuating her blue kohl-ringed eyes, which peered out in a glazed, non-seeing manner from under her long, straight fringe.

"Hello darling, let me introduce myself," the elegant man in the cape stood up and dramatically offered me his gold embossed card, "I'm Prince Tcherbanev, astrologer and tarot reader to the stars. And this is my lovely wife, Anne."

"Pleased to meet you both," I jokingly curtsied without getting up, still looking out for Brian.

"But you may call me Erik," Prince Tcherbanev gushed, "And may I say what beautiful green eyes you have darling," he kissed my hand, "You remind me of Melina Mercouri."

I declined to correct Prince, whatever his name was, by pointing out that my eyes weren't in fact green, they were blue actually. I wasn't entirely sure if Melina Mercouri was still alive, and even if she was, she must certainly be knocking on a bit by now, but I let it go. I was beginning to experience similar doubts about Morticia's mortality to be quite frank, who if not dead already, was certainly giving off the impression that she was soon about to leave this mortal coil. But then she suddenly seemed to awaken from her corpse-like trance and, in slow motion, leaned jerkily forward to reveal even more of her startling white cleavage as she reached out her trembling hand to take a Benson and Hedges out of the silver box on the coffee table. She contemplated the long white tube of the cigarette clutched between her shaky fingers for quite some time, seeming surprised to find it there and not quite sure what to do with it. To help the poor woman out, I charitably lit up a cigarette myself and was about to offer her a light, but alas too late, because the next thing she did was to dunk her cigarette in her glass of red wine and begin frantically sucking on it as if it were a straw. I watched in fascination as the cigarette soaked up the wine like litmus paper and slowly turned red. Removing it carefully from the glass, Morticia then fumbled around in her bag, finally producing a box of tic-tac mints, which she flicked impatiently, trying to light the soggy end of the cigarette.

"Oh, don't worry about her darling," Erik saw my confused expression, "She's on medication and shouldn't really be drinking, but she was nervous about meeting the infamous Brian Mercer."

"Do you know him personally?" I asked curiously, "Or are you friends of his new wife?"

"Actually, I worked for Brian as a translator in Algeria," Erik informed me proudly, "I speak fluent French of course, a skill acquired during my time in Paris as a gay young man, such wonderful times," his eyes behind his glasses misted with fond memories, "And when the great inventor and entrepreneur requires spiritual guidance, as he so often does, I do his astrological chart and I also read his cards from time to time."

I was surprised by this last piece of information. I wouldn't have considered Brian to be the type to consult a fortune-teller and I certainly couldn't imagine him having his tarot cards read. Being a man of science, he was normally sceptical of such things.

"Yes, they all flock to consult the Great Oracle," Erik boasted, sensing my disbelief. "Shall I do your tarot cards darling, I have them right here in my pocket, or let me look into my crystal ball and all will be revealed."

"No, thank you," I quickly declined, wondering where he was concealing his crystal ball and if he carried it around with him in his pocket. "To be honest," I told him, "I don't really want to know what my future holds."

In retrospect, it's a pity I didn't encourage Erik to consult his crystal ball, wherever he kept it. All may well have been revealed and, forewarned, as they say, is forearmed.

"Well, I'm sure you have a wonderful future ahead," Erik predicted, incorrectly as it turned out, "Because you are surrounded by a rosy pink aura."

I got the feeling that the rosy pink aura he was seeing was probably more a direct result of the tinted glasses he was wearing, or maybe due to the amount of red wine he was consuming, but I smiled politely, took my leave and went off in search of Brian. He had to be there somewhere, unless Vera had deigned to host this whole garden party extravaganza on her own. I informed the 'impromptu' butler that I was in desperate need of some fresh air and escaped out of the front door, kicking my high heels off, which were killing me anyway, remembering the time Brian and I had done exactly the same thing on our first magical mystery tour of his secret gardens. The garden was as beautiful as ever, I noted with pleasure, as I crossed the immaculately clipped lawns lined with regimented beds of perfect blooms, carefully tended and constantly rearranged by the four gardeners, according to which plants were in season. I walked on until I reached the copse of tall leafy trees, Brian's magical forest as he called it, which at this time of year was ringed with clusters of golden daffodils. And there I found him, almost hidden from view, sitting slumped between an enormous tree root, with his head in his hands.

"What on earth are you doing here all on your own?" I asked him, causing him to jump guiltily; then a look of relief spread across his weary features. "I thought it was her," he shuddered, then smiled forlornly. "I'm so glad to see you. How are you?"

"I'm fine," I lied, "But whatever you do, don't ask me how I am *really* or I just might tell you," I cautioned him.

I sat down next to him and we stared at the spiralling circles of daffodils in contemplative silence, then he slowly turned to look at me.

"I think I've made a terrible mistake," he admitted sadly, twisting a bent, misshapen branch between his long, shaky fingers.

"Well, I did try to warn you," I said quietly, resisting the urge to take his trembling hand in mine, like I used to, to stop it from shaking.

"The marriage isn't going at all well," he sighed, tossing the branch into the air, watching it spin, then nose dive and disappear into the sea of yellow blooms. "In fact, it's a bloody nightmare. She's a prima donna and an expensive one at that."

I shook my head in feigned sympathy, but I was really thinking to myself that it served him right for being such a gullible, and dare I say it, old fool.

"I miss you Adrienne," he reached for my hand. "I should have married you, shouldn't I?"

He seemed to have completely forgotten, or blanked the fact, that I'd rejected his proposal in favour of my art career and the chance to go to St Martin's.

"How's the art work going anyway?" he asked me quickly, suddenly brightening up. "I'm coming down to London next week. Can we meet somewhere? I'd love to see your new paintings. In fact, I'd like to buy one."

It was now my turn to sigh. Somehow it always came back to the same old thing with Brian, money and his ingrained philosophy that anything and anyone could be bought. And perhaps it was true? I thought about the kipper plates and the trip Liz, Kathy and I were planning to take to Bali and told him that maybe I'd consider it.

"Actually, the painting I'd really like to buy is 'The Spider and the Fly'", he added slyly.

I shook my head resolutely. "It's not for sale," I told him, tactfully removing my hand from his. He'd tried to buy it from me many times before, but I'd always refused. To me that painting said it all. It expressed the true nature of our relationship and I was reluctant to sell it at any price. Anyway, I felt it was all I had left of him now. I reminded him, with more than a touch of resentment in my voice, that he always had his Dali to console him. In the portrait Dali had painted of Brian, he'd also placed emphasis on his unusual hands, but unlike me, Dali had portrayed Brian looking angelic, with a sweet, sickly smile on his lips and pale blue eyes (maybe he was colour blind like Erik?) sitting on a throne wrapped up in a white sheet, with Vera's face (at her insistence) painted on a small stone at his side. Although, I'm sure if she'd been allowed to have her way, it would have been a bloody great boulder

That night I stayed upstairs in my old studio at the 'Clog and Billycock'. Even though Brian had told me otherwise, I still tortured myself with jealous visions of the two newlyweds. I imagined them making love in the sunroom on the white sofas (or even the white piano!) after all the guests had gone home; Vera playing for him and singing opera arias, Brian standing proudly at her side with tears in his eyes. Beautiful music, especially opera, always made him cry I remembered. But my mum came up to tell me that in fact, he was downstairs, standing at the bar looking suicidal and insisting that he had to see me.

"Tell him I've already gone to bed," I told her harshly. I didn't want to hear any more about, as he put it, his nightmare of a marriage. But what I was forgetting was, I would always be involved, because like it or not, I was still in love with the man.

"I'll tell him you're not coming down then?" my mum was still hovering at the door. She took my silence as a 'no' and reluctantly went back downstairs to face him. But I couldn't relax knowing he was down there waiting for me. I was conscious of the fact that he wanted something from me, something apart from my mere presence that is and something I was not prepared to give under any circumstances; the painting of the 'Spider and the Fly'. I knew that he would not relent until he got his way, until I'd finally given in and agreed to sell it to him. Well, I would never give in, I thought decidedly and taking out my old diary, began to write.

I am upstairs hiding from you. You are downstairs waiting for me to come down. I am huddled in the corner of the bed hoping to be swallowed up by the mattress. I don't want to sell it to you -- oh please don't make me by tormenting your eyes, by shaking your body, by appearing to shrink. It would be like ripping a part out of me. It's there safe on the wall - my wall, where it should be and I'm crouching under it. I will move it even higher still so you can't reach it and take it away. I put every brushstroke on that body to make it my body. I won't sell you every brush stroke of my body. I know you are still down there waiting for me. I can sense you in every pore of my being. I can't hide for much longer. You won't go away until I give in. But tonight, for once, I am determined not to let you have your way.

I decided I couldn't part with the painting under any circumstances so the next day I sent him this poem.

There are some things, in this life, that money just can't buy
And one of them, just happens to be, "The Spider and the Fly"
Although it would be very nice, to sail away to Bali,
Stick it up your jumper Bri and make do with your Dali.
I'm sure your wife would not agree to hang it in your house
It's bound to knock her right off key when she's singing Faust
If you could make a promise from your wall it wouldn't stray,
I might change my decision and send the spider on his way.

Sheer financial pressure made me relent eventually and I had the painting delivered to 'Kenolbri'. Brian sent the money in a crisp, blue envelope (paying way over the odds) and I paid the electricity bill for the flat in London.

Liz, Kathy and I never did make it to Bali by the way.

CHAPTER 15

The Suicide of a Banana

Yes, if only dear Erik 'The Great Oracle', who over the years has grown to be one of my closest and most cherished friends, had managed to predict what would happen to me, maybe I could have escaped my fate. Although, he did manage to predict from the reading of Brian's cards that his unlikely union with Vera wouldn't last and he was right. Two years later and their marriage was in deep trouble.

"I'm divorcing her," Brian called me unexpectedly one evening while I was writing my thesis in the run up to my last few months at St Martin's and told me over the phone. I would be lying if I said I wasn't pleased by his dramatic announcement, but I kept my feelings to myself. I think I mumbled something trite, like, 'Oh dear, I'm sorry to hear that,' which of course I wasn't.

A meaningful silence hung heavy in the air between us, during which I could sense his presence, hear his breathing; almost as though he was right there in the room with me and not hundreds of miles away. I could picture him standing alone in his house in the darkened sunroom, a dark, lonely figure with only his art now to keep him company and afford him solace, and the ever present whisky bottle of course. For all his millions Brian was the loneliest and most unhappy man I had ever met and now more than ever it seemed.

"I miss you so much Adrienne," he broke the silence with a deep shuddering breath.

"I miss you too," I was tentatively forced to admit and it was true. For all the alleged glamour of living in the big city and the bohemian art student life, I had found it somehow lacking. Of all the new people I'd met here, there'd never been anyone who could even remotely compare to Brian and I didn't suppose there ever would be.

"I'd like you to come to New York with me," Brian suddenly blurted out, taking me completely by surprise, something he had proven over the years he was well adept at.

"I don't think that would be very wise with you in the middle of another divorce," I replied somewhat tartly, "I mean, do you?"

"I don't care," he said sadly, "I just want us to be together."

"It's really not a good time for me at the moment," I floundered. "I'm right in the middle of my final exams."

Why was I making excuses? Why was I even considering the possibility? Why the hell didn't I just tell him no, straight out?

"We'll also be going to Grenada," Brian added quickly, ignoring my last comment. "You've never been to the West Indies, have you, or seen my boat 'Bahari'? I'd love you to come. If nothing else, it would be inspiration for your painting." There he was, at it again: dangling the bait, enticing me, laying temptation directly in my path, disrupting, distracting and alluring me all at the same time.

Bugger!

"I'm not sure," I wavered, sorely tempted, gazing down out of the dusty window of my bedroom in the top floor flat I shared with Liz and Kathy, watching a red double-decker bus splash by in the driving rain. "Who else will be going?"

As if that mattered.

"Only Ted and his wife and Keith and Irene; You like Irene. Please come Adrienne, I need you. I don't want to go without you."

How could I resist?

A chauffeur driven car arrived to pick me up at the flat to take me to Heathrow airport, where Brian and I had arranged to meet. Liz and Kathy waved me off enviously from the upstairs window.

"Lucky cow," Liz shouted down.

"Don't forget to bring me some Jamaican rum," Kathy adjoined.

"I'm not going to Jamaica," I yelled back, but they'd already shut the window.

My heart skipped the traditional beat when I saw Brian waiting for me at the premier check-in desk at Heathrow. He looked just the same, perhaps a bit older, but what did I care about a few more wrinkles? He was there and so was I and that's all that mattered. What's more we were going off on an amazing adventure together – at least it was an adventure for me. I'd never been to America or the West Indies, unlike Brian who'd spent most of his life travelling to exotic parts of the world. I secretly wished it was just the two of us going on this trip, but Brian could never go anywhere without his personal entourage in tow. At least we would be alone together on the plane I consoled myself, which would give us time to catch up on all that had happened since we'd last seen each other.

"I'm so happy you came," Brian sighed as he handed our tickets and passports to the girl on the check in desk. I noticed that he seemed exceptionally nervous and that his hands were still shaking; but then so were mine.

It was the first time I'd ever been on a Jumbo jet or flown first class. The glamorous British Airways stewardess served us champagne and caviar and then attended to our every need as we soared through the brilliant blue sky heading towards New York – the big apple! Brian held my hand tightly as we came in to land at Kennedy airport, where a silver limousine was awaiting us, to drive us to the hotel. We sat side by side as the limousine purred through streets, which I'd imagined to be a mass of crowds and filled with the sound of blaring taxi horns like I'd seen in the films, but were, in complete contrast, strangely silent when cocooned inside the car.

We were staying at the Hotel Pierre, which was the ultimate in luxury, although very different in its way from the jaded opulence of the Savoy. Here, everything sparkled and dazzled; glittering chandeliers dangled their icicle-like clusters of crystal stalactites from the high ceilings; gold leafed pillars framed huge bevelled mirrors reflecting the elegant images of the elite guests. Illuminated display cabinets glowed like treasure-filled Aladdin's caves with jewels and diamonds to tempt them.

After we'd checked in, the porter took charge of our bags then accompanied us to the elevator, where 'Major Tom,' as we later christened him, complete in livery and white gloves, pressed the button with his gloved finger for 'lift off' to our suite on the thirty-ninth floor.

The thirty-ninth floor! I'd never been in such a high building in my life. I'd never even been to the top of Blackpool Tower. In fact, I was scared of heights. My legs gave testament to the fact as they swayed and appeared to give out on me as I looked out of the window over Central Park, the sensation of vertigo making me feel light-headed and dizzy. I sank down to the floor and got down on my hands and knees, imagining that the floor was moving beneath me.

"I see I can still make the earth move for you," Brian coined the old joke. But it was true; he could and always had been able to, in more ways than one. Following my example, he knelt down on the carpet to join me and we sat side by side, our legs stretched out in front of us while he popped the cork from the bottle of champagne, waiting there for us on ice, alongside the enormous basket of fruit and huge arrangement of exotic blooms with the welcoming note addressed to Mr and Mrs Mercer.

Once I'd found my feet, I rushed around the rooms excitedly, like a child, looking in drawers and cupboards, flicking through the telephone directory to see if there was anyone with the same surname as me living in New York. There was one listing. I dialled the number but nobody answered; not knowing what I would have said if they had.

As luxurious as it was, Brian and I felt too restless to stay confined in our suite with the undiscovered delights of New York beckoning to us from below. Grabbing our coats, we ran hand in hand back along the plush orange carpeted corridor to re-board the space shuttle elevator where we dropped the thirty nine floors back to planet earth. With our feet once again planted on terra firma, we strolled arm in arm along Fifth Avenue, window shopping in the fabulous shops and huge department stores. We passed by the world famous Tiffany's and Brian showed me the Tiffany diamond. He joked about buying it for me, which, with all his millions, perhaps he could have done. But even if he could, diamonds and jewellery have never really interested me. We found a tiny art shop nearby, which was far more in my line, where we bought some handmade paper and a big bunch of sable brushes. The owner, an old Polish man, with half-framed glasses perched on the end of his nose, told us sorrowfully that he had been burgled four times in the last week.

After meeting up for the first time that evening with the rest of the party, we dined at the resplendent 'Maxwell Plums' with its unique style of interior design. Magnificent stained glass Tiffany lights adorned the walls and lit the tables with mystical mandalas of coloured light and rows of brightly painted china chickens hung from the ceiling. Huge china horses and leopards stood guard at the base of the sweeping stairwells, the gleaming brass rails exploding into art nouveau mermaids with coils of metallic hair. The restaurant was packed to overflowing with animated diners, mainly Americans, with the odd bunch of slightly more restrained English tourists, like us, thrown in for good measure. Wily waiters rushed to and fro, balancing silver trays over their heads, pandering to our every need. Then after a wonderful meal, during which Ted for once managed to restrain his foul tongue, mainly due to the fact he was too busy employing it for eating rather than slandering purposes, we all went back to the hotel, slightly drunk. Brian and I, by now feeling the effects of the earlier bottle of champagne, followed by even more champagne and wine at dinner, unsteadily boarded Apollo 1 and launched ourselves up to our suite way, way up in the sky, only to fall tipsily asleep in each other's arms, then drift off to dreamland, somewhere in another galaxy.

The next day, because I am taking time off college and in order to further my artistic development, Brian decides it is his duty to take me on a conducted tour of the Museum of Modern art, then on to the Guggenheim. We begin our tour at the very top of the building, then waddle down the spiral gallery like two flat-footed plastic ducks. Art was in the form of *'Perry Como'* – a drawing of a pear, a comb and an 'o' and *'The Suicide of a Banana!'* We then take a yellow cab back to the Pierre so Brian can indulge in an afternoon nap (taking in all that art has exhausted him) and I can prepare myself accordingly for my role as 'mistress' to man of wealth and substance when we go out for dinner later that evening.

Once again I'm not entirely sure how comfortably this particular role of 'mistress' sits with me, because after all, by rights he is still legally a married man, which makes me some kind of guilty party, doesn't it? But then again, it wasn't exactly the first time I'd been, to put it politely, 'between wives' with Brian, so I supposed I should be used to it by now. At least I was able to appease my conscience with the fact that he'd been officially divorced from his first wife by the time we'd embarked upon any kind carnal relations.

Carnal relations, or relations of any kind, were obviously out of the question at this particular moment in time however, because Brian, who was obviously knackered, had already laid himself down on the enormous king- sized bed, put his silk mask over his eyes and was now fast asleep.

Mmmm – what should I wear I ponder? I pop a seedless grape in my mouth as I pass through the mirrored dressing room into the white marble bathroom, turning on the gold taps to run a hot bath; liberally pouring in the bubbles. When I finally immerge, I make use of every spotlessly white warmed towel, dropping them on the floor for the maid to pick up. Then as an afterthought and in consideration for Brian, as well as the poor maid's probable lumbago, I pick them all back up and hang them neatly on the heated towel rack to dry. I'll never make a spoilt Diva, I think to myself, which is perhaps a good thing, especially after Brian's recent fiasco with the ill-fated wife number two. A taste of luxury could be a dangerous appetiser, I feared, and one might just get accustomed to it.

Next on the beauty agenda, down a few floors in the space craft for a previously booked hair appointment, where after roaming up and down the plushly carpeted corridors, disorientated and confused, I finally come upon a mysterious door that looks like any other but conceals a mysterious labyrinth of yellow cubicles, where aged women sit in a line with towel turbans wrapped around their tulip-shaped heads, reading glossy magazines. I am plonked down in front of a huge, ornate mirror, then swung around in something resembling a dentist's chair by a transsexual Cuban, who after shampooing my hair with his/her bony fingers and long painted fingernails, strategically arranges lines of drainpipe sized rollers across my head. Miss Cuba then beckons me to follow her/him and I am isolated under a long-armed, salmon pink hair dryer, with nothing to look at but my own face.

It's a long time since I have been to a hairdresser. Artists tend not to pay too much attention their locks and neither can they usually afford the luxury of a hairdresser. I suddenly feel very out of place, not to mention out of character and amazed to find myself here, in New York, in the Hotel Pierre, having my hair 'dressed' and living the life of luxury. It was a far, far cry from the impoverished lifestyle of an art student, that was for sure. Oh well, when in Rome I thought to myself.

We were obliged to meet up once again with the rest of the party that evening, but this time we dined in the restaurant at the very top of the Hotel Pierre. From our elevated vantage point, we were able to look down through the ceiling to floor windows at the glittering lights of Fifth Avenue way below us, carving a straight line through the towering buildings to infinity. A girl with a long ponytail sat at the grand piano, singing softy to herself. Busy waiters glided past, weaving their way amongst the blindingly white tablecloths laden with crystal glasses, shining cutlery, bottles of champagne in silver buckets and platters of food bursting into flames. I looked dreamily out at the New York sky to see the glitter of the candles and the sparkling chandeliers mirrored in the darkened windows of the facing skyscraper. How the other half live I thought, a touch resentfully, even though at that moment I was living that very same life myself. I put my hand under the starched white tablecloth to find the underneath of the table was covered with lumps of chewing gum.

It was freezing cold the following morning as Brian and I set off arm in arm in our long winter coats to watch the skaters in Central Park. There was a bitter arctic wind attempting to bowl us over with its icy intent, forcing us to bow our heads and clutch tightly on to each other. Any form of conversation strictly out of the question, we scurried along in silence; Brian's arm protectively around my shoulder as we huddled together for warmth. Suddenly stopping dead in his tracks, Brian swung me round to face him and shivering, demanded, "Let's get married."

I don't know whether it was the bitterly cold arctic wind that had taken my breath away, robbing me of words and rendering me completely speechless or Brian's unexpected, not to mention totally unrealistic, proposal.

"We could go to Las Vegas," he suggested hopefully, his impetuous words turning into vaporous mist and quickly disappearing like smoke in the frosty air. We bowed our heads and continued on our journey in silence. There was no need for me to remind him that he was already married and as yet to start divorce proceedings.

We managed to escape the others that night and had dinner at a small restaurant called 'Applause', where the waiters and waitresses were part of the performance. As they passed our table with plates laden with food, they burst into rousing songs from musicals. Brian performed an impromptu tap dance on the small stage as we left and everyone clapped. He took a sweeping bow, laughing.

The following day and another Limousine carried us grandly back to Kennedy airport. We left the towering skyscrapers of New York far below us and flew over strings of tiny, jewel-like islands, floating like necklaces in the azure sea. We landed in Barbados with the heat blasting. A stoned West Indian, with a matchstick balanced in the corner of his mouth, was the single, non-convincing representative of our next airline.

We boarded a tiny aeroplane and sat next to the pilot. After waiting for a huge jumbo to land, we were off, skidding along the runway and climbing into the sky. Cotton wool clouds shook us roughly from side to side then spat us out, only to be swallowed up by the next fluffy formation. We came into land over the aquamarine sea on to what looked like a dusty road, surrounded by palm trees and jungle hills with a skeletal black dog idling its way across the makeshift runway. A dilapidated huddle of buildings welcomed us to Grenada.

Martin, the captain of Brian's boat 'Bahari' and his wife Christine, were waiting to greet us, accompanied by a bodyguard and 'Miss Grenada' herself who was the bodyguard's girlfriend. No sign of a limousine this time, instead we clambered into the rickety old minibus, already loaded to overflowing with our suitcases, and we set off on our perilous drive to our destination, which was called 'Secret Harbour.'

It was late afternoon by this time and I didn't know which way to look first, it was so incredibly beautiful. Lush green palms covered the undulating hillsides, interspersed with bamboo groves, banana trees, bushes laden with flowers and small wooden shacks painted bright colours balanced on precarious wooden stilts. Open doors and windows revealed scenes of family life; jet black men and women, old and young, reclining or slouched in somnolent postures over wooden chairs and tables. Young girls sat on the steps, parting each other's hair into tiny plaits. Children with round, naked bottoms, their luminous eyes gazing at us with open curiosity, watched as we rattled by. Young men, lounged on walls wearing skimpy white vests revealing bulging muscles, glistening like wet granite; women crouched on the kerbside, nursing their infants, idly lifting a hand to wave at us as we passed. I waved back, smiling. We were drinking champagne out of plastic cups as we bumped along the pot-holed roads as the bus made its tortuous journey up into the mountains.

Stopping at a roadside bar to refuel, Brian and I climbed out to go looking for a loo in the tumbledown shack that was also a disco. Dancing our way to some funky reggae music, dancing back together hand in hand, then into the minibus and off again. It was dark by now as the minibus negotiated more isolated roads, then over the top of the mountain and down the other side, with the twinkling coloured lights of the town spread out below us. Our hotel was called 'Secret Harbour' and it nestled on the palm-fringed shores of a secluded bay and consisted of a line of separate bungalows on stilts, with balconies resting over the sea. Carved wooden doors opened into our tastefully decorated but sparse, almost church-like room. Arched stained glass windows, lit from behind by the balcony lanterns, cast slanting kaleidoscope patterns across the floor and coloured rainbows over the starched white cotton sheets on the two huge four-poster beds. Leading off from the balcony was an en suite bathroom with an enormous, round tiled bath, from which you could look directly out, through a glassless window, to the sea and the immense West Indian sky. A tropical breeze perfumed the air and even though it was night, you could still feel the soporific heat.

Brian and I stood on the balcony with our arms around each other and looked up at the millions of stars twinkling across the dome of the midnight blue sky. The only sound I could hear was the beat of his heart, along with the ebb and flow of the gently lapping waves as they alternately soaked, then blotted, the paper white sheet of sand spread out below us. Brian held me very close and it was a strange and unaccustomed feeling to be standing there, locked in each other's arms on a wooden balcony overlooking a tropical sea, somewhere on the other side of the world. As we stood there, lost in the time warp of our separate thoughts, I felt Brian try to disguise the shudder of a sob as he abruptly turned his head away, not wanting me to see him cry. When I asked him what was wrong, he told me that nothing was wrong and that was it. He was crying because he was happy and because I was happy, but most of all because I loved his island.

Dawn - a restless night confused and full of dreams, the sound of the sea through the open doors and the stultifying heat. I awoke to find I was alone. Brian must have left my side sometime during the night to sleep in the other four-poster bed. Still half asleep, I looked over at his motionless body, framed by the billowing curtains of the mosquito net draped from the huge wooden frame of the four-poster bed. Luminous red and green shafts of light from the stained glass arches, lit now by the early morning sun, dappled his slumbering form, highlighting the sculptured folds of the tightly draped sheet mummifying his body. Not really knowing where I was, thinking I was in a cathedral and this was the tomb of a knight or a bishop. Expecting to hear ethereal music, but there was silence, apart from the sound of Brian's regular breathing in time to the accompaniment of the waves constantly lapping on the sandy beach below us.

We spent our first morning on this magical isle exploring the bustling town, entranced by all the different sights and sounds; smiling faces full of character, open buses packed with people: some sitting on the roof, black arms and legs hanging over the sides and poking out of the windows. The buses had charming idiosyncratic names roughly scrawled on the sides, *'Carefree'* – *'Hummingbird'* – *'Comfort'* - *'Dignity.'*

The busy streets of the town were lined with brightly painted bars with signs hung above the door, proclaiming, *'The lord is my shepherd', 'Lileth's Snackett', 'No obscene language.'*

The smell of fish and rotting fruit pervaded the air emanating from the crowded market place, which was lined with stalls stacked high with huge bunches of bananas and strange looking fruits I had never seen before. It was stiflingly hot and bodies were sprawled on the floor, some under makeshift canopies, or lounging in the shade of doorways. Steep streets and rows of pink, blue and yellow houses wound their way up from the busy hub of the market place to the jungle-covered hills. Women walked proudly on their way with baskets of washing or bananas balanced on their heads, followed by groups of small children carrying pails of water. I smiled at anyone who would smile at me.

Afternoon, dazed by the heat, lying with Brian in a hammock strung between two palms on the private beach at 'Secret Harbour' with the hot wind rustling through the swaying palm fronds, making long shadows dance on the white sand. Black feather patterns, chasing each other across the sandy ripples, interlocking, becoming one, dancing over my body - a caress of cool shadow to soothe the scorching kiss of the afternoon sun; the familiar scent of Brian at my side and of hot, clean cotton. Then later, when the afternoon heat had abated somewhat, we took a leisurely stroll through the tropical gardens, where tiny hummingbirds cooled vivid flowers with the whirr of their wings, feverishly flying from bush to bush. I tried to follow one, placing a magenta flower behind my ear, hoping it would follow me.

"I would love a tiny hummingbird of my own," I told Brian, "To sit on my smallest finger and nestle in my hair."

Brian and I learned to love each other again in those magical days and dark, steamy nights, hidden away in our 'Secret Harbour' hideaway, only more tenderly now, with a deeper understanding of each other's inner sadness. His tired, drooping shoulders and rapidly aging body, shrunken now with sorrow; those familiar long, white hands that couldn't lift without trembling, reaching out to touch me. His haunted and often inebriated eyes, blurred with unshed tears as he thought of the past and all the years we'd wasted by being apart. When he was being his true self, as he could only be with me and he allowed me to feel the inner soul of him and not the person he projected to the outside world, I loved him in a deep part of myself. The part of me that is as deep and mysterious as the unexplored fathoms of the sea, where the creatures do not need eyes and ears to find their way, they simply float and feel by the vibrations of the black water moving over their bodies. Brian was my black water, my fathomless sea. And I was his.

We hired a battered old taxi for the day and set off to explore the less populated regions of the island. The taxi driver drove us along the rugged coastline and with every twist and turn of the winding road the scenery became more and more beautiful. We drove all the way to the other side of the island, over steep hills densely covered with palms and seemingly impenetrable, lush green foliage. At times our passage was hindered by the tangled wreaths of bright pink and yellow flowers which were sprawled all over the road, entwined in colourful profusion. For most of our journey we saw little evidence of civilisation, but now and then we would suddenly chance upon a cluster of rickety wooden houses with ragged curtains blowing in the warm wind, looking out across the tropical valleys to the turquoise sea. We caught fleeting glimpses of people living their day-to-day lives, lost in this tropical time warp. Children, washing themselves by the roadside; women stood balancing pails of water on their heads, their eyes sliding sideways to stare at us as we drove by. We passed through fields of sugar cane as high as the men who were cutting it; circles of workers wearing hats woven from palm leaves resting on the cut cane, eating and drinking. They waved at us and lifted their hats in salute. We journeyed on through miles of banana groves to the spice farm, where the taxi driver gave us a guided tour of the hot shacks packed with women and men sitting open-legged on the floor in between piles of ripening bananas. Old, wretched faces, others young and smiling, sorting spices into huge baskets, they ignored the swarms of flies that plagued them. Bats swooped around in broad daylight and the air was pungent with the smell of sweat mixed with sweet spices.

We went further down the makeshift road to a tiny village, where we encountered less friendly and vaguely hostile feelings from the people there. Some children shouted "white tourists" as we climbed out of the taxi to have a drink in a small roadside bar. A woman glared at me and offered me her baby. We quickly finished our drinks, got back in the taxi and drove on, passing huddles of people, sitting on walls, on steps, in doorways, or walking slowly along the road, swaying their hips lazily to avoid the car. I suddenly felt very out of place with my designer sunglasses and white skin and Brian (a man rich beyond their wildest dreams) at my side.

Later, back on board 'Bahari', the captain had invited a select group of expatriates for drinks. Tight knots of smartly dressed couples, sipping their Bacardi and cokes and dry Martinis, clustered around Brian, making small talk - the kind of social gathering I had spent my life trying to avoid. I imagined this same scenario could be found in any marina in the world frequented by the rich and famous, with their yachts and gin palaces. The novelty of luxury soon wears off it seems. My mind wandered back to the hostile village and the resentment clearly etched on the faces of the impoverished people and a feeling of guilt crept over me.

The next day, and a very different scenario, as Brian and I sneak off together to take a ride on the glass-bottomed boat. The boat stops to pick up American tourists from the cruise ship, all aboard for the first rum punch at 9.30 in the morning. Wrinkled, sunburnt men with faces like pickled walnuts; loud women with bright slashes of orange lipstick and over-powdered faces sporting hats and headscarves from Haiti; cameras clicking and whirring. Merchants crowd the dock, selling hats and fans woven from palm leaves. Steel drums clang; a wizened old man rows around us in his dilapidated wooden boat listing under the weight of its cargo of bright pink conch shells, '*Grenada*' scrawled in red on the lips. An enormous black policewoman jumps aboard as the steel band plays us out of the harbour, with a badly timed conch shell accompaniment from the old man in the boat. Brian and I laugh as the surreal humour of the whole thing hits us. Swaying from side to side, the glass bottom boat negotiates the headland and swings around into the next bay. A loud splash and the creaking of rusty chains as the glass bottom is lowered for us to gaze at the wonders of the deep. Two small ultramarine fishes swim past then the glass bottom is quickly raised and the boat heads for the shore, aiming its gangplank at the long, sandy beach. Glistening black bodies swim out and hang onto the ropes then disappear under the boat. On the shore, a crowd of smiling turbaned women wave brightly coloured dresses and sarongs, which they display for sale, rapidly changing them from their seemingly endless source, and once again, the shells and the drums and the woven hats.

The tourists straggle off the boat, one by one, along the rickety gangplank in their assorted beachwear, clutching snorkels and flippers. They flap excitedly into the turquoise sea, where chaos briefly reigns, until a sudden tropical downpour sends them scuttling back onto the boat. They cover their heads with towels although they are already soaking wet. Some of them have managed to get stung by sea urchins, so a line of deathly white feet are presented to skilled black hands to be treated accordingly, as the huge policewoman looks on with a bored expression on her face. She'd obviously seen it all many times before. The crowd of merchants on the shore are now in a bedraggled state, huddled under the huge leafy umbrella of an old, gnarled tree, sheltering from the downpour. An old man on a flower-decked donkey spurs it on, clutching his hat and trots off into the steamy jungle. Young boys, oblivious to the rain, slither up the ropes and grinning, offer us more shells. Brian and I decide to walk back along the beach, leaving the boat to make its return journey without us. We are followed by a crowd of happy, smiling children singing calypsos, *"Grenada is a beautiful island and de population is small,"* a young boy croons as hurriedly as possible, his little sister occasionally joining in, outstretching their tiny pink palms for money.

We rejoin the rest of the party and have lunch on a sunlit terrace with the light dancing through the leaves and lizards, almost transparent in the sunlight, scaling the walls. A polished grand piano stands in pride of place in the centre of the room, a silver bowl of shocking pink flowers dropping heart shaped petals onto its shiny surface, while overhead, two huge bats chase each other round and round in circles.

During lunch, Brian is called away for a phone call from England. He seems upset when he comes back and immediately dashes off for a conference with Fat Ted. I decide not to go out fishing with them that afternoon on 'Bahari' as planned. Instead, I walk around the market by myself taking photographs, which I hope to use as reference for paintings when I get back.

"Hey white girl," A huge black woman bellows at me from under a striped umbrella, making me jump, "Don't come round here wid your camera, snap, snap, snapping."

I scuttle back to the safety of the marina and sit in the harbour bar, scanning the horizon, waiting for 'Bahari' to come back.

When they finally arrive, Brian is in a sombre mood. Vera has apparently found out I am here with him in Grenada and has refused to leave the marital homestead, saying she now wants double the amount of money to settle the divorce. Brian promised me before we set off that all the papers had already been signed. Now there is a strong possibility that I will be cited in the proceedings. I am justifiably angry with him for lying to me, but he doesn't see it that way, so I take a taxi back to 'Secret Harbour' by myself. A storm is brewing and the rain is battering the roof and flooding on to the balcony. I suddenly feel frightened and a long way from home.

When they all come back to 'Secret Harbour', later that night, Brian informs me that they have discussed what should be done about the 'delicate' situation in regard to Vera and have decided that I should stay on in Grenada and they would go home as planned. Vera would probably be waiting at the airport armed with a photographer they said, and my name would be on the passenger list, so they would fly home without me and I would follow on in a few days. Brian and I argue all night long in our separate four-poster beds. I don't want him to go back without me, leaving me there on that beautiful but at times openly hostile island on my own.

"You won't be on your own," he shouts impatiently at me, "You'll be with Martin and Christine."

"But I want to be with you," I beg him, trying to hold back the tears.

He is very drunk by this time and rises up angrily out of his sheets, like a huge, monster from the deep.

"For God's sake woman," he bellows at me. "I am not a fish and chip shop man, so don't expect me to think like a fish and chip shop man."

"What on earth have fish and chips got to do with it?" I sniff tearfully, totally confused by his obscure reference.

"I am not an ordinary man," he pronounces pompously, "As well you know and if you want an ordinary man, you'd better go out and bloody well find yourself one."

I am now at a total loss for words, so I lay there in the dark, crying quietly to myself, hoping he will fall asleep. But after a few minutes, he gets out of his four-poster bed and comes over to mine. He tries to somehow make amends, but I am too upset. I push him away and turn my back on him. He clings like a limpet to my hostile shoulders, shaking and sighing, his breath wheezing and rattling in his throat; his trembling hands caressing my body. Revulsion suddenly wells up inside me and I find myself shrinking away from his drunken advances. I have to brace my shoulder to receive his short, sharp, noisy kisses, the neat arch of his cupid's bow, wet with desire and salty beads of sweat. His breath smells of whisky and his brittle black whiskers scratch my sunburnt skin. I roughly shove him away and he lies panting on his back.

"Don't turn me away Adrienne," he begs, "I want you so much." he points to his limp manhood,

He tries once again to make love to me, but I lay there impassive and unyielding.

"Was '*She*' happy?" he asks breathlessly, finally giving up.

"Who's '*She*'?" I retort sarcastically, "The cat's mother?"

He shuffles back to the other four poster bed, defeated, but still arrogant.

I agree to stay on in Grenada, even though I don't really have a choice, and I am given over to Martin and Christine's care. I move out of 'Secret Harbour' and on to 'Bahari' and they all fly home without me. The harbour is rapidly filling up with new boats from Trinidad, arriving for the Easter Water Parade which is due to start the following day. I sit alone on deck surveying the scene. It all looks incredibly beautiful at this hour of the evening, with the lights of the boats reflecting on the water and the luminous yellow sky silhouetting the palm trees. But I am feeling restless, so I tell Martin and Christine I am going ashore to have a drink in the bar. They tell me that I am not a prisoner, but warn me to be careful. However, I feel too conspicuous sitting in the bar on my own, so I soon scuttle back to the safety of 'Bahari.' I lie in my solitary bunk, listening to the rhythmic splashing of the water under the boat sounding like someone softly playing the drums, and dream of Brian.

It was the night before the great Easter parade and the bulldozers were attacking the quayside, which was still piled high with black mud. When the great day dawned, miraculously the new artificial beach was in place and we were all rudely awoken at the crack of dawn by the Prime Minister's opening speech blaring out on the radio. We were eating breakfast in the harbour bar when the Minister of Tourism pulled up in his enormous car; the doors were flung open and several officials jumped out then frantically ran up and down the quay looking for the 'World Champion Kite Man' who was supposed to be performing his fantastic flight. When he was finally located (in the bar) he was towed out to sea in a brash looking speedboat called 'Cigarella', only to make a disastrous fall and had to be rushed to hospital unconscious.

Christine and I spent the afternoon wandering up and down the market stalls where I purchased a brightly coloured rag rug to take back to the flat. Drunken old men and young boys were dancing outside the noisy bars, gambling and spinning wheels. I was really missing Brian, although I didn't want to admit it, even to myself.

That night we set off on another boat called the 'Rum Runner' just as the sun was going down. Rows of coloured lights had been strung from the trees on the shore and the motionless sea was like shimmering purple silk. All around the water's edge, hundreds of people were sitting on seats and benches, dressed in brilliant colours: fluorescent orange and bright greens mingled with electric blues and radiant reds. As the light began to fade, the faces of the exuberant throngs blended in with the night, leaving only the vibrant colours still glowing. The outline of the mountains gradually disappeared and the static loops of coloured lights hung suspended in the sky like a psychedelic galaxy of stars. With the onset of darkness came the throbbing, clanging music of the steel bands. The gangplank of the 'Rum Runner' was lowered (after several failed attempts) and a bevy of young girls in frilly, coloured skirts and flowered headdresses flounced aboard, followed by men with guitars and banjos. We had to walk over the makeshift stage to join the crowd on the shore and we were the only white faces there. Spirits were high in every sense of the word and everyone was dancing, an undulating mass of writhing bodies and outstretched hands waving in the air as though possessed by the music. I tried to imagine Brian in this wild, frenzied scenario, but somehow, I couldn't.

Martin and Christine flew back with me on the little plane to Barbados. On the drive to the airport to catch my flight back to Heathrow, we were stuck behind an old estate car painted a garish lilac colour, which was swerving from side to side of the winding road, a line of black arms reaching out of the window clutching onto a yellow coffin hanging precariously out of the back. We got drunk on banana cocktails as we waited for my flight to be called and I only just made the check in gate in time. Martin and Christine waved me goodbye then I was on my way back home. I slept through the entire journey, missing all the perks of first class and woke up as we were circling over a grey and dismal looking Heathrow. Then it was all over, the wheels were down and as I made my way through customs and on to the meeting point.

Brian was nowhere to be seen.

CHAPTER 16

Faithful Flagship

As in the words of my old school song, I continue to fight the good fight with all of my might against this deadly virus, this Hitler-like enemy; the oppressive force that has not only taken control of my body, but is attempting to commandeer my very soul. I have good days and bad days and we battle for power, for domination, for supremacy. Some days I feel as though I am in command and other days I lay defeated on the battleground, about to wave the white flag. But up to now I have refused to give in, although every day is a new and constant battle, even with the medication, my 'little soldiers.' They are supposed to be on my side, but at times it doesn't feel that way as they wreak havoc on my innards with their toxic poison and affect my mind. The battle scars, the afflictions of war, are starting to show themselves both mentally and physically and I think I am suffering from that thing soldiers get called Post Traumatic Stress Syndrome.

Aside from the internal battles, the enemy lurks all around me in the form of society's stigma and prejudice, forcing me to constantly lay low, deny my status, my HIV nationality. I live in exile and fight for victory behind the enemy lines, like the French resistance. There had been times in the past when Brian had felt like my enemy, a power-crazed dictator determined to reign over my life and direct my creative soul, and now he was no longer here to wield his power over me, it seemed the virus was acting on his behalf. Or maybe it was just Brian in another form. His was always a controlling love - out to destroy the object of its affections, like the female praying mantis who eats her lover, but in reverse. How could I have loved such a man? I have no answer to that question, other than I did, with all my heart. My flesh may have been weak but I fought his controlling influence over me to the bitter end and so it would be with this virus. It may well have taken control of my body, but I was buggered if I was going to let it take over my life.

It's the run up to World AIDS day on December 1st - a special day for me now and I await it with anticipation, like a birthday or an anniversary. In a way it is, because every one I survive from now on will be a personal victory.

My health advisor Janet from the GUM clinic at Blackburn hospital called me this morning and asked if I'd be willing to take part in some publicity to raise awareness about HIV in the form of a radio interview. In other words, be their 'flagship' as she described it, although I've never been called one of those before. Of course I agreed to take part without hesitation; after all, it was what I wanted to do, to help make the general public, especially women, more aware of the dangers of this deadly disease. So a 'flagship' I was and off I sailed, without a lifejacket but with all flags flying, to do my bit. The interview was to be strictly confidential, but I called myself 'Amy' just in case the executors of Brian's Estate heard me and died from premature heart attacks, because I hadn't quite finished with them yet. I was introduced as 'Amy from our county' which I thought had quite a quaint ring to it and spurred along by occasional prompts from the interviewer, I talked for about twenty minutes. The interview was broadcast the following morning between seven and nine (plus a sound bite delivered by 'Amy from our county' every half hour during the news.) It was heard by people driving to work, mothers getting their children ready for school and, apparently, quite a few other people who could identify with me. According to an email I received from BBC Radio Lancashire, there has been amazing feedback and the local newspaper has just called and asked me do something for them. So it looks as though I am now officially launched (albeit as poor Amy) on the high seas of public prejudice and possible condemnation. Off on my valiant voyage to raise awareness, while hopefully tossing a lifebelt or two to a few lost positive souls on the way. Well, awareness definitely needs to be raised and who better to do it than someone like me – or maybe 'Amy' should get the credit.

I read in the paper that the man who caused the recent train crash near Reading had just been diagnosed as HIV positive, so decided to take his own life (and quite a few others while he was at it). Had he not felt so isolated and alone, maybe he would not have been reduced to taking such a drastic action, and the lives of those totally unconnected people, as well as his own, would have been spared.

'Amy from our county' has also been doing her bit in other ways by becoming a mentor for an eighteen year old girl, diagnosed only two months ago. Her first thought on hearing that she was HIV positive was also to take her own life. Fortunately, she didn't, and we are going to try to form a support group, something which is desperately lacking in this area (in fact, in most areas). Every day now, in every town and in every country more and more people are being diagnosed HIV positive, so there is a great need for support groups and an even greater need to make people aware of the danger lurking out there. That means everyone, not just gay men or drug users, but ordinary people, living ordinary lives – people like me. Not that my life has ever been ordinary, but at least I have had a life and I suppose quite an interesting one at that. But that young girl, hers had only just begun.

We went ahead and held our first HIV support meeting last night at my house and although there were only the three of us, it turned out to be a humbling as well as totally inspiring experience. It's hard to put into words the sheer relief we all felt at being reprieved from our usual isolation and of being with other people who have been, and are still going through the same horrific circumstances. The only thing I can maybe compare it to, is a documentary I once saw about a convention of dwarfs (if that's the right collective description) - all meeting for the first time in an American hotel. A strange comparison perhaps, but as I imagine the dwarfs must have felt, it was like finding kindred souls, although we were all from very different walks of life and of different ages - and obviously not dwarfs. But the fact that we were so different didn't matter in the least and before long, we were imparting our various horror stories of how we found out, showing each other our deadly cocktails of pills and peering with great interest at each others' spots. My magnificent shingles scars, it has to be said, stole the day.

What amazing resilience those two young girls have and, I don't know why, but I didn't expect such strength of character from the 'youth of today.' Katie, for example, is only eighteen, tall, elegant and very pretty, with long blonde hair and an angelic smile. Her ambition had always been to become a nurse. To her immense joy, she'd been short listed for interview the day after going to the GUM clinic for routine health tests. These days, they are advising all young girls to test for HIV along with everything else, so Katie had agreed, thinking nothing of it, not considering for one moment that it would apply to her. When the results came back positive, her first thought had been to kill herself, believing she was shortly going to die anyway. She went home in a complete daze, totally traumatised, but refrained from tell her mother, who'd recently been ill herself, fearing she wouldn't have been able to take the shock that her beautiful daughter was HIV positive. For two months Katie lived with the knowledge that she was HIV positive on her own. She felt totally isolated and alone but only allowed herself to cry in the shower, so that her mother couldn't hear her, or witness her tears.

Paula is the mother of three young children, although still only a young woman herself and thought she had her whole life ahead of her. Her husband had been, what she described as a control freak, so they'd separated for a while and during that time she'd had a one night stand with someone else. She was later reunited with her husband, but over the course of time she began to feel ill. Being the mother of three demanding children, she soldiered on, but found herself getting weaker and weaker by the day. Her hair started to fall out and so did her teeth and she was constantly suffering from flu-like symptoms, but her doctor did little more than prescribe antibiotics and send her on her way. Then one day, she was going upstairs and she passed out. Her father had found her unconscious at the top of the stairs. She spent three months in hospital and at one point, was pronounced clinically dead. But somehow she survived, only to be informed that she was HIV positive, at which time she wished she hadn't. She was put on a cocktail of anti-retroviral drugs and at one stage was taking over a hundred pills a day. She'd suffered the dreaded shingles like me, but on her face and also in her eye. The worst day for Paula had been the day she'd had to take her three children to the clinic to be tested for AIDS. Luckily, they were all clear.

These were two very inspiring stories but I couldn't help but feel there must be so many more out there just waiting to be told. If only those people could find the same support that we were now able to offer to each other - this gathering together against adversity, like the great British public did in the war. True British grit as my mum called it, the spirit that would overcome everything and anything.

Apparently, the three of us were all party to the same paranoid thoughts. We would stand in the queue at the supermarket, or in the chip shop, ordering fish and chips twice and a portion of mushy peas, thinking, I am the only person here who is HIV positive – or am I? Maybe one or even two of those people in the queue were also positive and didn't even know it. And what would they do if they knew we were positive? Move out of our way; keep their distance in case they 'caught' it. The question we were all asking ourselves of course and each other was: why me, why not her, why not them? If only I hadn't done this, that, or in particular 'the other', then I wouldn't be in this position now. By the end of a very long night, which none of us wanted to end, we were telling ourselves that we were strong, that if we could survive this we could survive anything. There was a reason for everything and something good would come out of it and of meeting each other. We would make a difference, change things for the better; that was our mission in life now to survive and to raise awareness.

After they'd gone home, feeling inspired and also a little bit drunk after all the wine, I started to think of other things we could do when the support group really got going and we had more members. I could maybe start another dancing group, like the one I had in Ibiza, with a slight difference of course. A troupe of positive dancers! We'd perform my infamous 'Carmen Circle' but instead of red flowers in our hair, we'd sport red ribbons, the universal symbol for HIV/AIDS. Our wonderful specialist Dr Gayed could strut amongst us in his white coat, rattling boxes of pills instead of maracas, singing 'Toreador' and wearing one of those daft bullfighters' hats. My mum could rewrite the words to the song as she'd once had to do in Ibiza because our particular 'toreador' had originated from the East end of London and couldn't speak French. Unfortunately, she'd got a bit confused between her patriotic English hymns, the Second World War and Robin Hood as well as not being really sure what a toreador actually was. So instead of slaying bulls, she had him valiantly going off to die for his country while shooting arrows straight and true from his mighty bow.

'Toreador oh toreador..... off he goes to fight the war'

Carried away by my idea of a troupe of Positive Dancers, my mind ran on to other productions I could possibly choreograph. The possibilities were endless. Andrew Lloyd Webber would be begging to write the new score of course and the theatre would be booked out for years in advance. We'd raise awareness and huge amounts of money at the same time, which would enable them, whoever they are, to discover a cure. Instead of having "HIV" after our names, we'd have "OBE" like Brian.

Or, alternatively, my creative juices were flowing as fast as the wine in my newly refilled glass, we could make the 'Positive Women's Calendar', where we'd be pictured peeping coyly from behind our hospital robes, red ribbons perched on our nipples, or frolicking merrily in baths of multicoloured pills. They'd make a film about us, which would be a huge box office success and Julie Walters would take my part. Oh dear, I really was getting carried away now - and soon would be, literally, if I went on like this.

I poured myself yet another glass of wine, even though I knew that drinking alcohol was strictly not advisable in my condition and could react badly with the medication, especially at this time of night and particularly just before I took the dreaded stuff. With all the excitement of meeting the girls, I'd gone way past the allotted hour for my second dose of pills. I slid them reluctantly out of the special bag in which I kept them hidden and laid them out in a semi circle, then twirling them round one by one, positioned them in a neat line like formation dancers. This was probably the nearest thing to choreography I was going to get in my sorry state of health, I sighed sadly. I reached under the coffee table and took out my old photograph album of my dancing days in Ibiza. There I was, pictured in all my glory, wearing my black and red spotted flamenco dress with geraniums in my hair, surrounded by my troupe of little dancing girls. I looked so happy and the girls looked so beautiful in their brightly coloured outfits, they brought a tear to my eye.

Those girls would be all grown up now and as for me, who would have thought back then that I would have ended up like this? Certainly not me: I thought I would go on valiantly dancing till the end of my days, like the old saying, 'he died with his boots on'. Well, I thought I would die, (at least metaphorically), with my flamenco shoes on. But I had to face the fact that in all probability I would never dance again. My flamenco shoes and dresses would lie redundant in the attic, with the plastic earrings, the embroidered shawls, the wilted flowers; those treasured adornments reminiscent of another time, along with the fiery, passionate music and what the Spanish called the duende.

That time and those happy days before Brian had come to snatch me away from my carefree life in Ibiza and convince me to come back to Blackburn. The only dance remaining for me now, I thought self pityingly, an effect of the wine, would be with my memories and in my dreams, along with the swirling and twirling of crazy hallucinations resulting from the medication. I gulped the offending pills down with the last of the wine, then made my way unsteadily upstairs to bed and waited for the show to begin

CHAPTER 17

IBIZA 1995

The red telephone in the corner of the flat was ringing madly. I plied my way through the huddled cluster of shrieking little girls who had just arrived for a dancing lesson and were battling over the flamenco skirts on the floor.

"You wore the spotted one last week," Sasha was screaming, "It's MY turn."

"Let Sasha have it Sky, there's a good girl," I separated them by the scruffs of their necks like a pair of puppies and reached over and grabbed the receiver.

"Hello?" I screeched over the high pitched racket, attempting without success to untwine Sasha's arms, which were now strung around my neck like a baby monkey as she clung on to me in floods of enraged tears.

"Darling, how are you?" the voice on the other end of the line boomed. It was Erik, the 'Great Oracle' himself, as camp as ever. The sound of his deep, familiar voice was a welcome relief compared to the shrill little voices surrounding me.

"You've caught me at a really bad time, heart," I tried to make myself heard over the background din, while at the same time bending my neck sideways at an awkward angle in order to prevent Sasha from wiping her nose on my shoulder, "I'm literally right up to my neck in it at the moment." I managed to prise her bony little arms from around my neck, untangle the telephone cord which was snaking its way around her tiny brown ankle and endeavour to give Erik my full attention. It was so good to hear his deep, dulcet tones. I pictured him back there in England on the other end of the line, sitting at his carved wooden desk piled high with open books and packs of scattered tarot cards and his crystal ball of course. He would probably be adorned in one of his ornate embroidered silk smoking jackets, totally impractical for rainy Lancashire, but then, that was Erik. I'd really missed him since I'd moved to Ibiza, as over the years, from that very first day I'd met him at Vera's infamous garden party at 'Kenolbri', he'd become one of my closest friends. But even though it was great to hear from him, now wasn't exactly a good time to talk. Twelve overexcited little girls were clamouring around my legs, anxious to start dancing, hoisting frilly skirts around their miniscule waists and arming their feet with nail tipped flamenco shoes.

As a rule, I didn't usually teach the girls in the flat, this was a definite one- off, but we were rehearsing for a charity show in aid of the disabled children of the island and the younger ones were in desperate need of the extra practice. I was beginning to wonder if, by agreeing to do this show, I'd maybe bitten off a bit more than I could chew. But it was way too late for second thoughts now.

I'd become a flamenco dancing teacher completely by chance, although throughout my life I've always been involved with dancing in some form or another. In Ibiza, or the island of dreams as it is otherwise known, you could be anything or anyone you wanted to be. Back then, Ibiza was the place where you could literally live the dream, you could take on a whole new identity if you so desired, and I suppose that's what I was attempting to do. My role as a dancing teacher had come about by chance. I was officially employed as an art teacher at the local hippy school and, because I'd been taking flamenco classes myself, it just sort of happened one day and had carried on from there. My troupe of little dancing girls had multiplied along the way and now numbered twenty in total. Fortunately, at least as far as my neighbours were concerned, they weren't all assembled in the flat that particular day, as there was no way the floor would have been able to withstand the strain.

My now famous 'flamenco' troupe had acquired a certain celebrity on the island and we were often called upon to perform at functions. They were beautiful young girls of mixed nationalities, Spanish,

English, German, Indonesian and a stunning black beauty called Deva. I loved every one of them as though they were my own daughters, but they could be a bit of a handful at times. Like now for instance! The noise of their shrill little voices was ringing in my ears and I could hardly hear myself think.

"How's Ibeeeeeza corazon?" Erik asked over the high-pitched din, then without waiting for an answer announced dramatically, "You'll never guess who's just phoned me."

"Quiet a minute please chicas," I implored them, putting a hand over my other ear, "Who?"

"Have a guess darling," Erik taunted me.

"Erik, I haven't time to play guessing games right now," I reproached him, "The tax collector?"

"No silly," Erik replied short temperedly, "It was Brian," he breathed his name reverentially down the phone.

"Brian?" I repeated stupidly, my heart beating like a pair of castanets and doing a few flamenco steps of its own.

"Yes, Brian darling," he repeated with a frustrated sigh. "He wanted to take us out for dinner."

"Dinner?" I echoed dumbly.

"Dinner darling," Erik snapped a trifle impatiently, "Are you going a bit deaf dearest?"

"But I thought he'd absconded to Bermuda with wife number three." I refused to call Brian's latest wife by her name so we'd nicknamed her number three.

"Well, he's back in England now," Erik continued hurriedly, in a rush to spill out his news, "On his own and he desperately wants to see you. I reminded him you were in Ibiza, but he said that wasn't a problem, we'd come out to you. So we'll be arriving on Wednesday," Erik fluttered excitedly, "And he told me to tell you to book us a suite in a five star hotel for a week."

"Impossible," I snapped, "On two counts. Firstly the small Spanish village in which I live does not have anything remotely resembling a five star hotel, and secondly, even though I would love to see you, I don't particularly want to see him. In fact, I don't even want him here on the island."

"And you'll never guess what's happened darling," Erik carried on regardless, dying to tell me, "Number Three has left him - she's only gone and buggered off with the temporary captain of his new yacht."

"Fancy that," I uttered with a weak attempt at sarcasm, pausing for a second to let the impact of Erik's revelation sink in, then putting my hand over the receiver, screamed at one of the little girls who was in immediate danger of falling off the table, "Melissa, get down this minute will you, and take my shoes off."

"Are you still there heart?" Erik's voice boomed down the telephone. "Speak to me corazon."

"I'm lost for words," I told him honestly, "Brian? Here in Ibiza," my voice faltered, "I just can't picture it somehow. Anyway," I snapped, feeling as though I'd been put on the spot, "I've just told you, haven't I? I don't want him to come here, simple as that."

"I don't think you'll be able to stop him darling," Erik bossily pronounced, "You know what he's like when he's got his mind set on something and his mind is set on seeing you."

"How is he?" I threw in casually, attempting to appear blasé.

"He's having a nervous breakdown of course," Erik sighed dramatically. "But I'm sure he'll tell you all the sordid details when we arrive, though I have to warn you darling, he's on the Prozac and hitting the bottle."

One of the girls was tugging at my skirt, "I'll have to go Erik. I can't take it in right now. I'll have to phone you back later."

For the next hour I mechanically went through the motions of trying to teach twelve little girls how to do the rumba, but my mind was in a total whirl. As they stamped their tiny feet and frenetically swished their skirts, my thoughts were doing a wild dance of their own, whirling back in time to when I'd last seen Brian. In some ways it felt like only yesterday, but in fact it was several years ago. So much had happened since I'd last seen him. My own marriage (which had turned out to be a terrible mistake) was also on the rocks. That's why I was now living in a small flat in Santa Eulalia with my son Ben, the only good thing to have come out of that disastrous union as far as I was concerned

Now here I was, a single mother, struggling to get by and in order to make ends meet, I was giving flamenco lessons and teaching art at the local hippy school. Every now and then I sold a painting or two and somehow or other, Ben and I were managing to survive without any financial help from my ex- husband.

Brian had never forgiven me for marrying Dave and to be quite honest, I wasn't really sure why I had. I'd met him on a two week package holiday. My mum had roped me into going with her to Spain, not long after I'd come back from the West Indies. It was during the time Brian was going through his messy divorce from the opera diva.

Dave was a totally different kettle of fish to Brian, and maybe that's why I'd fallen for his dubious charms. He was young for a start, well at least more my age and he was wild and carefree. He was a bit of a jack the lad with a lust for life (as well as anything in a skirt it later transpired) and a wandering spirit, which eventually led him to wander off and leave me. Good riddance as it turned out.

After the girls had finally gone home, feeling drained and exhausted, I grabbed myself a glass of wine and slumped down on the sofa, surveying the aftermath of their departure. Flouncy petticoats and multilayered spotted skirts lay strewn around the floor in colourful profusion, tangled up with long fringed shawls and strings of tacky plastic beads. Over in the corner, the Moroccan rug loomed menacingly like a huge, saggy sausage, waiting for me to unroll it. But I neither had the energy nor the desire to get up from the sofa, where I continued to lounge with my flamenco shoes kicked off and my swollen feet splayed out on the cushions. It could bloody well stay there till tomorrow; as could the empty cans of coke and half eaten biscuits lined up on the coffee table, crisp wrappers littering the black and white tiled floor and the solitary abandoned red and white spotted flamenco shoe. Probably Sasha's, I thought to myself, she was always forgetting things. The whole room looked as though a bomb had hit it, even the curtains which had been drawn to shut out the glare of the late afternoon sun, now hung in disarray, permitting a long shaft of sunlight to intrude and catch the million particles of dust, disturbed by the previous frenzy of activity and hold them suspended in a swirling tunnel of golden light.

I would tidy it all up tomorrow, I thought to myself lethargically, but then the panic-ridden realisation suddenly hit me that I would have to tidy up if Brian was on his way. Brian couldn't bear untidiness or things being out of their rightful place, no matter where he was. I smiled ruefully to myself. He would be suitably horrified by my hippy Ibiza lifestyle and wouldn't be too pleased about my teaching activities either, especially the dancing, as he'd always insisted, in order to become a great artist one should devote oneself entirely to one's art. That was all very well, but there were times when artists had to support themselves financially by other methods, such as teaching art. And as for the flamenco dancing, I think I'd taken that up as a mode of expression to release the pent up frustration of being trapped in a marriage to the wrong man.

My ex-husband had been decidedly derisive about the idea of me as a flamenco dancer, as he'd been about most things concerning me. I'd been strictly prohibited from practising in the house we had lived in, especially with my flamenco shoes on. I'd refused to abide by his rules of course, at least when he was out. I remembered one time I'd been practising my twirls in front of the bedroom mirror, without my shoes on, forgetting the fact that I'd been painting in my studio beforehand in bare feet and had spilled some yellow paint on the floor. It was only later I noticed the twirled in yellow stains embedded in the pale grey carpet and had to spend the next few hours trying to scrub them out before he came home. I was a bit scared of him to tell the truth. He had once arrived home unexpectedly and caught me with the rug rolled up, practising my footwork on the newly tiled floor and had gone absolutely berserk.

"Do you realise, if you hit an air pocket, you'll cost me thousands of pounds," he'd raged. But the man did come from Yorkshire after all and we were never really suited.

In retrospect, I think I'd probably only married him to prove to myself that I could escape from the control Brian had over me. Or maybe it was just to spite Brian after the way he'd left me alone in the West Indies. Whatever the reason, I soon found out I'd made a dreadful mistake, but I was locked in holy matrimony by that time and heavily pregnant with Ben.

Brian had come to visit me in hospital just after Ben had been born and looked at him lying there in the crib next to me and cried, saying he wished it had been our baby. Not long after that, he got married again to number three, a distant cousin who, according to him, had turned up one day on his doorstep. Because of his enormous wealth Brian was never short of women turning up on his doorstep (or anywhere else for that matter) and wanting to marry him. I hadn't seen much of him after that. His new wife had been insanely jealous of our past relationship and had barred him from seeing me. Not that that had stopped us of course. Brian told me she'd even insisted that the painting of "The Spider and the Fly" be removed from 'Kenolbri', so he'd hung it in pride of place in his office instead. There he could look at it without her jealous eyes accusing him of still having feelings for me. At least, that's what he told me.

Despite our disastrous marriages, Brian and I had always managed to somehow keep in touch over the years and he'd never lost interest in my progress as an artist. He'd always attended my exhibitions and had continued to buy my work, although we still had a volatile relationship of course and he'd been most displeased about me moving to Spain. But I knew he would always be there for me should I really need him.

The burning question was, did I need him now - and my immediate reaction to that was no. I didn't need any more complications in my life; my disastrous marriage had been enough to cure me of any romantic aspirations.

Brian's marriage to number three had also been through its rocky times and at one point, while he was away on business, she'd allegedly tried to commit suicide. Luckily, Mrs Coombs the housekeeper had found her in time, after which Brian told me she'd spent several months in a psychiatric hospital. She desperately wanted to have a child, the one thing he couldn't provide her with, and maybe there were other reasons. Brian was not an easy man to live with, as well I knew. But no matter how much water had flowed under our various matrimonial bridges, there was no denying the fact that I was curious to see him again; needed to see him again in fact. I had so much to tell him and it sounded as though he had a lot to tell me, so I picked up the phone and booked the nearest thing I could find to a five star hotel; then waited in anticipation (and a certain amount of dread) for Wednesday to arrive.

When the day of Brian and Erik's arrival eventually dawned, I turned up at the airport way too early and paced the shiny marble floor, sick with nerves. How was I going to feel when Brian walked through those doors? A mixture of emotions: anticipation, dread, longing, anger, all battled their way to the forefront of my mind. Then there was an even stronger feeling, something more akin to hope; the hope that he was coming to rescue me. But that was ridiculous. Rescue me from what? I was happy enough wasn't I? Of course I was. I didn't need Brian coming back into my life and disrupting me. I was over him, I would be glad to see him again of course, but I didn't love him anymore – or did I?

The announcement finally rang out over the tannoy that the Iberia flight from London Heathrow had landed and the passengers had now disembarked and were making their way to the baggage hall to collect their luggage. I rushed excitedly to the arrivals gate and peered through the sliding doors, trying to single Brian out in the crowd, or at least Erik, who by virtue of his eccentric choice of wardrobe was always easy to spot, but there was no sign of either of them. The passengers came flooding out in their droves, dragging suitcases and wheeling trolleys piled high with bags, only to be instantly swamped by excited friends and relatives then quickly shepherded away. I watched with a feeling of nostalgia coupled with envy as reunited lovers flung their arms around each other in a welcoming embrace, oblivious to everyone and anything else, and even though it was all those years ago, I could still remember the terrible sense of abandonment and disappointment I'd felt when I'd arrived back from the West Indies and Brian hadn't been there at the airport to meet me.

Perhaps he'd changed his mind this time I worried, and he wasn't going to come after all? I wouldn't have put it past him: to build up my hopes, only to knock them down again. But then I spotted Erik making his way through the sliding door, pushing the luggage trolley and looking dashing in a navy blue double-breasted jacket with gold buttons (obviously new) and a white panama hat. Shuffling behind him, looking his age and hiding behind a pair of yellow tinted sunglasses, was Brian. He looked terrible. In fact, he looked like an old man; his shoulders slumped and his once jet black hair now intermingled with strands of silver. But the worst was, that he seemed totally confused, as if he didn't know where he was – or even who he was.

"My car is on the car park," I informed them breathlessly, after we'd kissed politely and said our hellos, "It's a bit of an old heap," I apologized.

"Wait there with the luggage and I'll go and get it."

I think it still hadn't registered with Brian that he was now on terra firma and about to have his first sighting of Ibiza. Erik did most of the talking as I drove them to Santa Eulalia while Brian sat hunched in the front seat at my side, hiding behind his tinted sunglasses. He seemed not to notice the sights of Ibiza, the old Moorish town with its ancient streets winding their way up to the magnificent cathedral looking down over the lines of boats anchored in the harbour. The picturesque countryside dotted with white farmhouses, or fincas as they are called, and the old, square churches dangling their rusty bells. The trees laden with oranges and lemons silhouetted against the brilliant blue sky or the odd horse and cart jogging along at the side of the road, as though in some strange time warp.

As soon as we arrived at the hotel and I'd helped check them into their rooms, Brian immediately ordered a bottle of wine, although it was plain to see that he was already drunk. I presented him with the welcome gift I'd bought for him, a small box neatly tied with a sky blue ribbon, his favourite colour, complete with a handpicked flower from my balcony. Inside the box was a tiny pair of handmade crocodile shoes, just like the ones he always used to wear, apart from the fact that they were bright pink! They even had tiny pink shoelaces. I watched nervously as he carefully un-wrapped them, not sure how he would react to this almost childlike offering and feeling slightly foolish in the process. But he cupped the miniature shoes in his long, shaky hands and his eyes filled with tears, at which point all reserve on my part was abandoned and I threw my arms around his neck as he broke down and sobbed in my hair. After a while, conscious that there was somebody else in the room, I looked at Erik over his shoulder and we exchanged meaningful glances.

"I'm rather drunk darling," Erik slurred; then in his way trying to be tactful, added, "Maybe I should go to my room and have a little siesta."

But Brian, making a swift effort to pull himself together, wasn't having it. If he wasn't having a siesta, no one was – so still the same Brian then. Instead, he ordered Erik to call room service for another bottle of wine to be sent up and by the time we had to leave for dinner at the posh restaurant I'd booked at Brian's request, they were both legless.

Over dinner Brian told me the story of wife number three's betrayal in all its litigious glory, although he was obviously still finding the whole sorry business very distressing. She'd apparently persuaded him to sell 'Netlon' (although how she'd managed to do that I'll never know) and move to Bermuda, where she was still a resident. Brian told me he'd gone along with the idea mainly for tax reasons. Once decided, not being a man to do things in short measures, he'd purchased a beautiful mansion on the island, which he'd refurbished to the tune of several million pounds. He'd then shipped his most treasured possessions from 'Kenolbri', which, fortunately, he hadn't sold, as it was his old family home and he couldn't bear to part with it. So at least he still had that, because, as he was soon to find out, he was about to lose everything else. Returning to England to tie up some loose ends, he told me that he'd only been back home for a day, when to his shock and horror, he shuddered at the only too recent memory, wife number three had served the divorce papers on him.

"She'd obviously been planning it for months," he told me bitterly, "If not years."

"How did you find out find about her affair?" I asked him curiously.

"I had absolutely no idea she'd been carrying on behind my back, otherwise she would have been out on her elbow long before now," he declared righteously, "Although apparently, everyone else knew what was going on. I only found out through a bundle of mail which had been forwarded to 'Kenolbri' from the West Indies. By chance, Erik was here with me when the parcel arrived and when I opened it I nearly had a heart attack. It was crammed full of letters to her lover, the temporary captain of my yacht Corinthian who I'd been obliged to employ while my regular captain was on leave."

"You should read them darling," Erik pronounced dramatically. "You know I'm not easily shocked, but they were enough to make even me blush."

"There was even a photograph of our king-sized bed," Brian gritted his teeth angrily, "With the sheets all tousled from their lovemaking and she'd scrawled something underneath, calling him darling and begging him to please be patient because it would soon be their bed once they'd got rid of me."

"So you didn't suspect anything was going on when she suddenly persuaded you to up sticks and move to Bermuda?" I asked him outright. "You must have had your doubts."

"None whatsoever," he shook his head sadly, "Why should I, although I have to admit, things weren't going too well between us in the sexual sense and hadn't been for quite some time."

This last comment at least afforded me some kind of solace in that he hadn't been enjoying the kind of passionate relationship I'd imagined him to be having with his now, about to be ex, wife.

"Anyway, thanks to those letters," Brian continued resolutely, "I now have plenty of ammunition in the form of written evidence for the divorce. I'll fight her every step of the way. She'll not get a brass farthing if it's up to me."

Two more bottles of wine and several Grand Marniers later, Erik and I had to practically carry him back to the hotel. Looking down on him lying on the bed, with his mouth open and his white belly protruding out of his shirt, I couldn't imagine that this was the love of my life; the man I could not forget, or escape from, no matter how hard I tried.

"I'll see you both tomorrow for breakfast," I told Erik and hastily made my escape.

But I couldn't sleep a wink that night. My mind was in turmoil. Why did he have to come back into my life? Why wouldn't he just leave me alone? I was happy here in Ibiza. I'd forged a new life for myself. I had lots of new friends and there was my son of course and my little dancing girls. I didn't want all those old feelings for Brian to come surging back. It was too painful. Well, I wouldn't have them I tried to convince myself. I wouldn't let him ensnare me back in his web. But I'd forgotten just how manipulative Brian could be.

The next day, I picked them both up at the hotel and took them to my studio which was in a tiny house on the outskirts of the village. I couldn't wait to show Brian my new paintings. I was desperate to hear what he had to say about them; his opinion still mattered to me more than that of any art critic. We had to stop off at the bodega on the way of course, to buy some champagne and several bottles of wine. But Brian hardly even looked at my paintings. He was in a Prozac-enhanced daze and more interested in the wine to be honest. It ended up with the three of us, me included, getting as drunk as lords and we spent the blazing hot afternoon sitting round the rickety wooden table on the patio shaded by the curtained fronds of red, purple and gold bougainvillea; then acting silly and dressing up in the theatrical costumes I stored there for my dance productions.

Erik was in his absolute element, a glass of champagne in his hand and a white net tutu wrapped around his head. "I can see an open grave," he ominously joked, pretending to read the crystal ball. I was hoping the open grave he was referring to wasn't Brian's, because as my mum would say, he was starting to look a bit like death warmed up as a result of all the alcohol he'd imbibed. But to my surprise, Brian also seemed to take great delight in dressing up and had determinedly squeezed himself into a tight, blue ruffled dress with a long billowing tail and was managing to give a good impression of 'The Little Mermaid' - or at least trying to, as not being a fan of Walt Disney or having any children of his own, he didn't really know who she was.

Brian wasn't impressed with Ibiza. He didn't like the hotel (it only had three stars) and he was jealous of all my new friends. He seemed to be in a complete daze but that was probably the Prozac, and he was certainly hitting the bottle with a vengeance. I tried to show him the more beautiful parts of Ibiza; I drove him right up to the top of the old Moorish town, through the perilous winding streets, steeped with history, to visit the ancient cathedral. I took him on a magical mystery tour through the beautiful countryside carpeted with bright yellow flowers and sprinkled with poppies and wild irises. We drove as far as the very tip of the island to view the mystical rock of 'es Vedra', where, according to legend, the sirens would summon the ancient mariners to their deaths. I drove him all around the island's rugged coastline, lapped by crystal clear waters and indented with ultramarine bays; then on to Beniras to watch the renowned, and much photographed, sunset. There, against the backdrop of a magenta sky, the hippies drummed their tribal lament to the God of the red sun as it slowly dipped its head and disappeared into the darkening sea. But nothing seemed to get through to him. Every day, the three of us met up in the morning for breakfast after which we'd move on to some restaurant or another for seemingly endless lunches, during which Brian drank bottle after bottle of wine, then eventually on to dinner where he drank even more. The week passed with him in a drunken stupor and, as usual when he'd been hitting the bottle, we spent most of the time arguing.

On their last night, Brian and I left Erik at the hotel and we went out for dinner on our own.

"Come back to England with me Adrienne," he begged after we'd finished our meal, most of which he hardly ate, his hand shaking as he clutched his glass of Grand Marnier, "I need you to be with me."

"I can't," I told him firmly, "I have a life here now and you're still a married man don't forget. I'm not going through all that again. You're just using me between marriages."

"You know that's not true," he hung his head, "I've never stopped loving you. We were made for each other. I've never met anyone remotely like me and I've never met anyone remotely like you."

Oh, not that weary old chestnut again, I sighed to myself! If he wanted to convince me to come back to him, he'd have to try a new tack.

"I still love you and I think you still love me," he stared at me intently, "And besides, I could do so much for you," he tried to bribe me. "I could help you with your art. You know I'm still your biggest fan."

"You hardly even looked at my new work," I accused him bitterly.

"There are so many things I want to do," he ignored me and quickly carried on, "And so many places I haven't seen, that I want to share with you and only with you."

"You've got Erik now, your new minder and travelling companion," I told him a touch resentfully, "Take him with you. He'd love it."

"It's not the same and you know it isn't," Brian said sadly. "Anyway, Erik's gay."

Although Erik had been married and had begotten three lovely children to his name, in his heart he was a homosexual and as camp, as they say, as a row of tents.

At the click of Brian's shaky fingers, the obsequious waiter who had been hovering discreetly in the wings, slunk up to our table and reverentially presented Brian with the carved leather box which concealed our bill, hoping for a huge tip no doubt.

"Can you read that for me?" Brian took the flimsy piece of paper out of the box, peered at it then pushed it over to me. I told him how much it was, some ridiculous figure that would keep me and Ben in food for a week, then pushed it back.

"You know I'm having trouble with my eyesight," Brian took out his magnifying glass and squinted at the bill in the candlelight.

I looked at him for the first time that night with genuine sympathy as I knew only too well what it felt like to lose the precious gift of sight. Although it had happened many years ago when Ben had only been a little boy, recalling the traumatic occasion still made me tremble with horror. We'd been at Heathrow airport at the time, waiting to board our flight back to Ibiza and I'd been putting a battery in the new remote control car I'd bought him from the duty free shop, when the car exploded in my face, completely blinding me.

I was rushed in an ambulance to Moorfields eye hospital and there had been some doubt as to whether I would ever be able to see again. During those horrific few weeks while I waited to find out if my eyes would ever recover from the acid burns caused by the exploding batteries, I'd experienced firsthand what it felt like to inhabit a world of darkness. A world where other people had to do things for you; pass you a cup of tea, hand you an ashtray, cut up your food and spoon feed you like a child, lead you around by the hand. I was forced to consider the unthinkable fact that I might never paint again. If that were to be the case, I'd decided philosophically, I would resign myself to becoming a sculptor instead. At least it hadn't happened to my beautiful son, I'd consoled myself, because that would have been unbearable.

As it turned out I'd regained my sight a few weeks later, but Brian it seemed, would not be so fortunate. He told me he was suffering from some kind of degenerative eye disease and had been told by the specialist that he could soon go blind, but unlike me, his sight loss would be permanent.

I tried to imagine what losing his sight would mean for a man like him. It would totally destroy his life. He would no longer be able to work on his new invention which he professed would solve the world's energy crisis; look through his huge library of illustrated art books or even read for that matter. He would be forced to cast unseeing eyes on his fabulous collection of art and only feel by touch his bronze and marble sculptures. No longer would he be able to revel in the changing seasons, so theatrically presented and meticulously choreographed down to the last tiny leaf by his team of dedicated gardeners in the beautiful gardens that he adored. He could not glory in the spectacular sunsets framed by the long glass windows in the sunroom, see the stars twinkling through the domed hatches in the ceiling, or even see me for that matter. He'd be lost. He'd need someone to help him. He'd need me to be his eyes. I looked at him fussing with the bill and sighed.

"Make sure I've only added the minimum tip," he ordered, passing the bill back to me. For all his generosity in other ways, he hated leaving tips. The hovering waiter was about to be bitterly disappointed I feared.

"Well, you know where I am," he said finishing the last dregs of his Grand Marnier, "All you have to do is pick up the phone."

They took a taxi back to the airport.

CHAPTER 18

Ocean going cruise

My life had carried on as normal after Brian and Erik had left, at least as normal as life can be in a crazy place like Ibiza, which by normal standards I suppose wasn't normal at all. I hadn't heard anything from either of them since they'd gone back to England but a few weeks passed and then I got a phone call from Erik.

"I've been on Brian's yacht darling," he gushed excitedly. "It was wonderful. Do you know, it cost over two million pounds and it has six crew members? What luxury, I was waited on hand and foot and my every desire was pandered to."

"Well lucky old you," I snapped jealously. The fact that Erik had been on the yacht was annoying me more than I was prepared to admit, even though I knew he'd temporarily moved in with Brian and was acting as a kind of personal companion. A bit like those rich old ladies or aunts whom nobody can stand and are therefore obliged to pay someone to keep them company.

"We flew to Paris first and stayed in the George V," Erik pronounced boastfully, "I've always wanted to stay there and you know how I love Paris darling," he sighed, "It reminded me of my youth."

"How's Brian?" I cut him off mid flow before he stared reminiscing. I wasn't in the mood to listen to him waxing lyrical about his misspent youth, as fascinating as it undoubtedly had been. I had more important things on my mind, like how Brian was getting on for example. "How's he coping?" I enquired, trying to sound casual.

"Oh, you know," Erik sniffed dismissively, "still drinking heavily and threatening to put the perfidious number three and her lover in a lead casket."

"Does he talk about me?" I asked him, unable to help myself.

"He talks about you all the time darling, in fact, he never stops. It's becoming a bore to be quite frank. Why don't you call him and put him out of his misery?"

"He can always call me," I answered sulkily, "But then again, why should he if he's got your ear twenty-four seven to pour his troubles in to."

"Don't be like that, heart," Erik tried to placate me, "You know I'm only second best because he can't have you. In fact, he asked me to call you. He's standing here right beside me now and we're both a bit drunk actually," he tittered, causing me to feel a surge of impatience with the pair of them, drunken fools. "He wants me to persuade you to come back to England," Erik continued Brian's directive, his voice starting to slur. "He says he still loves you and he can't live without you and for you to come back as soon as possible."

"No chance," I retorted defensively, "Anyway, why can't he tell me that himself?"

A week later there was another phone call, but this time from Brian. "How are you?" he asked me in his deep, sad voice, sounding thoroughly miserable.

"Fine," I chirped brightly, which I wasn't of course. I hadn't stopped thinking about him since the day he left.

"Don't answer now," he threw in quickly, "But will you come for a cruise on the yacht with me? We won't be on our own. I've invited my nephew and his girlfriend and my niece. I don't want you to feel compromised in any way. You can have your own cabin of course. Don't give me your answer now, think about it and I'll phone you tomorrow."

He hung up on me before I had chance to turn him down.

My mum had come out to stay with us for a few weeks. She often came to Ibiza and loved the island life, revelling in the Mediterranean climate and the chance to be with her grandson and her eldest daughter of course. She'd become accustomed over the years to the ups and downs of the ongoing relationship Brian and I shared, so was not at all surprised by the fact that he'd called me to ask if I'd 'accompany' him on his yacht. I could tell that she was totally in favour of the idea even though she wasn't saying so outright. But I had other ideas on the subject.

"I don't want to go on his yacht with him, I don't care how luxurious it is," I declared bad temperedly. We were sitting on the sea front in Santa Eulalia having a coffee in a bar we called 'pink tablecloths' for the simple reason it was one of the few bars that actually had tablecloths and was therefore slightly more upmarket, a fact which appealed to my mum. We were watching Ben and his Spanish friends happily kicking a football around on the beach. With his long, blonde hair he stood out amongst the crowd of budding Ronaldo's and Ronaldinos and looked a bit like David Beckham when he was a young lad, without the tattoos of course and before he shaved his head. I watched him proudly from afar wondering how I had managed to produce such a good-looking son.

"The last thing I want to do in this world," I tore my eyes away from Ben and dunked my croissant messily in my milky glass of coffee, "is to swan around the Mediterranean on a luxury yacht."

My mum sipped her coffee in a more ladylike manner and slowly nibbled round the edge of her croissant like a refined bunny rabbit.

"All those snotty rich people sitting around on gin palaces drinking cocktails," I pulled a face, "I couldn't stand it."

"I thought Erik said it was a real sailing boat," my mum briefly stopped her nibbling to chip in.

"Huh!" I retorted. What did she know about boats? "Gin palace, yacht; what's the difference?"

"I could think of far worse things in life," pronounced my mum, whose biggest fear for me had always been that I'd end up in a council flat.

"Does he think he can just come back into my life and sweep me off my feet?" I fired my inquisition at her, "I don't care if he is having a nervous breakdown. I don't care if he is going blind. He should never have married wife number three. It serves him bloody right."

"You don't really mean that," my mum contested.

And I didn't of course, apart from the marrying number three part.

We both sipped our coffee in silence thinking our separate thoughts.

"Well, I don't care what you say," I muttered, "I'm not going to be lured back into his web, ever again."

"I didn't say a word," declared my mum defensively.

"You didn't have to," I retaliated.

"It's only a cruise after all," she pointed out, "It's not for the rest of your life. You'd only be going on holiday with him and just imagine, all that luxury," she sighed enviously. "Think of the interesting people you'd meet and all the new places you'd see. Where did you say the yacht was going?"

Brian had faxed me a map and a copy of the itinerary. I took the crumpled piece of paper out of my bag and spread it out on the table.

"The south of France," I traced it with my finger, "I hate the south of France it's so pretentious. Then on to Sardinia according to these arrows and then the southern coast of Italy, ending up in Portofino, supposedly the home of the International Jet Set. How bloody boring."

"Mmmm," my mum hummed wistfully and who could think of nothing nicer than being pampered to death on a luxury yacht, not to mention mingling with the International Jet Set (whoever they might be!). "You've never been to Italy have you?" she added craftily.

"No I haven't and it looks like I'm not going to," I retorted emphatically, "At least not with him."

"Suit yourself," she sniffed sulkily.

We sat there in stony silence.

"I've always wanted to go to Italy though," I eventually had to admit, looking wistfully at the boot shaped coastline pictured on the map and picturing myself in Rome, "And maybe I'd be denying myself as an artist if I didn't take this opportunity."

"Opportunity only knocks once," my mum quoted a line from the once popular television programme aimed at showcasing new talent, long before Simon Cowell and the X Factor had hit our screens.

"So maybe I should consider it." I finally relented

"Well, I wouldn't consider it for too long," advised my mum, finishing her coffee and standing up. "I'd phone him right now if I were you, before he changes his mind and takes someone else."

In the end, I'd given in of course and agreed to go on the cruise with Brian, with a bit of a push from my mum. It seemed I was incapable of saying no to him and it had always been that way, although I was not alone in that respect. Few people could say no to him, and he always seemed to manage to get his way in the end

My mum stayed in Ibiza to look after Ben, and after meeting up with Brian in England, we flew directly to the South of France to join the yacht in Antibes. I'd been a bit wary about meeting him on my own, especially after our last debacle in Ibiza, but from the outset, Brian seemed in much better form and more like his old self. However, I remained constantly on my guard, conscious of the fact that he was being on his very best behaviour and obviously terrified to put a foot wrong.

The captain of Brian's yacht was waiting at Nice airport to greet us. He was a distinguished looking Englishman called Graham Pearson who chatted amiably to Brian over his shoulder as he steered the Mercedes confidently through the traffic-logged coastal roads to Antibes, then through narrow streets of the old fortress-like town to the marina. Here the heavy polluted air suddenly lifted and turned crystal clear, bathing the endless lines of glitzy yachts and motor cruisers, manacled to their pontoons, with the translucent light you only find in the Mediterranean. Brian, usually so constrained in the presence of members of his staff, had started to fidget excitedly in his seat, filled with an almost childlike anticipation at the thought of seeing his boat again. The captain drove us regally along the quay, the long silver bonnet of the Mercedes imperiously nosing aside the strolling sightseers as we passed alongside the rows of expensive looking boats, most of them devoid of their occupants apart from an odd member of crew hosing the decks or polishing the brasses. We pulled up directly alongside a magnificent white yacht, sporting the tallest mast in the harbour and which had the most stunning aspect of any of its sister ships or neighbours – the other yachts all paled into total insignificance beside her.

"Is this it?" I breathed in stunned disbelief.

Brian smiled smugly and reached over to squeeze my hand. The captain opened the car doors for us and as we got out, a crowd of people gathered on the quayside to watch as we strolled up the lowered gangplank like film stars and climbed aboard.

Corinthian was everything Erik had said it would be and so much more. It was, without doubt, the most spectacular sailing boat in the marina and it was absolutely immaculate. The pale teak and maple decks were spotless, the white paint work sparkled in the brilliant sunshine and the glossed varnish gleamed. The uniformed crew were expectantly lined up waiting on deck to greet us as though we were royalty. Brian officially introduced me to them one by one and I felt like Lady Diana as I politely moved along the line and shook all their hands. Then the Captain's wife, Ollie, (who was also the cook) presented us with a tastefully arranged tray of lobster canapés and a glass of icy cold champagne.

Graham proudly explained that Corinthian is what people in the know would describe as a 'super yacht' - in other words she was a real sailing boat and a fast one at that - the kind you could enter in the America's cup and probably win.

But aside from that, Corinthian was pure, unadulterated luxury and I'd like to say that I felt out of place surrounded by such sumptuous decadence, but somehow I didn't. Maybe that was because Brian was so overjoyed that I'd finally given in and agreed to accompany him, that he was going out of his way to make me feel at home and at ease, and I was more than glad now that I'd decided to join him. Not only because Corinthian was so beautiful, but because the simple fact of my being there had made him so ridiculously happy.

Brian took me on a conducted tour of the rest of the boat, including the crew's quarters and the galley, which seemed luxurious to me but then I saw that they had their own stairway to the deck and access to the engine room to ensure that the guests (and that meant the likes of me) were not disturbed! The engine room resembled something out of a futuristic science fiction movie and housed the huge Orca marine power system, which, according to the captain, enabled extended periods of quiet ship state. I didn't have a clue what he was talking about to be honest or what an Orca marine power system was, an Orca sounded like some strange space creature from out of a Steven Spielberg film to me, but whatever, it all looked very impressive.

Brian told me proudly that there were only three other super yachts such as Corinthian in the entire world and that she'd been built in New Zealand by Alloy Yachts and designed by the world famous Dubois Naval Architects. The design of the interior was sleek and modern, the curved maple wood fittings blending in tastefully with the pale beige carpet. In the main dining area, eight cream leather chairs were placed in line with the long polished table and huge white lamps and concealed lighting illuminated the sculptures ensconced in the alcoves. In the lower seating area, a leather sofa curved around a low coffee table which held a beautiful floral decoration which had been arranged by Ollie. All in all, it was more like a posh hotel really than a boat, and I tried to imagine myself sitting on that smooth leather sofa while being tossed in a gale on the high seas.

Continuing with the conducted tour, Brian then led me down some polished wooden steps and along a corridor to the guest cabins or staterooms as they were officially called, each with its own marble finished en suite bathroom and entertainment centre. Then finally to the master stateroom, which was Brian's of course and which boasted a huge king-sized bed and a mirrored bathroom with a marble floor and a full sized bath with gold plated fittings. The Stateroom was carpeted in pale gold with mirrored wardrobes running the length of one wall, a film star-like dressing table against the other, and a low, blue sofa under the slatted wooden blinds covering the portholes.

After the conducted tour was over, we went back up on deck where we were served more canapés and champagne and I felt myself start to relax a bit. This cruise might turn out so much better than I'd anticipated I thought happily to myself. I looked at Brian and he smiled back at me beaming with contentment, delighted that he finally had me all to himself. We sat together, a bit self-consciously under the watchful eyes of the crew, side by side on the white leather seats in the cockpit, under the shade of the canopy to protect us from the sun, only it wasn't called a canopy; it was called a Bimini.

Everything seemed to have a special name on a boat and I would have to quickly familiarize myself with all these strange nautical terms, for a start which was port and which was starboard, if I was going to be a true sailor. Although, the fact that there was a competent captain on board supported by his able members of crew, signified that there would not be much, if any, actual sailing involved as far as the guests were concerned. A fact which suited me right down to the ground, as I'd never really known what do with all those ropes and fenders.

Brian and I weren't on our own for long, however, before we were joined later that afternoon by his nephew John and his girlfriend Leslie (both psychiatrists) and his niece Jane who I already knew from the 'Clog and Billycock' days. After knocking back their welcoming glasses of champagne, they all disappeared down below to their cabins to freshen up; but Brian and I stayed up on deck watching the sun slowly start to set over the marina, reluctant to part. True to his word, I had been allocated my own cabin, which was affectionately nicknamed 'nanny's cabin' because it had two extra bunk beds and its own ensuite bathroom.

When it was time to leave the magnificent sunset and go down below to change for dinner, I found my clothes had already been unpacked for me and there was a bowl of freshly cut flowers on my dressing table. It wouldn't be hard to get used to this decadent lifestyle I worried to myself as I got dressed up in my 'finery' for pre-dinner cocktails, I would have to be very careful not to let it all go to my head.

Brian remained on his best behaviour throughout dinner, which was served to us up on deck by the crew, and after coffee and liquors, which Brian altruistically declined, we all went off to our separate cabins to sleep. It seemed strange for Brian and I to be acting like virtual strangers, but we had made a pact and had both agreed that we would let 'things' (if there in fact should be any) take their natural course, After his drunken behaviour in Ibiza, I wasn't about to take any chances. At least, not yet.

The next morning, with the minimum of fuss, and with absolutely no involvement from we guests whatsoever, Corinthian slid majestically out of the marina and we left Antibes and set sail along the coast to San Tropez, where a berth was waiting for us on 'Millionaire's Row.' We breakfasted on deck with hordes of people looking on from the quay, thinking that we must be famous celebrities. The worrying part of it for me was that I was beginning to feel like one.

While Brian planned our itinerary with the captain, Jane and I disembarked and took a stroll in the marina to investigate the trendy bars and boutiques. En route, I confessed to her that I was rather a nervous sailor and although excited by the prospect of our forthcoming voyage to Corsica and Sardinia, I wasn't particularly looking forward to being out on the high seas. This fear was being exacerbated by the fact that I couldn't swim. Well, I could manage a few pathetic strokes but that was about it. I went into a total panic if my head went under water, or if my feet couldn't touch the ground. In fact, I was finally forced to admit, I was terrified of water full stop. Jane, being of a sporty nature herself, the type of person who would relish any given challenge and who unlike me, felt perfectly at home on the high seas, shepherded me directly into a tourist shop selling lilos and rubber rings. She helped me select two bright green arm bands, designed for a child, with matching floats to go round my waist. As we were making our way back to Corinthian with my embarrassing purchases tucked under my arm, we were nearly mown down by the fluorescent vision of Brian hurtling along the quay on a bicycle, wearing a bright orange lifejacket.

"I wondered where you'd gone," he smiled at me nervously, obviously not wanting to let me out of his sight for an instant in case I jumped ship and disappeared back to Ibiza, which I'd threatened to do if he didn't behave. "It's years since I've been on a bicycle," Brian grinned at me spinning the pedal with his foot, "Do you want a ride on my crossbar?" he winked.

"He's in his second childhood," Jane whispered in my ear, "Showing off for you."

"See you back on board, the Captain is ready to set sail," he peddled off, swaying erratically from side to side, nearly knocking an old man off his crutches as he went.

Brian deposited the bike with a member of crew, then hurried back to reclaim me and after dismissing Jane, suggested we went for a coffee on our own.

"I thought you said the Captain was ready to head off," I remonstrated.

"He can wait," Brian took my arm, "In fact they can all wait. I want you on my own for a bit."

We sat down at a small café and watched the passing crowds as we talked about the past and our misspent relationships and how much it had meant to him that I'd finally agreed to come on this cruise. Then feeling much more comfortable and at ease with each other, we meandered back to Corinthian, arm in arm.

Back on board, the two psychiatrists were having a heated debate about belly button piercing. From the moment they'd arrived, they'd been busy arguing about something or other, or worse, canoodling, which really seemed to get on Brian's nerves. Lesley, or so it appeared, could not leave John alone. She was forever clinging to his side and 'pawing' him as Brian described it. In direct contrast, Brian and I were keeping our hands strictly to ourselves (at least in company) and still withholding a polite distance. This seemed to be causing Brian some frustration, which he took out at regular intervals on the two irksome love birds.

"For God's sake put him down will you?" he shouted at Lesley who was clinging on to John like a limpet. "You don't know where he's been."

Lesley blushed and clung on even tighter. She was obviously terrified of Brian.

Anchors away and we sailed around the coast to Port Grimaud where the Captain ferried us ashore, whizzing across the bay in the white tender with Corinthian written on the side. The port was a bit like a modern day Venice and after navigating the sluggish canals in the heat of the midday sun, we pulled up directly alongside an ice cream parlour where we were spoiled for choice for flavours. We then cruised up and down the picturesque Venetian like waterways, licking our ice cream cones and singing *'Just one Cornetto, geeeev eeeet to me.'*

Back to Corinthian and on to a tiny bay hiding behind the rocky headland, where once again the Captain ferried us ashore, but this time to a deserted pebble beach for an evening swim. I braved the deeper crystal clear water for the first time and proudly learned to turn around with my water wings on. When it was time to leave, we wrapped ourselves in the huge blue and yellow towels handed to us by the crew, then clambered back into the dinghy to be ferried back to Corinthian, with the red sun sinking majestically on the horizon.

The crew served us dinner on deck by candlelight with the lights of San Tropez to the left and Port Grimaud to the right. As we dined, Jet skiers whizzed past in the moonlight, rocking the boat and causing slight ripples in our wine.

"Fuck off," Brian shouted after them.

The next day we set sail for Corsica.

I woke up in nanny's cabin at 5 am with a slight hangover, thinking I was on some sort of roller coaster. I staggered out of my bunk, slipped on the white cotton Kimono with the blue embroidered birds I'd bought at a flea market in Ibiza just before I left and went up on deck. It was just starting to get light and Corinthian was already way out to sea and seemed to be sailing all by herself like a ghost ship. I sat hunched by the wheel wrapped in my kimono with the warm, salty wind ruffling my hair watching the deep ultramarine waves whizzing past, revelling in the feeling of aloneness and the new and unaccustomed sensation for me of being at one with the sea, with Mother Nature. There was no land in sight, no other boats to be seen and not a bird in the sky, only the insistent swish of the waves as Corinthian ploughed her way determinedly onwards. This feeling of solitude, of not really knowing where I was going or what would happen on the way made me feel like an adventurer taking part in a voyage of discovery.

Eventually, a member of crew sleepily appeared from the crew's quarters down below and dispelled my reverie by asking if I'd like some coffee. I sipped my coffee in a china cup and watched the sun slowly rise over the horizon as Corinthian gracefully rode the waves.

I recalled the strange dream I'd had sometime during the night in which the Captain had turned out to be a junkie and Jane and I had been pumping his arm, laughing and saying that it was the most work we'd done all day. This peculiar dream had probably come about because the two of us had been making jokes the day before about our fears of becoming the 'idle rich' as the only work we'd had to do since we'd been on the boat, was lift the tea pot.

Brian was the next to surface and he made his way unsteadily to join me on deck, his face rumpled with sleep. We sat together side by side, in companionable silence, watching the sun slowly roll like a golden pinball with the boat's motion against the background of a cobalt blue sky, until the others finally deigned to arise; then the crew served us breakfast. By that time there was a terrific swell and we had a rough eleven hours at sea. My earlier feelings of being at one with the sea and Mother Nature were quickly dispelled and replaced by sheer terror. It was like being in the America's cup with the boat completely on its side, skimming through the waves at a rate of knots. I was gripping onto my seat and feeling seasick, but Brian loved it. The sea air seemed to revive him and he suddenly looked ten years younger, without a care in the world. He put a Frank Sinatra CD belting out on the stereo and had a mad half hour, tap dancing along the sloping deck, dangling from poles, climbing up the boom and grinning down at me.

Later, when the waves had calmed somewhat and we could make our precarious way to the front of the boat, we sat huddled together under a blanket, drinking chilled white wine as we scanned the horizon looking for our first sighting of Corsica.

"You're completely mad you know," I told him, laughing, "You could have been swept overboard back there."

"Would you have missed me?" He asked, taking my hand.

"A bit," I smiled.

"I suppose I am a bit odd," he admitted. "I don't know anyone remotely like me."

"Neither do I," I agreed heartily.

"And I don't know anyone remotely like you," he added. "We were meant to be together. You know that don't you?"

I tactfully removed my hand from his, pretending to tie back my hair in an attempt to both evade his question and at the same time avoid any physical contact. Luckily, at that moment Jane staggered along the outer deck, clutching onto the rails to join us.

"Where are John and Lesley?" Brian barked at her in headmaster-like tones, as if they were errant school children playing truant.

"In bed," Jane informed him directly, then quickly added by way of an excuse,

"Having a siesta."

"Having it off more like," Brian sneered with a possible touch of jealousy in his voice. "If they roll out of bed in this swell, they'll still be stuck together. That bloody Lulabelle never lets go of him. Go and get them up," he ordered Jane.

"Why do you call her Lulabelle?" I asked him when Jane had obediently gone off to do his bidding.

"Because she looks like one," Brian laughed superciliously.

The weather had taken a sudden turn for the worst again and a flash of lightning lit up the sky, followed by a loud rumble of thunder.

"Shall we go down below?" I tugged his arm nervously. I was terrified of thunderstorms, especially out at sea.

"No, let's stay here," Brian reached for my hand again and clung onto it, tightly this time, so I couldn't withdraw it. "Nothing bad will happen to you when you're with me."

"I wish I could believe that," I sighed, cuddling up a bit closer to him and putting my head on his shoulder. "Just look at that sky. It's full of sheets and forks."

"Sheep and hawks?" he misheard me.

"Sheets and forks, cloth ears," I laughed.

The misty blue shores of Corsica gradually appeared on the horizon and I felt my spirits suddenly lift, for the first time in ages and I started to sing. Brian joined in and we harmonised along together, our voices floating back to the crew as they scurried around battling with the flapping sails, lifting the hatches, squeezing out the huge fenders as we approached the entrance to the port, then winding the anchor chain, preparing to berth. Brian and I just ignored them and carried on singing.

When Corinthian sailed majestically into port, crowds of people stood on the dock to watch us berth.

After such a long stint on the boat, Brian decided that we should have dinner that night in a very upmarket restaurant in the marina called 'Emil's.' We all got dressed up to the nines and shakily disembarked, suffering from sea legs.

Much to Brian's disgust, Lesley was a strict vegetarian. To further add to his disdain, she hailed from the tenements of Glasgow, which didn't help matters, because, aside from holding a certain contempt for the working classes, he also had trouble understanding her accent. After struggling with the menu, which was all written in French, Lesley asked the snotty waitress if they had anything that was meat free. The waitress, who was also having trouble understanding Lesley's Scottish brogue and obviously didn't have much time for vegetarians either, scribbled something disdainfully on her order pad and sauntered off in the direction of the kitchen. She eventually ambled back, long after our meat contaminated meals had arrived, bearing aloft a silver platter which she haughtily placed under Lesley's nose, then lifted the silver dome with a smirk to reveal a few slivers of carrot. Brian thought this was hysterical and chuckling away to himself, tucked into his raw steak with gusto.

Back on board Corinthian, Brian and I sat up on deck long after the others had gone to bed, looking at the floodlit castle across the bay and sipping our Grand Marniers.

"I can hear music," I suddenly noted, cocking my ear to catch the distant strains of something vaguely reminiscent of bagpipes, "Can you hear it?" I asked Brian, "It sounds like someone playing the bagpipes and seems to be coming from the battlements of the castle, come on, let's go and see what it is."

We grabbed our shoes and crept furtively down the gangplank like guilty children, scuttling along the quay until Corinthian was safely out of sight, then strolled arm in arm through the deserted cobbled streets of the old town.

"I love it when you take my arm," Brian beamed at me, staggering slightly from the uneven cobbled streets and the half a bottle of Grand Marnier he'd consumed, "It fills me with happiness."

The music was finished by the time we made it up to the castle, the battlements guarding the streets of the old town deserted, so we meandered back in a leisurely fashion to the boat, where Graham the Captain was anxiously waiting for us on deck.

"You shouldn't go off alone sir, madam, without a member of crew," he scolded us. "People can just disappear around here."

We are stuck on a sand bank trying to leave port. Crowds of people have gathered on the quay to witness this embarrassing spectacle like voyeurs at an accident, smugly thinking thank God this hasn't happened to them. Alarms are sounding and there are clouds of diesel fumes contaminating the early morning air. The smug voyeurs are forced to cover their faces with hankies or scarves in order to breathe. The Captain is frantically trying to rectify the situation as the crew cower nervously on the aft deck, clutching the huge fenders to their bosoms, fearing Brian's wrath. Brian is pacing up and down in his shorts, the veins on his forehead bulging with anger. Helpful nautical types from other boats and from down on the quay are shouting advice. The Captain pretends not to hear.

"The poor boat will need some nappy cream for its sore bottom," Jane tried to make light of the situation.

"Pathetic," Brian glowered at her, pacing back and forth. "If you've got nothing constructive to say, don't bloody well say it."

The psychiatrists don't even bother to look up from today's Times. Brian tuts in their direction and gives them a disgusted look.

"Just look at them," he snarled to me, "Joined at the bloody hip."

When we finally get out to sea, the cliffs of the Corsican mountains look like a row of pirates' faces in profile, gradually getting smaller and smaller in the distance as we head off to circumnavigate the island. For all its majestic beauty and quaint nickname of the 'scented isle', the rugged shores of Corsica somehow bore testament to the centuries of invasion and political violence that have dogged its history and moulded its character. But now, softened by distance and the haze of the Mediterranean sun, the island looked more mystical than threatening.

Skimming gracefully over the ocean waves, the captain now confidently back in control at the wheel, Brian's mood relaxes. We eat lunch on deck as we breeze along, delicious goat's cheese, pasta and salad accompanied by several bottles of Corsican wine. When the crew have cleared the plates and retired to their quarters, Brian takes out his big sketchbook and starts making notes for his latest invention.

"I love paper, don't you?" he looks up and asks me questioningly.

"Mmmmm," I reply dreamily gazing out to sea, searching for dolphins. A member of crew scuttles by, ducking down as he passes in order not to disturb my view.

"Especially paper with squares," Brian continues, stroking the page with his long fingers, "And I get very excited by a certain grey paper. I wonder why?"

"I'm sure there's some deep underlying meaning. Why don't you ask the psychiatrists?" I suggest sarcastically. But they were down below playing Scrabble, missing all the magnificent vistas of the receding coastline.

The Captain came up to give us our daily history lesson as we sailed passed a small deserted island, informing us that a ship had gone down on the craggy rocks and hundreds of bodies had been washed up on the shore and were buried there in makeshift graves. For that reason no one would live there, believing it was haunted by the ghosts of all the drowned sailors – all those poor lost souls. Brian was fascinated and immediately summoned Graham to turn the engines off and stop the boat so we could go ashore. Graham anchored Corinthian off as close as he could get and Roger, one of the crew members, took us out in the dinghy to get a closer look at the surreal formation of rocks clustered around the bay like huge, uneven teeth. To everyone's great amusement, before boarding the dinghy I'd insisted on donning my fluorescent green armbands and matching floats, as the sea was a bit too choppy for my liking and I didn't want to become yet another lost soul. But as we bobbed ever closer to the shore, surfing the waves, we saw that the island was not entirely uninhabited, because splayed out on the molar like rocks and camouflaged like lizards, were the naked forms of a young couple offering themselves up to the midday sun. Roger slowed the engine till it was little more than a soft throb, then expertly steered the white dinghy in between the slime coated foundations of two enormous slabs of rock jutting out of the water like rugged skyscrapers and leaning in towards each other as if they were locked in a stony embrace. Emerging out of the other side of this prehistoric geological birth canal, we found ourselves in a tiny secluded cove; an enchanted grotto, the entrance guarded by the monstrous rocks which from behind had now taken on the appearance of sentinel giants.

"Those rocks look like two lovers kissing," Brian looked back and remarked to me, excitedly getting his camera out.

Roger cut the engine and we all fell silent as he steered the dinghy in a slow circle around the tiny cove and it seemed as though we were somehow floating suspended on the mirror-like water. The secret cove felt magical, almost sacred, like the sensation of reverence that overcomes you when you first walk through the doors of an ancient church and your eyes have trouble adjusting to the dark. Over the passage of time, the ecclesiastical rocks surrounding us had formed a cathedral-like cave but with its top cut off, allowing a halo of neon turquoise sky to eerily light our way.

Brian stood up, balancing precariously on his wobbly legs and pointed his old-fashioned camera this way and that, and to where I directed, until his film ran out. Then Roger allowed the dinghy to drift slowly towards the half moon crescent of the shingle beach, where we all clambered over the side and into the water to help drag the dinghy over the smooth black pebbles.

John, Lesley and Jane immediately put on their snorkels and flippers and waded back out into the soundless bay, then disappeared under the water. Roger wandered tactfully off, and climbing up the steep rock face, sat at a discreet distance with his back to us, looking out to sea and pretending he wasn't with us. Brian and I sat side by side on the shingle shore with our legs splayed out in front of us, selecting pebbles and skimming them across the crystal water, competing to see whose pebble could make the most bounces. It was eerily silent in the cove apart from the gentle plop of the pebbles as they bounced across the mirrored sheet of water, causing silver ripples to orbit over the aquatic marine galaxy. You could almost sense the presence of the ghosts of the dead mariners, watching over us from their watery graves.

Brian put his flippers and mask on, then holding my hand, led me into the shallow water. We were clinging on to each other and laughing as we slithered on the slimy stones coated in layers of sap green seaweed beneath our feet.

Then he let go of me and swam off to explore the rocks and I floated contentedly up and down like Myrtle the Turtle in my bright green armbands, paddling my feet under water and letting my head spin round and round. I was looking up at the blue dome of the sky and revelling in the silence; staring at the shapes of faces in the rocks and imagining they were those of the dead sailors.

A white hand suddenly clutched hold of my foot and Brian reappeared from under my legs and shot up from out of the water to face me, removing his mask.

"God, you gave me a fright," I spluttered, trying to regain my floating position, "I thought you were an ancient mariner about to pull me down to join him in his watery grave."

"Well, I am an ancient mariner but very much a living one," he cradled his hands under my back to help me float. "And you look just like a mermaid," he removed a strand of seaweed from my hair. "In fact, I think I prefer you with your hair wet."

"Then I shall always keep it wet," I laughed, twirling around in a circle and slithering out of his grasp. But he caught me in his arms and pulled me towards him to kiss me and I could taste the salt on his lips. Then he ducked back down in the water and quickly swam off again.

The red sun was slowly disappearing behind the 'kissing rocks' as we climbed back into the dinghy and Roger started up the engine. He manoeuvred the dinghy back through the narrow entrance to the cove then headed out to sea, but Corinthian was nowhere to be seen. The waves were getting rough and Roger began to look concerned. He'd lost contact with the mobile and we all started to get a bit worried, all apart from Brian that is, who never seemed to show any signs of fear.

At last, we saw the tip of Corinthians' tall mast peeking out from behind a cliff and we all let out a huge cheer. We gratefully climbed aboard with helping hands from the crew, as the dinghy rose and fell and crashed against the bow.

Once safely onboard, the Captain fired up the engines and we sped along the coast to anchor off for the night in another deserted cove, which was sheltered on three sides by towering red rocks.

"Those two would say it was like being back in the womb," Brian gestured towards the psychiatrists, who were busily working away on their laptops, "A womb with a view."

"There was no womb in the next cove," joked the Captain, "Otherwise I would have anchored there."

Brian pulled his face in disdain. Only he was allowed to make the jokes; especially the corny ones.

The next day, the bewildered crew, who clearly were not endowed with the same artistic natures and therefore rapidly coming to the conclusion that Brian and I were stark staring mad, were ordered to get the tender ready at the crack of dawn to take us out to photograph the rocks in the early morning light. Brian set up his various cameras and lenses and we cruised around the cove locating the best shots as the sun slowly turned into a blazing ball of fire, setting the red rocks alight and making them glow like burning coals. As the sun rose higher in the sky, the rocks, like dying embers, began to take on a more subtle bronzed patina, their jagged edges gilded in gold leaf. Then it disappeared on its never ending journey and the rocks reverted once again to just being rocks, at which point Brian put his camera away and ordered the relieved crew to take the tender in.

Back on board Corinthian, we sailed around miles and miles of jagged coastline, until finally, sick of the sight of rocks and needing to see signs of life and civilisation, we anchored off what appeared to be a small harbour, where the tender was prepared once again for us to disembark. We climbed precariously down the ladder, one by one, clutching our shoes and squashing in together on the wooden seats; then clinging on to the ropes, sped across the entrance to the harbour and pulled alongside a small beach bar called "Le Bloody", where we sat in white deckchairs, drinking cocktails until dusk.

When it was time to leave, Graham gave full throttle to the engine and we seemed to fly back over the now calm mirror-like sheet of violet water as the cerise sun slowly sank into the sea and then disappeared from sight. I sat at the upturned front of the dinghy between Brian's knees, clutching the rope to my chest, the force of the wind nearly blowing my earrings out. I was laughing and smiling back at Brian, filled with exhilaration.

"I think you've had a dose of happiness today," Brian shouted in my ear.

"I think I have," I grinned back at him, suddenly realising that I hadn't felt as happy as this for years. But then, I suppose it would have been impossible not to feel happy in such an idyllic situation.

We dined that night on deck in the moonlit bay, sheltered by the eerie formation of rocks. It was Brian's favourite meal, roast lamb, gravy and mint sauce, but that night something must have gone dreadfully amiss in the kitchen because Ollie's attempt at conjuring up a soufflé turned out to be a bit of a flop.

"It's like eating shredded tyres," Brian complained, flinging his over the side where it hit the water with an ominously loud plop.

"I hope she didn't hear that," I worried. Ollie usually worked wonders in the galley and managed to produce meals equivalent to any five star restaurant. Besides, I really liked her and didn't want to offend her in any way. But in his usual arrogant manner, mindless of anyone's feelings other than his own, Brian reached over and grabbed my uneaten soufflé off my plate, then tossed it over his shoulder to join his. Silvery crescents of fish circled the boat, flapping their tails excitedly, but tonight I think even they were in for a disappointment.

After dinner, Brian and I padded barefoot along the deck and sat in our favourite hideaway at the bow of the boat with our legs dangling over the side, gazing at the full moon and laughing about John and Lesley who had disappeared down below to the privacy of their cabin.

"She can't keep her bony hands off him," Brian complained in exasperation,

"She's like a bloody skeleton. All she eats is carrots."

"Psychiatrists?" Brian muttered, "Trick bloody cyclists more like."

"Oh leave them alone," I smiled, "They're in love."

"So am I," Brian sighed quietly.

CHAPTER 19

The Longest Pause

The next morning we'd sailed to Bonifacio an ancient harbour and city situated at the southernmost tip of Corsica. It was a breathtaking sight as we approached the precipitous, chalk-white limestone cliffs sculpted into unusual shapes by centuries of battering from the ocean and the wind. The appearance from the sea was of a shimmering white city gleaming in the sun, suspended over the churning waters of the Mediterranean below. The city and its fortifications extended along the cliff tops so that the buildings which were situated on the very tip of the precipice appeared to overhang it. The deep cleft between the peninsula and the mainland formed a perfect natural harbour sheltering the old town behind the protection of the cliffs. As Corinthian regally approached the narrow entrance to the harbour, we all stood in a line on deck, marvelling at the sight of the houses perched perilously on the side of the luminous white cliffs, looking as though they were about to slither off into the sea.

Once again a crowd gathered to watch us berth, but we were getting sick of that by now. Graham artfully slid Corinthian into position between two other luxurious yachts where her beautiful sleek lines and high towering mast made her stand out from the rest of the boats in the harbour as the gathering crowds gazed at her in awe. For all Brian hated being in the public eye, it was impossible to be inconspicuous on such a magnificent vessel as Corinthian.

We had dinner for the first time that night down below because Brian didn't want to be watched by the 'hoi polloi' as he called them. It was all very grand with candelabra, gold edged plates and crystal glasses. But Brian was in a strange mood. He kept fussing around, making sure that everything was absolutely perfect, that the napkins were straight and correctly folded, the cutlery was laid out in the right order and the candles were all lit to the exact same level.

"Would you like some Segovia?" he asked Lesley as he walked over to the stereo to select some music.

"I've never actually tried it, Dr Mercer," she answered nervously, mishearing him and thinking he was talking about a white wine.

"Thick as a bloody plank," Brian muttered out loud.

Tension grew at the table as everyone tried to appease him, sensing that he was about to go off on one. We all knew by experience that that would mean a difficult few days for all of us.

"Could somebody please pass the salt?" Lesley whispered, hunched over her plate of vegetables. Brian scowled and passed it to her, but woe and betide, she failed to put it back in its right place.

"No manners whatsoever," Brian yelled and plonked the salt cellar back in its rightful position.

Fortunately, at least this time, Brian's bad mood did not extend to me. Since the 'dose of happiness' we'd been getting closer and closer every day and I suppose it was inevitable really and only a matter of time before something happened between us. I knew that he was waiting for me to make the first move, so that very night, when we went down to bed, I slipped on my nightdress, grabbed my pillow and quietly opened the door of nanny's cabin hoping that no one would see me, then crept into his cabin. He was lying there in the dark, waiting for me, as I knew he would be. His heart was thumping dangerously as he threw back the sheet on the enormous double bed and enveloped me in his embrace. The passion we'd shared all those years ago was still there, only stronger now than ever and afterwards, we slept curled up together, lost in our separate dreams of now and long ago.

I woke up to the gentle rocking of the boat and noticed that it was starting to get light, so I picked up my pillow and went back to nanny's cabin before anyone saw me. For the time being, I didn't want anyone to know Brian and I were back together in the physical sense and that's why I took my pillow, in case Ollie or any of the crew could smell my perfume or see traces of my mascara on his. I also wanted to see what my feelings were going to do by themselves, without any influence from anyone else.

****

The island of Elba – Midnight. Brian knocked softly on my cabin door and as I'd been doing every night since that first time, I picked up my pillow and crept into his cabin. I loved sleeping in that big bed with him. When he turned out the light and enfolded me in his embrace, I felt safe and loved. He would stroke my arms, my head, my neck, with long, lingering caresses I could feel deep inside me, right down to my toes.

"I still love you Adrienne," he whispered tonight into my hair. "I've never stopped loving you, you know."

I didn't respond. I was waiting to see if our newly rediscovered passion would evaporate and suddenly disappear like sea mist when the time came to abandon this floating paradise.

Able was I ere I saw Elba – the famous palindrome, a sentence that reads the same backwards. But would I ever be able to go back; return to a normal semblance of life once we'd left Elba and when this cruise of a lifetime was finally over. I didn't know; I didn't care to be honest. For now I was enjoying the moment and the future, whatever it was going to bring and whether or not it was going to involve Brian, would take care of itself.

Early next morning as we sailed away from Elba and watched its mystical shores fade into the distance, Brian and I listened to the new 'Nuevo Flamenco' CD we'd bought at a record shop in the local town. It had sounded fantastic back in the shop, but now to our disappointment, it sounded tinny and flat up here on deck. But then we made a discovery. We found that if we crawled under the table and lay right next to the speakers, the acoustics were perfectly balanced and the sound didn't get lost and carried away by the wind.

"Can I get you both a drink, Dr Mercer?" Ollie peered under the table. A born eccentric herself and that's why Brian and I liked her so much, Ollie saw nothing odd about the fact that we were huddled under the table listening to flamenco.

"Yes, we'll have two gin and tonics please, Ollie. Oh, and tell the Captain to put 'Julio' on." Brian had obviously got bored with flamenco by this time, new or otherwise.

"Bloody Hooolio," Graham grumbled, but he reluctantly did as he was told, then disappeared down below to check the charts.

The crew will think we're crazy" I laughed, sipping my gin and tonic from my cramped position squashed against Brian's legs.

"Let them," he pulled me even closer and kissed me. It was nice kissing under the table, hidden away like guilty teenagers, feeling the passion starting to grow, but having to keep a watchful eye and restrain ourselves for fear of being discovered.

When we finally crawled out from under the table, Brian let me steer the boat and I felt like a real sailor for the first time, standing there at the wheel with sea spray on my face and Brian smiling proudly at my side.

Corinthian, with me the 'captainess' at the helm, sped across the bay where, according to legend, Byron swam back and forth twice a day to visit his mistresses and then out onto the open sea where poor Shelley drowned. His corpse when it was eventually recovered was burnt in a funeral pyre, along with the volume of Keats found in his pocket; and his poet's heart, snatched at the last moment from the hungry flames, deposited with his ashes in Rome along with the inscription –

'Nothing of him that doth fade, but doth suffer a sea change into something rich and strange.

I had always loved Shelley and all the romantic poets, but here spanning this same ocean in which he drowned made me feel somehow connected to him.

As we cruised along the coast of Italy with the sails billowing in the wind and the huge spinnaker casting its dark shadow replica on the water, I kept thinking about the words of that inscription and somehow transposing them to Brian. The constant sea changes of our relationship, the fact that, for me, he would never, ever fade and whatever our relationship was, it could never be described as dull, or boring - more rich and strange. Brian was certainly strange and he was undeniably rich. Maybe the two things went together, I thought to myself, because this kind of luxurious lifestyle was by no means normal. It would be bound to influence your personality. It was starting to affect me if only by the fact that it was affording me another kind of luxury of the time and space to allow my creative mind to once again come to the forefront. There is nothing like love, or being in love, to spark the creative fire and that's what Brian had rekindled in me. Just in time, he'd snatched my withering poetic and artistic heart from the flames of normality.

Lulled into a trance-like state by these romantic thoughts and the hypnotic rock of the boat as it cradled us over the ultramarine waves, I thought my eyes were deceiving me as I noticed what I thought to be snow-covered mountains on the distant shoreline. I nudged Brian who was lying in a similar somnolent position on a cushion at my side and pointed to the white-tipped mountains. The Captain, now back at the helm, reached over and passed me the binoculars informing us that they were in fact the marble quarries of Carrara.

"How I would love a slice of that to sculpt," I breathed longingly to Brian, zooming in for a closer look, "A big scoop of white marble like a great dollop of ice cream."

"Why don't I buy the mountain for you and then you can have as many scoops or dollops as you like," Brian joked. Or at least I think he was joking. I never really knew with him, especially where my art was concerned. Money seemed to be no object.

"I do believe your surreal artistic vision would transpose well into 3D," Brian grabbed the binoculars and peered at the marble topped mountains, "Besides, I've always wanted to try my hand at sculpture. We could work together as a team." He was getting quite excited by the idea and our earlier torpor was instantly dispelled by this new creative vision. "Many artists do work together you know?" he looked at me meaningfully.

"Mmmm," I frowned. I wasn't too sure about the idea of working together as a team. I liked to work strictly by myself, but I humoured him nevertheless. "We could start by making a sculpture of the 'Kissing Rocks'," I suggested, suddenly feeling inspired. "We could carve it out of sandstone which supposedly is much easier to work with, although it wouldn't be as beautiful or as stunning as in white marble." I looked longingly at the beckoning line of mountains just waiting to be quarried.

"I love sculpture," Brian remarked thoughtfully, "I think I love it even more than painting."

"So do I," I sighed, "I love painting because it involves the use of colour but a sculpture is 3D, it has a front and a back and sides and you can touch it. For that reason it's more sensory. It's also more physical because it involves a lot of hard labour. I know, because I once tried to carve a lump of marble. I must have had a burning desire even back then to be a sculptress, but somehow it got pushed to one side by the painting. I remember looking in the yellow pages and seeking out a monumental mason called Mr Rock, funnily enough, and asking him if he'd teach me to sculpt. I went to see him at his workshop and he sent me home with a piece of old gravestone and a bag of tools. But after a week of continuous chipping away with my mallet, my hands were all blistered and bleeding and I'd still only managed to round off the edge of one corner. So I gave up on the idea."

"Captain," Brian suddenly interrupted me and ordered Graham, "Take Corinthian in to the next harbour. We want to visit the marble quarries of Carrara. Madam here is about to become a famous sculptress"

Even before Graham had had time to comply with Brian's orders, Brian had grabbed the cell phone and called his friend the renowned sculptor Ralph Brown, who was an old time colleague of Henry Moore. He was able to arrange for us to visit the most prestigious marble-carving studio in Carrara, and for Carlos, the owner, to give us a guided tour. This turned out to be quite an experience, mainly down to the dubious Italian charms of Carlos who was a distinguished and charismatic man in his early sixties but a born womaniser and eccentric to the point of appearing to be slightly mad.

He took us first to visit the main studio which was a huge warehouse-like room; an eerie, noisy place, crammed to the high ceilings with enormous dusty marble sculptures and plaster casts of dismembered body parts. Religious icons and statues of the Virgin Mary in various shapes and sizes crowded every corner and hanging from the high ceiling on chains were oversized casts of horses heads, like something out of the Godfather. Effigies of Jesus on the cross abounded of course and there was even a full size version of our own Queen Victoria covered in dust and seated on a marble throne, frowning down over the proceedings like a disapproving stone spectre. The swarms of workmen, who seemed tiny in comparison, resembled something out of a science fiction movie. Their faces were covered by masks and, wielding Luke Skywalker-like drills, they crawled over the huge slabs of marble like colonies of powdered ants. Others were mouthing directions over the deafening roar of the drills, shrouded from head to toe in marble dust and wafting around in the spectral dusty air like ghosts from a bygone age. It was totally surreal and for Brian and I, absolutely fascinating, as we followed hot on Carlos's heels with our cameras flashing, taking photos for reference purposes at every available opportunity.

After the guided tour of the workplace, things were to become even more surreal as Carlos took us upstairs to his private apartment, which was like going back in time to Renaissance Italy. The walls were crowded with dark, cracked oil paintings hung in huge, gold-leafed frames and sumptuous sofas adorned with tapestry bolsters and embroidered scatter cushions abounded. There was even an antique grand piano covered with silver-framed photos of his family and faded sepia images of his long deceased Italian relatives who resembled clans of Mafia. Carlos couldn't wait to show us his impressive collection of beautiful marbles which he kept on display in his private gallery and at this point I got the feeling that he was more interested in Brian as a prospective buyer than me as a prospective sculptor. But nevertheless, he made us both very welcome, serving us tea and cakes and he even played the grand piano for us. The melodies were totally unrecognisable, sounding more like something Les Dawson would perform, when he used to deliberately hit all the wrong notes.

"You ah musta knowa theesa a one," Carlos beamed at me and Brian, plonking away. "Come on, seeeenga alonga. You don'ta recognize eeet? You musta."

We didn't have a clue.

"I'll call my mum on the mobile," I told him, "And you can play it to her. Sheela seeenga alonga with you, my mother knows the words to every song in the world."

I stood over Carlos's shoulder, dangling my mobile phone in the direction of the discordant keys as Carlos played yet another totally unrecognisable melody to my mum. Poor Brian could hardly contain himself. He was doubled up with laughter.

"What a bloody racket. Never heard it in my life," my mum yelled back to me down the phone. "Tell him whatever it is, he's ruining it."

"My mother says you are a wonderful pianist," I lied to Carlos, "But she says could you possibly play a bit slower because her hearing is not what it was. She's getting on a bit you know."

My mum would have killed me if she'd heard. Luckily, his repertoire quickly came to an end and he got back to the business in hand which was to try to sell Brian one of his expensive marbles.

I wanted to buy a souvenir for Erik, a camp statue of Botticelli's Venus or Michelangelo's David, but Brian was too embarrassed to mention this to Carlos, who was still trying his very best to flog him one of his exclusive pieces, at a special discounted price of course. I gave Brian a meaningful nudge.

"Actually," he began tentatively, his hand conspiratorially on Carlos's shoulder, leading him towards the door, "We would like to buy something."

Carlos's eyes lit up.

"Nothing grand mind, more of a souvenir really and we only want something cheap."

Carlos's face immediately fell.

"The statue would not be for us of course," Brian quickly assured him, "It's for my auntie Doris who has very bad taste," then pulling Carlos closer, he whispered in his ear, "She hasn't got long for this world, you know, so we have to be quick."

Carlos sighed, then giving a despairing shrug, reluctantly took it upon his Italian shoulders to help us seek out this 'pisa of tack', as he described it, for Brian's mythical aunt.

Off we went in Carlos's car on a perilous drive up to the marble quarries, stopping along the way at all the tourist shops so we could choose a tacky statue for poor old auntie Doris, who was about to pop her clogs. At one point we were stuck behind a dilapidated old lorry, loaded with huge blocks of granite, which was experiencing great difficulty trying to surmount the steep mountain road, emitting strange farting like noises in its wake. Brian and I, both regressed to child mode by now, were hysterical with laughter in the back seat; what with Carlos's Les Dawson impersonations on the grand piano, Brian's mythical Auntie Doris who was on her last legs and now the farting lorry. It was all just too much for us.

In the end, Carlos having abandoned all hope of making a sale, chauffeured us bad-temperedly back to the marina on a death-defying drive and dropped us back at Corinthian in disgust. We had our naff statues of David, as well as a one-armed Diana for good measure, tucked under our arms. Carlos was obviously thinking to himself, "These mad eeengleeesh people with a strange a sense of humour and no taste in art a whatsoever."

But what did we care what Carlos thought of us, or what anybody thought about us for that matter. Something wonderful had happened. We'd fallen in love all over again. We were so much more comfortable in each other's presence now and felt a great sense of peace at having found each other again. Brian called it a double sigh.

"We've merely had a pause in our relationship," he told me, taking my hand as we sat on deck sipping champagne and admiring our camp statues.

"A bloody long pause," I joked.

"It could get into the Guinness book of records," he laughed, "As the longest pause."

And that's the difference. We never used to laugh much together before. It had all been too serious and angst-ridden. But now we'd found we shared a surreal sense of humour as well as a surreal taste in art.

We sailed into Portofino in the rain, towels wound around us like sarongs and draped over our heads Arab style, but the rain did nothing to detract from its beauty. For me it was the most beautiful of all the places we'd seen up to now. We could have been in Indonesia apart from the fact that the fringed, golden palms were interspersed with tall, green cypress trees and pink and terracotta turreted houses. The usual crowds gathered to watch us berth, huddled under their striped umbrellas as the captain manoeuvred Corinthian with great difficulty between two huge gin palaces; then the beautiful view was obscured. We sipped our welcoming cocktails in the rain as the crew tossed the ropes ashore and put out the fenders. The people on the next door gin palaces watched with casual disinterest, clad in their immaculate white towelling dressing gowns, obviously bored with life and everything it had to offer.

Brian got very drunk that night and, as he was prone to do, started picking on Lulabelle. "What did she say?" he kept asking me sarcastically, every time she spoke. "Speak up will you, woman."

"Leave the poor girl alone," I tried to defend her.

"I can't understand a bloody word she says," he muttered to me. "Why can't she speak the King's English?"

"Because she's Scottish," I reminded him caustically.

"Scottish?" he repeated. "Scot-twitish," he was really drunk. "She's a twit. A psychiatwit."

I tried to take his attention off Lesley by changing the subject and talking about Ibiza, but I should have known better. Brian got very jealous if I mentioned anything in my life that hadn't involved him and the atmosphere became heavier and heavier to the point where even I couldn't lift it. He then started having a go at me, accusing me of being an old hippy for liking Ibiza and falling in love with poets and pirates, then stomped off down to his cabin in a rage. I stayed up on deck with the others for a while, but we were all despondent. We sat around the table in the flickering candlelight, with our heads in our hands.

"It's going to be a rough day tomorrow if Uncle Brian's in a mood," Jane sighed.

"Perhaps he'll cheer up after a good night's sleep," I offered optimistically.

"When he's sobered up more like," sneered Jane.

"Why don't you go and knock on his cabin door," Lulabelle suggested snidely.

So they knew then?

"Don't do anything you don't want to," said Jane unconvincingly.

Oh dear, I thought dejectedly to myself, it looks as if I must obey the rules at all times or we will all have to suffer. However, I decided not to 'knock' on his cabin door that particular night.

As predicted, Brian was in a filthy mood the next day. John and Lesley stayed out of his way and got on with some work on the table down below. It was still raining so I was reading a book and Jane was chatting to the Captain.

"You have terrible handwriting," Brian growled at Lesley as he passed. "You can judge a person's character by their writing don't you know."

"That's not strictly true," I argued foolishly, putting down my book, "A person's writing can change with age or with mood."

"That is a sweeping statement," he denounced in his most royal tone. "You are always speaking before you think. Just listen to yourself. Play the bloody tape back and listen to yourself."

It was a long, long day. Brian spent most of it on the phone talking to his lawyers about his impending divorce, which made him grumpier still.

We ate dinner in stony silence then I went straight to nanny's cabin and locked the door. He knocked a few times but I pretended not to hear.

"Hello?" he knocked again. "Hello? Is anyone in there?"

I ignored him.

"Suit your bloody self then," I heard him mutter as he shuffled off.

There was a very strained atmosphere at breakfast as we left Portofino and sailed back along the coast. The 'sikes' crunched their bran flakes in silence, or at least as silently as it is humanly possible to crunch bran flakes.

Jane lifted the teapot and offered Brian more tea.

"No, thenk you," he declined pompously.

Ollie brought his two lightly boiled eggs, placing them apprehensively before him. Brian reached for his special egg-cutting tool, which probably has a fancy name, but I don't know what it is, and ceremoniously snipped off the tops, one by one. Then his face turned a thunderous purple colour.

"Overdone," he bellowed, pushing them aside in disgust. "Not exactly a difficult task is it?" he yelled at Ollie. "Three minutes exactly."

Ollie scuttled away with the offending eggs.

The boat's telephones weren't working which put him in an even worse mood. I avoided him all day and lay on a mattress on the deck, making the most of the sun, which had decided to reappear. I was aware of him padding up and down, taking photos of me but I pretended to be asleep.

As we approached land, I wrapped myself in the beautiful sari he'd bought me in Portofino and made my way to the front of the boat. It was a bit rough and I had to hold on to the ropes as I made my way along. Brian followed me, staggering along the deck, the wind nearly blowing him over the side. I stood there, the force of the wind whipping my hair away from my face and moulding the sari tightly around my body. Brian planted his feet firmly on the swaying deck folded his arms and stood directly in front of me.

"What are you doing?" he asked.

"I'm being a maidenhead," I laughed into the wind.

"Well, I'm a bowsprit," he replied, "In fact, I've got one this very minute. Shall we go down to the cabin?"

Things were back to normal after that.

It was John, Jane and Lulabelle's last night so we sailed to Monte Carlo to watch the legendary annual firework display. Corinthian crept along the coast in the dark, following the twinkling curve of lights on the shore, her bow slicing neatly through the luminous fluorescent waves. Other boats followed us, the nippier speedboats swishing ahead, all vying for the best position. Some huge Arab gin palaces were all ready anchored off, the armed guards pacing the decks, waiting for the display to start.

The Corinthian crew lowered the swimming platform and set about making us a barbeque. Brian and I took our glasses of red wine and sat on our own in the dark, watching the lights of Monte Carlo twinkling on the shore. After we'd eaten, we all took our places on deck and watched with wonder as the fireworks lit up the sky, cascading over our heads and falling like coloured stars around the boat, all to the accompaniment of rousing classical music. As the fireworks reached their spectacular climax, all the boats sounded their horns, renting the gunpowder filled air with a cacophony of sound like some kind of discordant modern symphony. Brian and I rushed to the wheelhouse and like a couple of over-excited kids, took turns at sounding the horn, determined to have the last hoot. Then seemingly of one accord, all of the boats turned around and sped off back into the night, swishing past us in the dark.

"Ships that pass in the night," I sighed to Brian from my perch at the wheel.

"That's not going to be us this time, is it?" he squeezed my hand.

We sailed back around the bay with the wind in the waves and the lights of the coastline now to our right. Brian put some Mozart blasting out on the stereo and we sat together at the wheel, glasses of chilled white wine in our hands, conducting the music with our feet. I don't remember ever feeling as happy or as in love as I did that night and I think Brian felt the same. I felt lucky, blessed in fact and glad to be alive.

Back in the harbour, with Corinthian safely anchored for the night, the others joined us and we all sat up on deck with the rows of tiny tea light candles that Brian loved so much, twinkling in the breeze.

"I feel like I'm about to have a stroke," Brian clutched his chest and winked at me. The other's looked a bit worried - or maybe it was relieved? But I knew what he meant. I said my goodnights, went down below, slipped on my long white nightdress, grabbed my pillow and crept into the master cabin as silent as a ghost.

John, Jane and Lesley flew home but Brian and I stayed on for another week, happy to be alone at last, revelling in every moment. We visited the island of monks and walked through the scented fields of blue lavender, hand in hand. We took surreal photographs of each other standing next to ancient statues or leaning on tombs of deceased monks. We took drives along the coastline and ate lunch in tiny French cafes. But most of the time we stayed aboard Corinthian, after all there was no better place in the world as far as we were concerned, so why would we want to leave?

Brian was happier during that last week than I'd ever seen him. He zoomed up and down on the Jet Ski holding a huge, blue and white-striped umbrella in the air, while I lay on deck on my stomach, taking photographs of him. At one point he disappeared from view, speeding off towards the coast until he was just a speck on the horizon. To my relief, I eventually sighted him speeding back, his hair whipped into salty curls and a huge beaming smile on his face.

I was happy too. In fact, I've never known such happiness, either before or since.

Some nights the Captain took us ashore in the tender and we dined in the most exclusive restaurants along the coast. When we were ready to leave, we called the boat on the mobile and one of the crew would come to ferry us home, back to Corinthian, our floating palace. We would sit up on deck, holding hands and talking late into the night; then blowing out the candles one by one, we would creep down below to make passionate love, after which we would sleep tightly wrapped in each other's arms in the gently rocking bed, spinning slowly round and round in the moonlit bay.

I didn't bother taking my pillow with me anymore, or try to hide the fact that we were sleeping together. The captain and the crew left us alone as much as possible, realising that we were very much in love and needed to be on our own.

Then sadly, it was time to come home. The crew lined up and waved us goodbye, although in truth, they were probably glad to see the back of us. The Captain drove us to the airport in the Mercedes then we were on the plane and on our way back to dismal, rainy Blackburn to recommence our love affair of twenty years ago.

Walter Downs my 'Irish Grandad and Guardian Angel"

Me as an early flower child

Alan Seed (my dad)

Doreen Seed (my mum)

NEW YORK
1977

THIS WAS TAKEN BY KEITH MARTIN ONE OF THE EXECUTORS WHO WAS WITH US ON THIS TRIP.

HELLO, I Like flying, I like Bermuda but my boiled egg was runny so I think I'll come home. No really SUPER time darlings, off to New York this afternoon. Hello from shaken Onassis. Our Pad. See you next year, love. Guess who from.

THE SEEDS,
CLOG & BILLYCOCK,
BILLINGE ENDRD,
PLEASINGTON,
BLACKBURN,
LANCS.
ENGLAND

GRENADA W.INDIES 1977

BRIAN AND I ON HIS FIRST BOAT BAKARI

Brian with Salvador Dali holding an example of Netlon

The portrait of Brian painted by Dali (right), and my portrait of him "The Spider and the fly"(left).

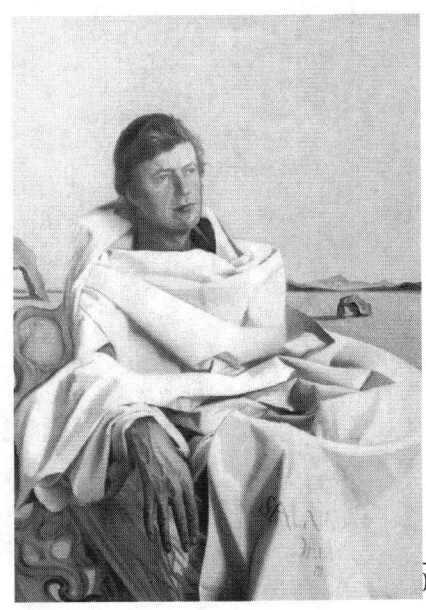

Brian and I on his yacht Corinthian

The two faces of a relationship.

CHAPTER 20

Big Brother

Blackburn, the same as it ever was, although there have been some changes since those halcyon days with Brian, if you could describe those days as such, as we were both highly complex characters and our relationship was always volatile to say the very least. And yet when I think back to those times, any day could be described as halcyon compared to what I have to live with now on a daily basis, thanks to HIV.

Blackburn's main claim to fame is that it had a mention in one of the Beatles' songs. Another is the Right Honourable Baroness Barbara Castle of Blackburn, now deceased; the erstwhile Labour heroine and champion of women's rights. She was otherwise known as the 'Red Queen' and afforded the womenfolk of the town the right to 'pee for free' – i.e. she abolished the paying toilets in the town. So at least there are some financial benefits to living here I suppose. Look after the pennies, as they say, and the pounds will look after themselves, although most of my pounds not to mention my pennies have gone down the pan. Barbara Castle's legacy lives on to this day, even though the expression, 'having to spend a penny' is still a common phrase. Now we've got Jack Straw of course, who sometimes holds his surgeries in the school just across the road from me and who we are freely invited to lobby if we thought for one moment that it would do any good.

If you are interested in the history of the Industrial Revolution, the 'Spinning Jenny' was invented here in Blackburn by a man called James Hargreaves, which enabled a single weaver, such as my poor grandma or my auntie Dora to work eight or more spools at once. Bet they thanked good old James Hargreaves for that! The story goes that he got the idea for his invention after his daughter knocked over her spinning wheel, although in point of fact, he didn't even have a daughter called Jenny and the invention was possibly down to another craftsman, who, in life's unfair pattern, never received his true acclaim.

Then of course there was Brian who in 1959, when I was only ten years old, invented the plastic mesh 'Netlon' the product which made him all his millions and subsequently left in his wake his huge carbon footprint. Another story goes that Brian got the idea for the process of plastic netting by stuffing a potato in his first wife's old fashioned steel mincer - and I can personally verify that on this occasion, the story is absolutely true, because I heard it straight from the inventor's as opposed to the horse's mouth.

With the ongoing passage of time, Blackburn is no longer that same industrial, working-class town of yore, home to the cotton mills and the colossal, smoke-belching chimneys that coated all the buildings and row after row of terraced houses with an impenetrable coating of black soot. The buildings have all been sandblasted now and the air is clear, although most of the rows of terraced houses have been knocked down, along with many other architectural structures of historical interest. Gone is the outdoor market, the Thwaites Arcade and the old shopping centre. Now Blackburn's shopping precinct looks exactly like that of any other nondescript northern town. Nothing like the gloomy industrial Blackburn of my childhood days, but still depressing nevertheless. There are too many memories here for me, especially of Brian and although most of them were happy memories, they have become tainted somehow because of what has happened to me.

It's just as rainy and as dismal as it was back then of course, but in those days, unlike now, I had still had hope for the future, a wonderful future with the man I loved. I also had the prospect, due to his commitment and belief in me as an artist, to realise my potential and become in his words, "A great painter, a great sculptor."

Well, all that's gone down the aforementioned pan, along with my pounds and pennies and I'll probably still be here twenty years on, that's if I'm lucky enough to survive that long of course. They say that the average lifespan of a person with HIV is eight to ten years, so probably not. But the medications are improving all the time and, you never know, maybe they'll come up with a cure. Hope springs eternal as my mum always says, but some days it's easier to muster up that hope than others and most days it's impossible to feel anything other than a numb kind of terror. Terror of the unknown quantity of this alien virus that is residing within me. Terror that when the unpredictable beast that HIV is decides, it will suddenly start to duplicate, propagate and wipe me out. Until then, I have to live with the worst terror of all: the terror that I will be found out.

Apart from this bloody disease, there's also my mum to worry about, not to mention my son who sometimes gives me cause for concern. What happened to those days when it seemed, at least in comparison to now, that I had nothing to worry about? In retrospect, those truly were my halcyon days, when Ben was a baby and I knew exactly where he was and what he was doing; the days before my mum suddenly started to get really old; those magical days when Brian and I were madly in love and all I had to worry about was what I was going to paint or sculpt next. The days, in fact, before I was diagnosed as HIV positive and my life changed there and then into a living nightmare.

These days, one day is pretty much like another and it's all about survival. My mum and I stumble through them as best we can; the difference is that I don't know who is taking care of whom anymore as her health continues to rapidly deteriorate and I find I'm having to do more and more for her, which of course I don't mind, but who is going to take care of me? And if I go down, who will take care of her? Oh dear, far too many things for one immune-challenged person, who is supposed to avoid stress, to worry about, so I just try to concentrate on the moment and get on with things as best I can and deal with each problem as it rears its ugly head. Plod on, best not to think about it, just take every day as it comes.

As has become our custom, I cook dinner at my house then cart it down to my mum's in the laundry basket. We watch Coronation Street and Eastenders, followed by an old black and white film on TCM starring Bette Davis. It features the usual obligatory bloke in a belted raincoat, peering out from under a trilby hat through hooded eyes, smoking an un-tipped cigarette. My mum loves these old black and white films with their haunting music and plots of unrequited or impossible love, although I don't know why, because they seldom have a happy ending. Rather like true life, I suppose, or at least mine. My mum enjoys them though because she say's they make her feel nostalgic and remind her of the good old days, when, in her words, life was so much simpler. Presumably she means before the nanny state set in and people felt free to puff on their Capstan full strength and pollute the air in peace. The days before additives in food were ever heard of and you could eat doorsteps of freshly cut buttered bread and not have to think about giving yourself a premature heart attack. Sometimes, ignorance is bliss I thought, as I stood at the kitchen sink and washed up. No dishwasher at my mum's; nowhere to put one in her tiny kitchen, although I've measured up and I think if we took out a cupboard, we could just about squeeze one in by the back door. My mum insists however, that it's not worth putting one in now at this stage in the game, whatever that means. I do wish she wouldn't say things like that, it makes me nervous and conscious of the fact that she won't be around forever, or even for much longer the way she is starting to talk.

 I help her upstairs to bed and after I've made sure she has everything she needs to survive the night without having to come back downstairs, I come back home. Even though it's late by this time I turn on my computer to check my emails. Nothing much, the usual offers from Amazon, or fly to Dublin for less than a pound if I book before midnight. Too late for that, not that I particularly want to go to Dublin right at this moment, or anywhere for that matter, although it wouldn't be a bad idea to get away from Blackburn for a while. But even if I did have the desire to go somewhere, I couldn't just swan off and leave my poor old mum to fend for her self and anyway, she usually accompanied me on my travels. Even after her mobility had become somewhat restricted, that hadn't stopped us and thanks to her wheelchair, we'd still managed to head off on our travels to not too distant places like Holland or Ibiza. But maybe it was now time to face the fact that my mum's travelling days were finally over, as she seemed to have done.

I carried on scrolling down my unopened emails then found to my surprise one from Endemol the Dutch television company responsible for 'Big Brother,' according to my sister, who was very excited when I called her and woke her up to tell her about it. They wanted to know if I was interested in taking part in a television production, employing my dubious skills as an art therapist for a reality show featuring a selection of well and lesser known Dutch celebrities who would be taking part in a detoxification programme scheduled to be filmed in Ibiza, called 'Patti's Fort'. Apparently, they'd found me on Google where in my blurb it mentions my connections with Ibiza and also that I'd studied Art Therapy at Goldsmiths University. What it doesn't say of course, is that I never finished the three year course because I'd foolishly left half way through to get married to that reprobate of an ex-husband of mine. But never mind all that, I was very interested in taking part and also, like my sister, quite excited, both by the prospect of being on television and also by the fact that it would give me the opportunity, or the excuse, to go to Ibiza again, all expenses paid, to see Ben who was still refusing point blank to leave the island and come back to England. There was just one problem – who would look after my mum?

The next morning I discussed it with her and characteristically, in typically unselfish mother fashion, she insisted that I go alone. That I had to go in fact; that I couldn't possibly throw up a chance to be on television. Who knew what would come out of it. I could become famous, every mother's dream, and that she would be perfectly capable of managing on her own, at least for a week. So off I went, after first making sure that my neighbours Willo and Paul, or Pavlito as I'd started to call him as a joke because he was so tall, would be around and close at hand to keep a constant eye on her.

It was great to be back in Ibiza, even though it was unseasonably cold for the time of year and the filming had to be postponed on three occasions due to the torrential storms. The celebrities were partaking in a range of therapies, from rebirthing to colonic irrigation, but unfortunately, my art therapy session was scheduled for the day after they'd all endured the indignities of the latter. Despite the inclement weather, the camera crew had decided to shoot the footage in a secluded wooded copse on a hilltop. The participants had no choice but to climb the steep hill, clutching cushions and rubber rings for their poor behinds, groaning and, uncharacteristically for the Dutch, decidedly bad-tempered. Aside from the celebrities' sore bums, the session went very well and the cameramen were pleased with the footage. I was duly paid in hand with a wad of euros by the director and informed that the programme was scheduled to be shown in Holland in a few weeks time.

As I had a wallet full of cash for a change, I decided to treat Ben for a nice dinner somewhere. We'd had a really good talk the night before, or at least I'd thought so, however my words of warning had obviously fallen on deaf ears. We ended up having a terrible argument and Ben rushed off half way through the second course to go and seek out his so-called friends, leaving me to finish the expensive dinner on my own.

"I've really had it with you," I told him the next day, "Enough is enough. You're coming home with me, whether you like it or not." I went into the bedroom and angrily started to pack.

"No way," he shouted back, "I'm never going back there, anyway, why can't you stay here with me? Ibiza is my home, not England."

If only he knew the awful truth, that I had to go back because of health reasons, then maybe he would understand. But there was no way I could tell him, maybe not ever. I felt far too ashamed. How could I tell my only son, who I loved unconditionally and with all my heart, that his mother had HIV? How could I tell anyone - and even if I wanted to, I couldn't, for the simple reason that I didn't want him to find out the shocking truth about me from someone else.

"Please come back with me Ben," I tried a different tack, "Your Granny misses you so much and so do I."

"There's no way I'm ever coming back to England and you can't force me to, I won't get on the plane," he shouted hysterically. "Anyway, you'll have to find me first," he laughed in my face; then stormed out, slamming the door behind him.

Oh dear, It will be my son that will be the death of me, not this bloody illness, I thought sadly to myself as I half-heartedly tossed clothes into my open suitcase.

I really thought I'd managed to survive Ibiza this time without being struck down, as I usually was, by some horrible bug or another. But the day after I got back, I came down with a nasty cold which later turned into bronchitis, to the point where I could hardly breathe and my congested lungs were wheezing like a pair of bagpipes.

My neighbours, Pavlito and Willo, were once again called into service as paramedics to whisk me down to the hospital, where I was prescribed a course of antibiotics and ordered to give up smoking. Due to the fact I was confined to bed for the next few days, which included my fifty-fifth birthday, I had no choice but to watch daytime television – Trisha, Good Morning, Changing Rooms etc. As soon as I rose from my sick bed, totally brainwashed, I felt obliged to get rid of all the colour in my house, leaving me one year older, a minimalist and thanks to the antibiotics, manically depressed. On my mum's orders, I also entered Richard and Judy's writing competition, 'How to get published'.

I'd taken the doctor's advice and given up the fags for two weeks, which was making me even more depressed, but unfortunately I started again in the anti-social smoking circle at college. I do wonder at times if I have the true makings of a counsellor, as you are obliged to merely listen to the client and not under any circumstances offer advice, just nod empathically at appropriate moments without joining in. The group always starts the first session of the day with what's called a 'round' where each one of us has to state briefly how we are feeling. I'm not very good at this either, a captive audience being too difficult to resist.

A typical 'round' might go something like this.

Eileen (nervous timorous type) – *Well, I've had a really tough day, week, month, life* (obligatory) *and I'm feeling very tired, stressed etc.* (compulsory) *and still feel nervous about being with group*

Me – (indecisive Libran) - *I've had a great day for a change actually, I've sold a sculpture and I'm really happy to be here and not feeling at all nervous about being in the group - but maybe I should be?*

Janice (down to earth outspoken type) – *As you know, I work in a car exhaust shop and some selfish bastard came in yesterday complaining that his exhaust was wobbly. Well, bloody 'ell, I told him, after the week I've 'ad - if that's all you've got to bloody worry about....*

Marvin (typical man type) – *I have to say, Janice, that if I had a wobbly exhaust, I'd also be very upset.*

One fellow student, a 'Hell's Angel', comes to class adorned in her bike leathers, with long, pink, furry rabbit ears stapled to her helmet, which fortunately (or unfortunately if the session is particularly boring) she takes off for the lessons.

"Do your ears rise up in the air when you're driving very fast?" I asked her with genuine curiosity.

"No luv, but mi lips wobble a bit," she replies with a completely straight face.

As a general rule, I am finding to my dismay that trainee counsellors do not seem to be endowed with much of a sense of humour, they are far too intense, but maybe that goes with the territory and the very nature of the job.

The sculpture I'd sold, at the buyer's request, needed to be mounted on a marble base, so off I go on a mission to a local Memorial showroom, where as luck would have it, I encounter a very handsome monumental mason; Italian, with blue eyes and unruly black hair, wearing a lumberjack shirt with packet of Marlborough lights poking out of the top pocket. After giving me a guided tour of the tombstones and reconstituted angels, he leans seductively against a headstone, lights up a Marlborough and looks at me meaningfully through his piercing blue eyes,

"Actually," he grimaces through a swirling plume of smoke, "I'm looking for someone to do a bit of carving for me."

"Oh, really," I reply, batting my eyelashes, forgetting momentarily that flirting for me is now strictly out of bounds and that due to health reasons and the very nature of the beast i.e. HIV, sculpting or manual labour of any kind has become physically impossible, "What exactly did you have in mind?"

What he had in mind was for somebody, presumably me, to carve a bloody great Range Rover complete with caravan out of a huge slab of black granite. Sadly, I had to decline. This peculiar epitaph had been requested, before he'd passed away of course, by a member of a rich gypsy family, who apparently wanted to arrive at the pearly gates (as you do) in his four-wheeled drive. The Italian told me people ordered all kinds of strange effigies to mark their passing - racing cars, for example were very much in mode at the present moment. Maybe he would come in handy when it came to carving mine, I thought, as I slipped his card into my bag. I don't know what I want for mine actually, although it definitely won't be a Range Rover. I have put in a preliminary request for my dancing troupe of 'mop ladies' who performed the routine I choreographed for a charity show at the casino in Ibiza to carry my coffin, bedecked with bouquets of feather dusters through a tunnel of mops.

My ongoing legal dispute with the executors of Brian's Estate seems to have come to a grinding halt. Since the day Brian died, for reasons best known to themselves they have constantly attempted to deny that Brian and I had shared an ongoing relationship, a relationship which in point of fact endured over twenty years. They have even tried to deny that Brian and I loved each other, which is ridiculous considering the facts.

I did write to them shortly after I found out the shocking news of my positive status to politely enquire whether they knew, in view of Brian's sudden and mysterious death, whether he had been tested for HIV infection. I'd received an outraged letter back declaring that it was a 'giant leap' to link my condition to Dr Mercer and that his family were totally outraged by my comments. I was used to receiving insensitive if not litigious comments from the executors by now, but why I constantly asked myself, were they so intent on denying that Brian and I had loved each other.

It didn't make any sense.

CHAPTER 21

Cinderella's Slippers

Although it's true that Brian had played a major part in my leaving Ibiza and coming back to England, he hadn't been the only reason. Ben, on his father's insistence, had been due to start boarding school in Yorkshire that September and in typically over- protective mother fashion I'd wanted to be nearer to him, so we'd come back to Blackburn. Initially I'd stayed with my mum at her house and not with Brian, much to his great annoyance, because even though we'd got on so well together on the yacht, I wasn't confident enough we could maintain that idyllic equilibrium if I moved in with him. So during the week I stayed at my mums, and at weekends I stayed with him at 'Kenolbri.' However, this wasn't nearly enough for Brian, who wanted me at his side twenty-four seven, so in order to entice me to spend more time with him, and also because I had nowhere to paint in my mum's tiny house, he converted the top floor of 'Pittarrow' the big house next door to 'Kenolbri' as a studio for me. I started working hard towards an exhibition he'd arranged for me in Belgium.

During this time, with Ben away and settled at boarding school and therefore free of my motherly obligations, Brian and I often went down to London on the train and stayed at the Savoy. Brian was having experimental laser treatment at Moorfields Eye Hospital and was becoming more and more concerned about the fact that he could soon go blind.

So that I would look the part at the Savoy and all the fancy restaurants Brian liked to dine in, he insisted on buying me an extensive wardrobe of designer clothes, which as a 'scruffy' artist with hippy leanings and a style all of my own went somewhat against my grain. To be honest, I would have been far happier spending all that money in the nearby Covent Garden boutiques or market stalls. However, off-the-rail clothing or bargains picked up in the sales and especially not in the second-hand or charity shops where I often chanced upon some of the more eccentric items which made up my wardrobe, would certainly not have fit in with Brian's exacting high standards. Although as rich as he was, he was always a one, as the rich often are, for getting something cheaper or money knocked off, but where clothes were concerned they had to have a designer label and nothing else would do. We often argued about this, but in the end, as in most things, I deferred to his wishes. This is not to say I didn't enjoy these expensive shopping sprees, what woman wouldn't? I took a certain dubious pleasure in spending hours in Harrods selecting the outfits and then modelling them for him, a pastime I both deplored and delighted in. Brian would sit straight backed on a gold embossed chair outside the dressing room, a bit like the Godfather in his long black overcoat, waiting for me to make my grand entrance and then watch me parade up and down in front of him like a reluctant mannequin. He took great pride in helping choose the 'right' clothes for me and had good taste, albeit a little old-fashioned at times. When, after careful consideration, a decision was finally arrived upon, the chosen garments would be whisked away to have their hems taken up or sleeves adjusted, and then delivered the following day to the Savoy in white cardboard boxes wrapped in layers of fine tissue paper.

I must say, for all my old hippy and socialist leanings, I loved opening those boxes and peeling away the tissue paper to glory all over again in the sumptuous materials and sheer extravagance of the garments. I would then spread them out all over the bed and try them on again, while Brian helped me to decide what went best with what and which accessories to wear with each particular outfit. The correct choice of shoes was imperative as far as Brian was concerned, and he insisted that I had a different coloured pair of ridiculously priced designer brands to go with every single outfit. He also liked to buy me fancy underwear and expensive nightdresses, his excuse being that it was to impress the maids at the Savoy. The underwear always had to be bought in duplicate because he wanted me to keep a spare set of everything at 'Kenolbri', his reasoning being that it would feel more like I was living with him all the time, which is what he wanted, if the cupboards were full of my clothes and the drawers full of my stockings and suspenders. Most men like their partners to wear beautiful undergarments and I suppose wearing them made me feel beautiful too. But were there more fetish-based reasons for his fixation with buying me all the silk and satin underwear – who knows? I sometimes had my doubts. Brian had many different sides to his nature and sometimes the more unpleasant aspects of his personality would shoot to the surface, especially when we were away and for some reason, while we were staying at the Savoy.

On one of these particularly unfortunate excursions, we'd travelled down to London with the specific intention of purchasing new accoutrements for Corinthian. We had been shopping most of the day, visiting the exclusive designer outfits in Canary Wharf to seek out fabrics for the new upholstery, then on to Thomas Goode & Co to choose the new china, then to Harrods to get me a new coat. After a quick visit to the barber, Brian had gone off for his eye appointment and I'd returned in the taxi to the Savoy alone.

I opened the door to our suite on the fifth floor with my special key, tossed the brand new camel coat Brian had bought for me in Harrods over the back of a chair and flung myself on the overstuffed velvet sofa. The sofa had been moved on Brian's orders to face the huge window looking down over the Thames so that we could sit there and enjoy the view while we sipped our customary nightcaps of Grand Marnier before we went to bed. I kicked off my elegant new shoes with a sigh of relief and thought how much my life had changed in the last four months. I remembered the first time I had been here in this very same suite at the Savoy twenty years ago and how much had happened in between. The feelings we'd had for each other hadn't changed in all that time, but I had. I was very anti-money back in those hippy dippy, art school days and now look at me, I thought. Lady Muck! Lapping it up.

I can see out along the river, three bridges then it turns the corner and disappears. A train with dusty orange windows slowly chuffs across Charing Cross Bridge, while a tugboat passes lethargically underneath, scissoring through the sluggish brown water causing ric racs of coloured reflections to decorate the curled ripples frilling out in its wake. The illuminated face of Big Ben, golden against the darkening blue sky, chimes six o'clock and I suppose I'd better get dressed for dinner. His Lordship would be back soon. But I stay right where I am.

In the centre of the room, the round table on wheels with its crisp, white cloth still stands from lunchtime. In this light, the two starched linen napkins have taken on the form of geometrical origami birds, about to take flight, and the huge half full, bell-shaped glasses of expensive red wine cast deep purple shadows on the snow white cloth. The silver domes covering our lunch plates, shine dully in the lamplight. Martin, Brian's valet has not been in to take the table away. Perhaps he thinks he would be disturbing us. He tells me he remembers me from all those years ago, but I can't remember him. He also confessed to me that he hadn't liked Brian's last wife much. Too many airs and graces, he said. Charlie Chaplin stayed in this suite years ago he informed me and so did Raquel Welch. He'd pointed to the ceiling where she had allegedly kissed it, standing on the shoulders of her tall lover, leaving her lipstick imprint there.

Brian has gone for his eye test at Moorfields. I offered to go with him but he didn't want me to. In two years, the specialists say, he could be as blind as a bat. I am practising in readiness to be his eyes, as well as everything else I seem to have become. I'm not sure what I've become to be honest; what role I've taken on. Sometimes my 'role' as it must appear to everyone else, of mistress, 'kept woman', artist and patron, or younger woman with much older man, doesn't sit well with me, even though I know it is so much more than that. Brian keeps hinting again about us getting married, but I don't think I could stand the strain; he is too unpredictable by far, although I suppose that's what's kept me interested all these years. Anyway, beside him other men pale into insignificance, so he's ruined me for anyone else. Not that I want anyone else, why should I, when at least to all intents and purposes, I have everything I need and so much more, right here with him.

I pour myself a gin and tonic and stay on the sofa a little while longer. The huge velvet curtains make a stage out of the window, with the rolling river and rippling reflections a constantly moving backdrop. I slowly gaze around the room. It's a bit like being in a time warp with its white mirrored doors and fringed standard lamps. But that's how Brian likes it. Old-fashioned, like him. Today, in Harrods when he was buying me the camel coat, he'd asked the assistant where the costume department was.

"Dear me, sir," she'd sighed, "I'm afraid we don't sell costumes anymore."

Earlier, we'd taken a taxi to Lobbs because one of his new crocodile shoes (how very dare it) was pinching. Lobbs, for those like me, previously not in the know, is the bespoke shoemakers for the rich and famous, where members of the Royal family and erstwhile celebrities such as Caruso and Frank Sinatra had their shoes especially made for them. A pair of Lobbs handmade shoes is unique to their owner and according to the head salesman, (who was asked by Brian to explain the history of the establishment to me), a work of art. Each individual shoe, he told me proudly, is created by a team of highly specialized craftspersons: the maker, the fitter, the pattern cutter, the closer, the last maker, the clicker, (whatever that was, although I wasn't going to ask) and last but not least the polisher. On Brian's insistence I was then taken on a tour of inspection of the cellars, ending up in the cave-like tunnel where all the wooden lasts were stored.

"We have 3,700 at the moment," the odd little mole-like man with the long apron told me proudly, "1,300 of which are for women."

"Fascinating," I tried to feign interest. "But what happens when the people die? Do you keep the lasts or do you burn them?" I imagined a huge pile of redundant wooden lasts, rotting away in another cellar somewhere, or an enormous bonfire, lighting up the London skies.

Dwarf-like men in long, beige coloured aprons were busily working away at dusty workbenches, looking as if they never got to see the light of day. One scuttled over and knelt compliantly at Brian's feet, fastidiously checking the adjustment to his shiny crocodile shoe. I excused myself and went outside for a cigarette. Being a smoker can come in very handy at times.

Brian needed a new lens for his camera so we'd taken another taxi to find the shop where he'd originally bought the camera, many years ago. The taxi driver cruised round and round the block.

"I'm sure it was there – right there," Brian insisted, pointing to a large billboard advertising the United Colours of Benetton.

"It's gorn, Guv," the taxi driver threw over his shoulder in his cockney accent, "It's moved, gorn out of business."

"Impossible," Brian shouted. "Drive round the block again."

"It's your bill, mate, but if you insist," the taxi driver swung the wheel.

But there was trouble that night at the restaurant, some fashionable eating establishment, haunt of the rich and famous renowned for fish dishes, although I cannot for the life of me remember the name. Brian and I went to so many fancy restaurants and they were all pretty much the same to me, pretentious and overpriced.

"Good evening, Dr Mercer, Madam," The headwaiter heralded us in. Brian was obviously a regular and I wondered if he used to bring any of the three wives here. Perhaps the headwaiter thought I was wife number four but had refrained from addressing me as Mrs Mercer, like they did in the Savoy, in case I was only a mistress.

The headwaiter shook the white linen napkins out over our knees with a magician-like flourish and I almost expected to find a rabbit sitting on my lap, or see a pair of doves flutter away, then he bowed reverentially and politely backed off, leaving us to peruse the menu.

Fish, fish and more fish! I'm not a great fish lover: there are too many perilous bones to contend with for my liking. I would have preferred fish and chips out of a newspaper any day to be honest, but what could I do.

I noted with pleasure that four young Spanish women were sitting at the next table to us, so I smiled at them and said good evening politely in Spanish. We ordered our meal but when our starters arrived, the enormous pink prawns still had their heads on, complete with their black beady eyes. I shuddered and asked Brian if he would decapitate them for me, but he was midway through telling me a story. He didn't take kindly to being interrupted, although it was a story I'd heard many times before, so to be honest I wasn't really paying him my full attention. I was more interested in listening in to the conversation of the young women at the next table and, hearing them chattering away in an animated fashion in Spanish, made me suddenly feel homesick for Ibiza and my old hippy life. I suddenly felt very out of place and bored out of my brains by this decadent rich lifestyle I was living.

Brian, sensing my sudden boredom, started to act silly in an attempt to regain my attention.

"Do you think that couple up on the balcony are about to have oral sex?" he leered, the juice from the garlic prawn he was guzzling dripping down his chin and a long pink prawn whisker stuck to his cheek, "They look as if they are."

"God, you're revolting sometimes," I told him, giving him a disgusted look.

"You simply don't understand my sense of humour," he smirked, passing me a headless prawn in his greasy fingers.

"I don't think that was funny," I snapped, turning my nose up at the prawn and smiling over at our Spanish neighbours, hoping they hadn't overheard Brian's lewd comment.

"Sometimes I think you're obsessed with sex," I chastised him primly.

We sat in stony silence for a while glowering at each other. Brian was the first to lower his eyes, then reaching over to dip his fingers in the fingerbowl, he carefully wiped his hands on the napkin, ceremoniously extracted his Cartier fountain pen from his inside pocket and started to write something on the back of the menu. When he'd finished, he passed it over to me with a flourish.

"I was smiling when I asked the question," he'd written in his spidery handwriting, "And I had a deep and loving feeling in the humorous side of my heart."

"Rubbish," I grabbed the pen and wrote back, "You've just got a one track mind and a dirty one at that."

"You obviously didn't notice," he smirked as he wrote, "That I was kicking the coddymuck off my boots as I asked the question."

"What's coddymuck when it's at home?" I scrawled, losing patience.

"I wear my heart on my sleeve for you," he'd drawn a series of hearts. "I can't help it. I wish that I didn't. I wish I could take it back, but I love you. Please bring me into the conversation. I am not a leper."

I couldn't be bothered to play this silly game anymore so I just pushed the menu back to him.

"Bugger you then." He wrote in big capitals, turning the menu back to face me. He slid the fountain pen back in his inside pocket, took out his wallet, tossed a wad of money on the table then stood up, scraping his chair back and stomped off.

I thought he'd just gone to the gents, but he didn't come back. Ten minutes or so passed by and the Spanish women started to look at me with curiosity, verging on sympathy, so I told them in Spanish that it seemed I had been abandoned by my hombre. In the spirit of sisterhood they invited me to share their wine and in a very short space of time, we were singing rancheros using the empty wine bottle as a microphone and receiving looks of extreme displeasure from the surly waiters, not to mention some of the more stuffy diners.

"How do you know all of these old, Spanish songs?" one of them asked me with interest, "You're not a typical Englishwoman by any means. You must have Spanish blood."

"Sí, tienes sangre Latina, chica y corazón del sol," said one of the others, who couldn't speak any English.

But I didn't feel like I had anything resembling Latin blood coursing through my veins or even a sunny heart! I felt like a typical snotty Englishwoman the way Brian had dressed me up, with my hair tied neatly back, my smart suit, camel coat and high heeled leather shoes from Harrods.

I couldn't believe he'd just walked out on me like that, leaving me to fend for myself in a strange part of London. I wasn't even sure where I was as we'd come in a taxi and I hadn't paid much attention to where we were going. I'd just placed myself in his competent hands, as ever. I swore to myself that I would never let that happen again and sighed. Bloody hell, what had gone wrong? I must have broken the rules again.

Rule number one – He must have my undivided attention at all times.

Rule number two – I must laugh at his corny jokes.

Rule number three – I am not allowed to mix with the 'hoi polloi' and I'm certainly not permitted to sing rancheros with Latin 'chicas' with my hair untied, sleeves rolled up and shoes kicked off under the table.

I declined the offer to go on to a club with 'las chicas' and walked back to The Savoy by myself, not having enough money left after paying the bill to order a taxi.

I quietly opened the door of the suite with my key and crept in. I didn't want to wake him if he was asleep and then have to listen to him ranting on at me for hours in a drunken rage, so I lay down on the sofa and threw the camel coat over me. All was quiet apart from the distant rumble of the London traffic down below and I was just drifting off to sleep, when I heard a persistent clicking noise coming from the direction of the bedroom.

Click, click, click – what on earth was it?

Suddenly I was wide awake, heart thumping, as I tried to work out where the sound was coming from. Then I froze as I realised what it was. It was the bony click, click of Brian's long white fingers, summoning me from the darkened bedroom.

Who did he think he was I thought angrily, I was not a person who could be summoned. I lay as still, as a statue, hardly daring to breathe, as his looming figure slowly emerged from the shadows.

Click, click - snap, snap…….

He was wearing the perfectly pressed, pale blue pyjamas he always wore to sleep in and his tall figure in the light of the adjoining corridor was reflected back at me a thousand times in the mirrored doors; a long line of Brians in pale blue pyjamas stretching to infinity, snapping their fingers, like something out of 'Chorus Line'.

Big Ben chimed midnight, boing….. boing….. boing….. making me jump out of my skin. I sat bolt upright clutching the camel coat under my chin like some kind of talisman.

"Come to bed, why don't you?" Brian ordered - snap, snap, snap.

At first, I stayed exactly where I was, refusing to obey his orders; then fearing reprisals the following day, I reluctantly got up off the sofa, trailing my camel coat behind me like Snoopy with his comfort blanket and followed him to the darkened bedroom. I reluctantly slipped on the new nightdress we'd bought that day in Harrods, which had been laid out on the bed for me by the maid in all its satin glory and shivering, tentatively slid in between the cold sheets beside him. But I couldn't fall sleep, try as I might. I lay awake for hours in the pitch black room, listening to him snoring softly at my side to the accompaniment of the constant rumble of the London traffic somewhere far down below.

The next morning, to my surprise he woke up in a really good mood, as though nothing untoward had happened and didn't mention the night before, so neither did I. It was best not to I had learned from experience.

After breakfast, wheeled into the room and served to us by the valet, we went to Harrods to buy tablecloths and napkins for Corinthian, then once again back to Thomas Goode & Co to make the final decision on the new china. Brian was adamant that he wanted to replace every single item on the boat in order to erase the bad memories of wife number three and her treacherous infidelity.

"I want you to help me choose everything," he told me. "I want you to think of it as 'OUR' boat and I want you and me to go back to it as soon as possible. On our own."

That was fine by me; I couldn't wait to go back to Corinthian as Brian was a different man when he was on the yacht and nothing like the critical, pompous, pretentious snob he would sometimes turn into in London.

After lunch it was time for my special treat, the one I was looking forward to most of all, which was going to Tirantis to buy some sculpture tools. We wandered up and down the cramped aisles, looking at all the different types of clay and Brian spent a lot of time examining and fingering the various tools, or rifflers as they are called in the trade, weighing them in his hands, helping decide which ones to buy for me. He loved tools of any kind and was really excited at the thought of making the armatures I would need to make the models, as that would call into play his engineering expertise as well as his creative skills.

When we got back to the Savoy, he laid them all out on the table in neat orderly lines and then we played shops.

Ding a ling

"Good morning sir," I played the game. "What can I get for you today?"

"I'd like some sculpture tools if you please. Do you have any rifflers by any chance?"

"Rifflers?" I enquired, routing through the regiment of tools laid out in their correct order of size and rank. "Now let me see. Italian rifflers do you mean or French rifflers? I don't seem to have any Italian rifflers today but I do have a fine selection of French ticklers here. Will those do? How many would you like sir?

"Half a pound."

"Half a pound of French ticklers it is then. I'll weigh them for you. Would sir like them in a brown paper bag?" And so on.

But on the train coming home we had another silly argument, which developed into a major dispute, about shoe trees of all things and the fact that I considered them to be a waste of money, resources and an unnecessary luxury. Not according to Brian however, who had downed half a bottle of wine during the first class buffet lunch and was feeling argumentative and determined to steadfastly defend his obsessive respect for shoes and anything to do with them. What was wrong with balls of rolled up newspaper, I'd asked him churlishly, which was me just being awkward by this time and wanting to wind him up.

"You can tell a lot about a person by their choice of footwear," Brian had responded pompously; then retreated into one of his mega sulks, refusing to speak to me for the rest of the journey.

Well, he might have thought so, I hid behind my magazine, but shoes weren't something I gauged people's character by, but then again, look at him with his bespoke bloody crocodile shoes. His shoes were always hand made for him at the aforementioned Lobbs, and when he'd taken me there, it had felt like going back in time. But then a lot of things felt like going back in time with Brian, due to our twenty year age difference. His bespoke crocodile shoes clearly said a lot about him, so what did my shoes say about me? I know that some women (and men if you include Brian) have an absolute fetish for shoes, especially powerful women. Think of Imelda Marcos, who had container loads of them shipped to her from America, even though her impoverished country was on the verge of total bankruptcy. I have to say shoes have always been at the very bottom of my list of fashion accessories, although I'm quite partial to boots. But now, thanks to Brian my shoes all sported a designer label and were usually purchased from Harrods where they came in little drawstring bags with 'Harrods' written on the side, complete with their own wooden shoe trees. I looked down at my feet. These days I was certainly well shod. In fact, I was probably the best shod artist in the north of England, if not the entire country. So what did that say about me exactly, or what I had become?

When we got off the train, still not speaking, Bob the chauffeur was waiting at the station to pick us up and, at my request, drove me straight back to my mum's and Brian went on to 'Kenolbri' in a sulk. We didn't speak to each other for days – and all over some bloody shoe trees.

He finally called me late one night and, against my better judgement as he sounded like he'd been drinking, I agreed to go down to 'Kenolbri.' Big mistake, I should have relied on my better judgement, because almost as soon as I'd got through the door we had yet another row, fuelled by the fact that he was drunk and I stormed off, yet again, back to my mum's.

I was far too angry with him to sleep, so after a wakeful night, as soon as it started to get light I got in my car and drove back down to his house. I parked the car at the top of the drive leaving the engine running so it wouldn't stall on me as it so often did and I nervously got out. Even at the height of my anger, I couldn't help thinking how beautiful the magnificent gardens looked in the dawn light. Long shafts of syrupy sunlight slowly pouring over the immaculate lawns and illuminating the yellow helmets of the tulips standing sentinel along the drive, guarding him whilst he slept; row after regimented row, straight and perfect, because, as my mum used to say, they wouldn't dare to be anything less. Luckily, the fortress-like gates had been left open after my hasty getaway the night before. For all Brian's supposed genius, he'd never managed to master the remote controls of the electronic gates, and neither could he set the timer to record a TV programme on the video recorder - but then, neither could I.

"You won't break my back, no matter how hard you try," he'd ranted after me the night before, as he'd chased me up the drive in his black silk kimono, "You'll never find another camel like me."

There's an old saying, isn't there, about it being easier for a camel to pass through the eye of a needle than for a rich man to enter the gates of heaven – so maybe that's what had been running through his whisky-soaked brain. Who knows, I certainly hadn't and neither had I cared. I'd just made a run for it.

"Never find another camel like him! Well, we'll see about that," I muttered to myself, as I crept down the gravel drive, trying my very hardest not to crunch - mustn't wake him or alert the staff. But it was Sunday. We always had the house to ourselves at weekends. Brian preferred it that way. He liked to keep me to himself.

The solid oak door with its resplendent brass knocker was firmly shut. I knelt down and took the seven odd shoes I'd brought with me out of the Harrods carrier bag and lined them up in a row on the step, then placed the note, written in great big letters between a solitary Charles Jourdan and a partner-less black stiletto I'd never ever worn and now probably never would.

"*Farewell prince bloody charming,*" the note read, "*I leave these glass slippers for my ugly sisters. Cinderella has gone off to have herself a ball.*"

Then I hot-footed it back up the drive, scattering gravel right left and centre, got back in my car and drove as fast as I could back to the safety of my mum's. It would not be long, though, before he would persuade me to come back.

CHAPTER 22

Cops and rubbers

Enough was enough, I decided. I wasn't going to let HIV rule my life and stop me from travelling or from having a good Christmas this year. So with the help of my mum's wheelchair and a pre-booked oxygen machine for her to hook up to in the flat, me and my mum managed to get out to Ibiza to spend Christmas with Ben.

Ben was in great form - he had even cut his hair and got rid of the 'wings,' much to his granny's relief, not to mention mine - which meant we could actually see his handsome face for a change. He also seemed to take a great delight in looking after his granny and, miracle of miracles, had got back in touch with his sense of humour, something he'd lost somewhere along the line.

I did everything a dutiful mother and a daughter should in regard to Christmas, to make it a good one for both of them, for all of us in fact, even down to making a trifle. I spent a fortune in the supermarket, bought three sacks of wood so that we could have a real fire and we even roasted chestnuts on it. I also bought a virtual fire for the times when I ran out of firelighters, or my mum wasn't up to making her famous plaited logs out of old newspaper like they used to do in the war. I bought Ben a stack of presents, as well as the two huge speakers he'd asked for.

He bought presents for me and my mum too, even though most of them came from the hundred peseta shop. But who cared, it was the thought that counted. He even played classical music, much to my mum's delight, through his huge new speakers instead of that horrible techno trance stuff. We went out together on family jaunts, which was a complete turn up for the books as he wouldn't have been seen dead with us before; or pushing his 'ageing granny' as we had jokingly started to call her (much to her annoyance) around in the wheelchair, stopping now and then to cover her up with a blanket and asking if her little legs were OK, which made us all laugh, especially my mum.

Although my mum was confined to her wheelchair, she typified the term glamorous granny and would not be seen in public without her face on or anything other than elegantly dressed. Even in her wheelchair she still drew admiring glances and people always commented on how beautiful she was and what piercing blue eyes she had. Nothing got past my mum's knowing blue eyes; she could see right through you and if she didn't like someone she could slay them with a glance. But, on the whole she got on with all of my Ibiza friends, and everyone loved her there, even the waiters.

When our two weeks were up, I tried every way I could to talk Ben into coming back with us, but alas no joy and as I had to get back for a hospital appointment, there was no other option than to leave him there.

As soon as I got home I decided maybe I would send off the synopsis of my book to various literary agents in an attempt to get myself published. I was encouraged to do this by the fact that Chris Smith Labour MP and former Culture Secretary had recently come out of the closet to the media and revealed his HIV status to the world. If he could do it, so could I, I reasoned and I would face the consequences of telling everyone else, including Ben, should I be successful, with (hopefully) the financial prospect of a book deal to soften the blow. Well, we can all dream can't we and at least it was giving me something to work towards, some kind of a goal.

I was so impressed by Chris Smith's courageousness in outing himself that I felt obliged to write him an email.

Dear Mr. Smith,

I just want to express my admiration and gratitude for your brave public declaration and message of hope for people (like me) living with the stigma of HIV. It is very uplifting to know, that as a respected and high profile figure, you are up there – and out there - raising awareness and keeping the taboo subject of HIV in the public eye, especially since they killed poor Mark off in Eastenders (not that I am comparing you to a barrow boy, heaven forefend!)

However, the public also needs to be aware that HIV is a problem which is now affecting more and more women – as in my case. You also did me a very great favour by 'coming out' just as my autobiography, which covers the dreaded subject, will hopefully one day soon lay brazenly on various literary agents' desks, with its pages open, hoping to sleep its way to the top.

Thank you once again and I'm sure I speak for many more women.

Adrienne Seed

Would you believe it? I have found myself a job and I am now teaching art again, albeit only one day a week and to ladies who don't really want to learn how to draw but would prefer to make decorative cards and the like.

However, as that's definitely not my forte, they will have to get their hands dirty drawing with sticks of charcoal instead. It's great actually, because as it's only term time work I will be able to take advantage of the half-term break to go to Ibiza again to see Ben. While I am there, I will also need to retrieve my flamenco shoes, my castanets and my red and black 'Carmen' skirt, not to mention the odd couple of fans (as in wave over the head as opposed to football) as I've been roped into doing a 'flamenco for fitness and fun' workshop at the Women's Centre where I've signed up as a volunteer in order to practise my counselling skills. The flamenco workshop is for International Women's Day and already eight women have put their names down for it. Will I be up to it one wonders? If someone had told me this time last year that I would be plotting to do my infamous 'Carmen circle' I never would have believed them. But the human spirit is a wonderful thing - and so are anti-retroviral drugs it seems. Talking of which, I got a nice email back from Chris Smith.

House of Commons

London SW1A 0AA

Dear Adrienne,

Thank you very much for your kind letter a few weeks ago, following my statement about my HIV status. It hasn't been as easy decision to make – as you will appreciate – and your support and encouragement mean a lot. Thank you. I do hope you are successful with your book! My very best wishes to you yourself for the future –

Yours sincerely,

Chris Smith

It was very nice of him to respond to my email, but I do feel, as former Culture Secretary he could have put a word in with one of his publishing buddies to help me on my way! But I suppose that was a bit much to hope for. At least he took the time to write back.

My new art class is in quite a surreal venue in which to teach art, because in the next room, through the open shutters of a Victoria Wood 'Dinner Ladies' style canteen, the old age pensioners hold their weekly tea dance.

Today, I was demonstrating, Rolf Harris-style, to my students/ housewives how to draw a human nose (not an easy task.) Suddenly, from out of nowhere, a sniffer dog (plus burly handler) came scurrying into the room, dabbing its dirty paw marks and dribbling all over the charcoal drawings we had just finished. The overpowering aniseed-like smell of the fixative on the drawings was sending the dog into a frenzy of olfactory hyperactivity and it was barking and yelping fit to bust. The noise overpowered the more relaxing strains of the music from the next room where the pensioners were shuffling across the lino, holding arthritic hands and doing the Valeta.

The sniffer dog and its handler were closely followed by some plain clothes (or clothed) detectives and a long line of policemen, all dressed in black, swinging their truncheons and mumbling into their two way radios. I think they thought a bomb had been detected by the way the dog was carrying on. But once they'd realized there was no immediate danger, apart from the housewives eyeing them up that is, the handsome coppers immediately commandeered the canteen and started making cups of tea, or 'brews' as they call them up here.

"What's going on? What's all the fuss about?" I asked a rather dashing officer of the law through the open hatch of the canteen.

"Jack Straw's holding 'is surgery luv," was his gruff reply.

That was all very well and good but what about my art lesson I wanted to know? I wasn't prepared to let politics interfere with art even if it was Tony Blair himself visiting the centre. Now, it just so happened that this was our last session before the break and I was about to award the housewives their certificates of attendance. I was in the process of inscribing their names in my best Italic, when I suddenly had a brilliant idea. Who better to present them with their awards than the Foreign Secretary himself? I informed the housewives of my cunning plan and they shook their permed heads nervously, muttering things like - you'll never get him to do it, he's far too busy, much too important, won't want to bother with the likes of us etc.

"Oh won't he now," I stuck out my chin in a determined manner and set off to elbow my way through the lines of towering policemen, undercover and otherwise, until I reached Mr. Straw's main henchman where I proceeded to try to sweet talk him into it. He finally agreed, how could he refuse and after all, we were coming up to the elections. I rushed back to tell the good news to the housewives, who immediately dashed off to the loo to wipe the charcoal smudges off their noses and titivate their hair. We then waited for the honourable gentleman himself to arrive, practising our curtseys, handshakes etc. while someone from the centre was sent out to purchase a disposable camera from the chemists next door.

Suddenly, there was a bustle of anticipation in the corridor and I saw poor Jack's pale and worried face, waning like a sad moon over his bright red tie, looming through the swing doors. He was shepherded in by his burly bouncers, but instead of going directly to his surgery as planned, he found himself being elbowed, on both sides, along the corridor and down to my room.

"Who are you?" he asked me, giving me a slightly annoyed but nevertheless quizzical look, as though he knew me from somewhere, or was supposed to know me, but couldn't quite remember who I was. Perhaps he had a vague and distant memory of me from Brian's funeral.

"Adrienne Seed," I announced in a loud, clear voice, so that should I need to call on him again for future favours, he'd remember my name. "Thank you so much for taking the time to present these awards to my ladies," I smarmed, "It means so much to them."

So, quite a political coup for the Women's Centre who employ me - not to mention the housewives. They will probably be queuing up for my next course.

CHAPTER 23

Pittarrow

It was all very well becoming a volunteer counsellor and being a mentor to the recently diagnosed, starting an HIV support group, not to mention teaching reluctant housewives how to draw noses. But I badly needed to start painting or sculpting again myself. Not least from the financial aspect. I had tried, but the heart had been knocked out of me somehow.

What I lacked of course was Brian here by my side (or even somewhere in the background, apart from in ghost form) to spur me on. It just wasn't the same without him. He'd been my inspiration for most of my life, even though at times he could be a thorn in my side, a slave driver and a hard taskmaster. He was also a workaholic and a total perfectionist and, somewhere along the way, he taught me to be the same. While I'd slaved over my paintings, high up in my attic studio looking down over the mighty oak trees in the garden at 'Pittarrow', Brian had worked on his new invention to save the world's energy crisis in his laboratory at 'Kenolbri'. He used to like the fact that we were right next door to each other, only a short walk away along the tree-lined path that joined the two gardens, and that we were both working hard to achieve perfection in our separate fields. He always said that he could work so much better knowing that I was close at hand and yet he couldn't wait to see me at the end of the day. I'd barred him from coming up to the studio or phoning me until after seven o'clock when the natural light had gone, so he would wait impatiently for the allotted hour – twitching, as they say, at the proverbial bit.

He constantly drove me to paint harder and harder. Not that I needed him to make me work any harder. I was totally into my painting and it was wonderful to have 'Pittarrow' all to myself. Every morning, I would unlock the huge door of the empty house and creep by what used to be Brian's old offices and boardrooms with their enormous desks and marble-topped tables, then climb the thickly carpeted steps to the top floor, which was all mine. I even had my own kitchen, bathroom and bedroom.

Sometimes, if we wanted to get away from Anne (Brian's secretary) and her husband Tom, who lived at 'Kenolbri' during the week where they were employed as housekeepers, we would sleep there. But more often than not, I stayed with my mum during the week and only stayed at 'Kenolbri' at the weekends, when Brian dismissed the staff, barred all visitors and there was just the two of us. Occasionally, an odd gardener or two could be seen creeping around the foliage, tending to the beautiful gardens and trying to keep a low profile, but on the whole we were completely on our own. In this way we could live totally undisturbed in our magical, creative and inventive world. For me as a painter this gave me the freedom to reach a far deeper level of inspiration than I had ever known before. Brian was the touchstone, the fuel for my creative soul, which once the spark had been cast, kept me raging like a forest fire. There was no stopping me it seemed and Brian was equally inflamed with that same creative passion as I was, both for his invention as well as for my art.

That same passion infused into our relationship and forged us together with the surety of the blacksmith's hammer – our creative molten souls merged into one.

'Pittarrow', was almost like a giant playhouse for us, where we could either live out our fantasies or where we could also be ourselves, our true selves, which was something Brian often found hard to do, unless he was with me that is. There were no bad memories here for Brian, no family ghosts, nothing and no one to distract us from each other.

For the purpose of painting 'Pittarrow' was an artist's heaven. The light was perfect in my studio and I could make as much mess as I wanted. A cleaner came in two or three times a week to clean the kitchen and bathroom and vacuum the rest of the house, but she was deaf and dumb so we'd just nod at each other if we chanced to meet on the stairs, which was hardly ever as she tended to come very early in the morning.

Brian designed a special table on wheels for me to mix my paints on and ordered me a huge wooden easel and everything else I needed to work with. We went to the art shop together where he bought me two tubes of every single colour of oil paint and acrylic on the colour chart, even the really expensive blues and carmines. We took them all back to 'Kenolbri' and before they disappeared into the chaotic artistic confusion which my studio had rapidly become, we laid them out in neat orderly lines on the Persian rug, like an army of soldiers, ready to go into battle.

"Just think of all the wonderful paintings that are going to come out of those tubes," I sighed in anticipation. It was every artist's dream come true and I was determined to make the most of it. For the first time in my life I had the space and the time, not to mention the materials, to work as much and as hard as I liked. Ben was happy at school and Brian had relieved all the financial burdens from my shoulders. The only fly in the ointment was Brian's occasional drinking bouts and the fact that he tended to interfere too much with what I wanted to paint, often selecting the subject matter for me. But on the whole, I let him; in fact I wanted him to. Anyway, what else could I do? Artists have always been subject to the whims of their benefactors and Brian was so much more to me than just a benefactor. He was the love of my life. Aside from that, I had a great deal of respect for his taste in art and his extensive knowledge of the subject and in relation to art at least, our minds were as one.

Every evening, during the working week, at seven o'clock on the dot, the front door of 'Pittarrow' would creak open and I would hear Brian politely shout 'hello.' He would continue to call out as he mounted the three flights of stairs. He'd caught me one time unawares and lost in concentration, I'd nearly jumped out of my skin - my paintbrushes flying through the air and landing at his feet. He always bought a bottle of wine with him and went straight to the kitchen to open it. Then we would sit and review the work I had done that day and Brian would offer helpful suggestions or point out obvious mistakes, which, with eyes blinded from staring at the same canvas all day, I had failed to notice. Sometimes, when I'd been so absorbed in what I'd been working on I hadn't noticed that the light had changed or how late it had got, my heart would sink when I heard him call out from the bottom of the stairs, because I wasn't ready to stop painting yet. Other times I couldn't wait for him to come so I could show him what I'd done. If he liked it I felt a sense of real achievement and if he didn't, at least I could benefit from his expert advice or see my work through the perspective of another pair of eyes.

It wasn't all smooth going of course. The process of creation calls for highly strung and oversensitive artistic natures, which we both had and neither of us took too kindly to criticism, especially what I considered to be negative criticism. But, in fairness to Brian, I was oversensitive on that score, especially where my work was concerned and far too quick to jump to the wrong conclusion and take offence.

On occasions like these we would often fall out, especially if I was really tired, or if Brian had started on the wine before he came.

One such night we had a terrible row, I can't even remember now what set us off. But in the end I'd stormed out, calling him a bully and a dictator, telling him he could stuff his bloody studio and find another artist to boss around. I grabbed some paints and a couple of canvases and went back to my mum's. I wouldn't answer the phone for days or answer his faxes, which arrived on the hour.

Adrienne,

For some reason a small flame was blown into a forest fire. Perhaps I am stupid but I really don't know how it happened. I am terribly sorry that it did.

Please, please continue to use your studio at Pittarrow. Don't let a few moments of anger wreck something which was becoming very special and seemed certain to become sublime. I am much more than willing to continue to help you Adrienne. Please allow me to do so. You surely know that working together brings a lot of happiness and comfort to each of us.

We should not blow up our world. I don't think that we could find another one even remotely like ours,

Brian

A week passed and a hundred more faxes rolled out of the machine and lay curled up on the floor, then late one night a hand written letter landed on my mum's doorstep.

Dear Adrienne,

I think so very often about Portofino – our rock pool – you driving us along the coast – dinner at Eden Roc and a million other things. During that period I was so much happier than I've been for very many years. I look at the photographs often. I am sure that you were also very happy, well, for much of the time. Perhaps most of the time. We shouldn't have blown it all up – should we?

I love you very much Adrienne. Nothing can wash that away, not even the sea,

Brian

Dear Brian,

Love was a smooth, white pebble, tossed into a breaking wave; a flat, skilled stone, skimming over a silvery bay. It was the roar of feelings in the blood, like the sound of a seashell, pressed hard to the ear. It was an ancient whisper, a forgotten song,

A pebble – a shell - a ripple – a roar- a whisper - a sigh………a lie?

Adrienne

Oh dear, how silly and childish it all seems now - and such a waste of precious time.

CHAPTER 24

Azertiva

When I got home from college this evening there was a message on the answering machine, "Hi Adrienne, it's Janet from the clinic; there's another young girl who would like to meet you. Could you please give me a call?"

Another one and there'll be many more, I know. This is just the start, but all good practice no doubt for my counselling skills, which are slowly starting to develop, even though they don't seem to be doing much good for coping with my own particular problems. Although, how anyone copes with this dreadful disease I will never know and it's not just dealing with the physical side of things such as the HIV-related illnesses and the side effects of the medication, it's having to live with the mental side of things that are the real killer, like the stigma and the prejudice and being forced to live a lie.

Neither do my new found counselling skills seem to be having any effect as far as my son is concerned, as he is still refusing to come back to England. I torture myself with the fact that, by funding him to stay over there, I am only confounding his problems by enabling him to carry on with his decadent Ibiza lifestyle. But then again, the first rule of counselling, or at least person-centred counselling, is to encourage people to find their own way because even if you try to tell someone what to do, they won't do it until they are ready to. Anyway, apparently it's unethical to counsel your own family or friends because your own issues get in the way and I can see now how that works. All I want for my son, as any mother does, is for him to be happy, but no matter how I try, I can't make that happen. The more I try, the worse things seem to get. People like me, in counselling terms are apparently named 'enablers' and are advised to use tactics like 'tough love' rather than make life too easy for them, otherwise they will never learn the harsh facts of life. This, by its very nature is a hard, if not impossible task for any mother, and I find it far easier to say yes and very difficult to say no to my only son. But maybe I was just trying to make things easier for myself due to the fact that Ben was far away from me. At least he didn't have to witness all the times when I was sick, or watch me struggling with my medication - or more importantly, find out about me.

I called Janet back the next morning and finally managed to locate her, as they are very busy down there at the clinic these days. She gave me the girl's phone number and I called her. She sounded really nice and we arranged to meet next week.

For World Aids day, there was a vigil in Blackburn Cathedral which appeared to be a private function where people were not allowed in without a special invite – like some kind of secret society. It's a strange thing, this whole HIV business, people forced to live in isolation at a time when they really need support the most - deprived of human contact and not even (on medical advice) allowed to touch a dog or a cat. We went to the vigil in Preston instead, my mum resplendent in her wheelchair, which we'd decorated with red ribbons and I'd invited the young girl, who, to protect her identity, I will call Karen, to come along with us. She loved my mum straight away and took great delight in pushing her in the wheelchair and sitting next to her in church. My mum loved her too and in no time at all they'd bonded and Karen was calling her, her adopted granny. It was a very emotional service, especially when it was time to light the candles for the people who had died from AIDS. We placed the candles in a circle under the altar. I thought about the people I had known who had lost their lives to this terrible disease, never dreaming back then that I would ever have it.

Karen is coming for a curry with us, her new adopted family. I thought it would be good for her to have a readymade support network. My sister was over for the weekend, Willo and Pavlito, my neighbours and last, but not least, my cousin and her girlfriend.

We went to 'Suki's' for the curry. Willo with her purple hair and baker boy cap perched on the top of her head, was sporting a black and turquoise sequined ra-ra skirt with co-ordinating stiletto turquoise boots. Me, in my new sophisticated dark green velvet orient express ensemble complete with imitation fox fur trimming. My sister in bright Caribbean pink with orange flowers and chopsticks pinning up her flyaway hair. Pavlito, as usual, in nautical role, with his piercing blue sailor's eyes and neatly clipped white beard wearing a navy blue fisherman's jumper and new blue denim jeans. The 'jolly' girls decked out in black leather with matching blonde ponytails. The conversation was as mad as ever when us lot get together. I had had an erotic dream the night before about Simon Cowell, so my crazy sister kept sending me fake text messages pretending to be him.

Driving home, all squashed in my car, Willo began to sing mournful African songs, learned during her years living in Zambia. My sister and cousin were determined to join in but didn't know the words and they can't hold a tune between them, so it was a rowdy ride home.

"Poor Karen," sympathized my sis, "She thinks this is what her life will be like from now on, full of weirdos and nutters."

The poor girl couldn't wait to get out of the car, or at least that's how it seemed. We worried for next few days that we'd all been a bit too much for her and she would no longer want to associate with us. My sister sent her a text message (not from Simon Cowell I hasten to add) but she didn't reply. She did send me a card however with a little plaque, saying, 'to a special friend' and I sent her one back with an angel, but I didn't write anything inside in case her mother opened it.

It's funny, but I've come to realise that, as long as I look after myself, my life is not necessarily over as I had first thought, in fact a brand new stage is just beginning. I went for my three monthly review yesterday to check on my CD4 counts and my viral load, which thankfully is still undetectable, although every time I go I fear the worst. After Dr Gayed had finished examining me for any physical signs which would indicate that the virus was once again rearing its ugly head, something it could do at any time if it wasn't being strictly controlled by the medication, he asked me if I would take part in a survey to choose a name for a new HIV drug that was just about to be launched on the market.

I felt quite proud that he'd asked me to perform this noteworthy task, so on the appointed day, I dressed very smartly in a black jacket with a crisp, white, ironed (no less) blouse and long skirt and in order to look that bit more official for my important role, carrying the black leather briefcase my mum had bought me for college.

When I got to the clinic I hardly recognized Dr Gayed who came out of his office to greet me wearing a suit and tie instead of his usual white coat. He shook my hand warmly, as he always does and thanked me for coming, then handed me a piece of paper with the suggested names of the new medicine, which I was to study.

The potential names were as follows –

DUENZA

ATRUVA

EZALTA

VYLASTA

ASERDIA

DURACERT

EZIRA

DOSADA

AZERTIVA

I had to list them in three groups – the ones I liked the least, the ones that weren't too bad and the ones I liked the most. I took the whole business very seriously and studiously made notes in my notebook with reasons for and against each one and after careful consideration I arrived at my final list. Dr Gayed called me back in to his surgery, where he left me alone to talk to a representative from the company on the telephone.

The conversation went something like this -

"Hello, my name is Jamie, thank you for taking part in this survey. Can we start with the names for the new drug that you liked the least?"

"Hello Jamie, my name is Adrienne and the names I like least are, 'Duracert', because it sounds like a condom, 'Vylasta', because it reminds me of a surgical stocking, 'Aserdia', because it sounds like a Russian state, 'Ezira', because it sounds like someone's aging Aunt, 'Dosada' brings to mind a dose of something horrible, which I've already got and 'Azura' and 'Atruva' because they sound like low cholesterol margarines."

Jamie laughed.

"The ones I quite liked," I continued, "Were 'Ezalta', because it sounds like a huge jump for mankind and 'Duenza', because it makes me think of Duende in Spanish, which is something to do with your inner soul. But my favourite is 'Azertiva', because it sounds really positive; although that word doesn't go down too well with people like me it has to be said."

Apparently, I will receive a cheque for ten pounds for contributing to this survey.

CHAPTER 25

Lamb Chops

Every night I continue to cook dinner for me and my mum at my house then cart it down to her house on my hip in the laundry basket. That's probably what's done my back in if the truth were known, but I'd never admit that to my mum, who feels bad enough that I have to do all these things for her in the first place and I know the last thing in the world she wants is to inflict any more health problems on me. In typical mother fashion she is always saying she would take them off me if she could, but is that typical – I don't know. I just think I've got a very special mum and I feel blessed, at least in that respect. Instead, I go along with the pretence that I hurt my back at Tai Chi, or typhoo as she stubbornly continues to call it and in this way she can convince herself that I brought it on myself by subjecting my body to some ancient foreign ritual that English bodies weren't designed for. In some ways she may well be right, but I knew for a fact that my weekly Tai Chi lessons were definitely improving my mobility and balance and giving me back some strength in my upper arms and wrists.

Battling the elements, in all weathers, I cart the food-laden basket the short distance (although it doesn't always feel that way) from mine to my mum's, always arriving just in time for *'Coronation Street'*, or *'Eastenders'*. The neighbours, peering out from behind their curtains (Lancashire folk are notoriously nosy although they would prefer to describe it as being curious) on seeing me pass by with my now famous basket at the same time every night and quite often now during the day, have started calling me 'meals on legs'.

As each cold and dismal wintry day passes, my poor mum is finding it harder and harder to look after herself. This is a continuous source of frustration for her because she has always been fiercely independent and the realisation that this is no longer possible makes her ratty at times, even with me. Unfortunately, the general norm in life seems to be that people only tend to do things for you if you can offer them some kind of favour in return. This may seem harsh but it's true and I was beginning to get an insight of what it must feel like for an old person who can no longer offer anything other than themselves, which sadly for most people is not enough. This was not the case, by any means, in regard to the way I felt about looking after my mum, but I could see that she felt powerless to do the same for me, which was causing her to feel useless and a burden. I tried to not let her see if I was feeling depressed or exhausted, but at times due to the effects of the medication, not to mention the disease itself, it was impossible to hide things from her. Anyway, being my mother, as mothers do, she knew everything about me, even down to what was going on in my head. At least it sometimes felt that way. I was really starting to get worried about her though, because even though I cooked her all her favourite meals, she was hardly eating anything and seemed to be fading away before my very eyes. She loved her lamb chops however, so those were often on the menu, even though she actually preferred the fat to the meat and I had to burn them to cinders before she would even look at them.

Brian had also loved his lamb chops or 'cutlets' as he used called them, but he of course, preferred them almost rare. Even when we ate in restaurants Brian would always choose lamb chops (or should I say cutlets) over anything else. He preferred eating at 'Kenolbri' to be honest and we mainly ate out for my benefit, so I wouldn't have to cook. It seems ridiculous now, thinking about it, that with all his millions he hadn't employed a chef. But then, he hated other people being in the house with us, even the staff.

Mind you, eating out with Brian, no matter how fancy or exclusive the restaurant, wasn't always a pleasure for me, because he was very pernickety. He would often throw one of his infamous 'wobblers', especially if the food wasn't cooked exactly to his liking, or the waiters weren't subservient enough, or worse still if I managed to annoy him in some way, which being me, was often the case. One such night, it was a Tuesday so I was staying at my mum's, Bob the chauffeur had arrived to pick me up at 8.30 and then driven Brian and I to a small restaurant we often frequented, called 'Solos'.

We'd made up after our last fight and things were more or less back to normal; but predictably, all that was about to change. Bob delivered us to the door then drove off after arranging to pick us up in a couple of hours. The maitre d' heralded us in and showed us to our usual table and Brian seemed in excellent spirits: he'd had a productive day and was making good progress with his latest invention. We talked about that for a while and then made plans for the coming weekend. The first course arrived and we carried on making our plans and discussing the possibility of maybe going out to Corinthian for a few days to supervise the refurbishment that was taking place.

Brian was in a jovial mood, joking with the waitress when she came to take away our plates and everything seemed to be just fine and dandy. The main course was served when Brian suddenly reached over the table to take my hand with the intention presumably of holding it. Not wishing to be distracted from my delicious dinner, I snatched my hand away, much to Brian's evident displeasure and carried on eating. Well, that was enough to set him off and his mood took a sudden and terrifying downward turn.

"Why won't you ever hold my hand in public?" he demanded accusingly, his eyes blazing, "Are you ashamed of me?"

"Of course not," I laughed, "I was just enjoying my dinner, that's all."

"Well, in that case I'll leave you to it then," he declared melodramatically and picking up the bottle of wine, (which I also happened to be enjoying,) he strode out to the adjoining lounge, slumped down in a chair next to the log fire and turned his back to me.

This kind of erratic and irrational behaviour was not uncommon as far as Brian was concerned, especially if the demon drink had passed his lips, so I decided to stay and finish my meal and ignore his comments. Brian could act like a spoiled child at times, which is exactly what he'd been, of course, and this pattern of behaviour had followed through into his adult life. It wasn't helped by the added power of his accrued millions which afforded him the right (or at least he thought so) of getting his own way at all times.

By the time I'd finished my meal and gone through to the lounge to join him, he'd emptied the bottle of wine and I could see by the look on his face that he was all set for a fight.

"Come on Brian," I tried to placate him, "Let's not spoil the night; we were having such a lovely time before."

"Lovely time before you fucking spoiled it," he spat at me furiously.

"How did I spoil it?" I asked incredulously, although I knew well enough what had displeased him, the fact that I'd not dropped everything i.e. my knife and fork to hold his hand.

"Sometimes I think you are psychologically disturbed," he accused me, "In fact, you're not only psychologically disturbed, you are fucking mental."

He was obviously very drunk.

"That's the same thing, isn't it?" I pointed out coldly, lighting a cigarette and deciding I wouldn't rise to his bait

"You really are stark raving mad," Brian refused to let it drop, "Bonkers. In fact you're a fucking looper."

"Me a looper?" I couldn't refrain from contesting, "Why, because I wouldn't hold your hand when I was eating my dinner? You're the one who's fucking bonkers if you ask me."

Luckily, by that time the other diners had all finished their coffees and liqueurs and left, and we had the lounge to ourselves. The log fire was blazing away and one side of Brian's face had turned dangerously red and was criss-crossed with veins.

"You'd better move away from the fire," I warned him, "Your poor face is starting to look like a piece of Netlon."

Well, that did it, he blew his top.

"I'm not a fucking leper you know?" he shouted, mopping the angry beads of sweat popping out from his brow like popcorn with the perfectly ironed handkerchief he always kept in his top pocket. "But I might just as well be," he snarled, "As you never show me any sign of affection."

The waiter nervously crept through to the bar, carrying a rattling tray of empty glasses, trying his best to be invisible.

"And what about last night then?" I asked caustically, referring to our passionate union of the night before.

"I'm not talking about between the bloody sheets," he spluttered. He was beginning to slur his words.

"Besheen the bloody tweets," I laughed in his face. The whole thing was so ridiculous I was finding it hard to take him seriously.

"I'm talking about in public," he bellowed furiously.

I thought you didn't like public shows of affection," I reminded him, "You were always moaning about John and Lulabelle canoodling on the boat."

"Never mind them, I'm talking about you," he quickly interspersed. "You wouldn't even hold my hand when I asked you to."

"Ordered me to more like," I corrected him. "And for your information, I don't do anything to order. I don't hold hands or kiss someone or do anything for that matter because somebody orders me to. The things I do, I do because I mean them and because I feel them. Not for public show."

I noticed that my own hands were shaking now and I was starting to get nervous, my previous bravado fast failing me. It didn't do to cross Brian, especially when he was drunk. He would only make me pay later, one way or the other

"You're dishturbed," he slurred, poking his long, shaky finger at me, "You're a dishturbed woman."

"Well, I won't 'dishturb' you any longer then," I mimicked him and taking a leaf out of his book stood up to leave. "I'll order a taxi and leave you in peace."

I went out to look for a phone and found the waiter crouching down behind the bar, trying to pretend he hadn't heard anything, although we both knew that this would have been impossible as Brian had been shouting at the top of his voice.

"Can I help you madam?" he tried to act as though everything was normal and completely above board.

"I just need to phone for a taxi," I smiled politely, also putting on an act, but I think it came out more of a grimace really. He passed me the phone but before I could dial the number, I saw Bob arriving with the car so I didn't bother.

Brian paid the bill and the waiter helped us on with our coats then saw us to the door, locking it behind us. I bet he was glad to see the back of us. Bob opened the car door for me and then for Brian and we sat as stiff as statues in the back of the darkened car. We drove all the way home in stony silence, sitting as far away from each other as was humanly possible, clutching onto the door handles so that we wouldn't slide into each other on the slippery leather seats every time Bob turned a corner.

"You can take me to 'Kenolbri'," Brian told Bob pompously, "But madam will be going directly to her mothers."

"I'll call you sometime," he shouted after me as I hurriedly leapt out of the back seat before Bob had chance to come round and open the door for me.

"Don't bloody bother," I yelled slamming the door with a bang and went inside and cried to my mum.

I swore to myself that I would never allow this kind of thing to happen again. There seemed to be neither rhyme nor reason in the way he behaved. One minute he was swearing his undying love for me and the next he was calling me a fucking looper. Well I'd had enough.

The next day I posted this letter through his letter box.

To 'Him' it must concern,

I'm sitting here and wondering why, I've let myself be taken in, allowed myself to fall again, be wrapped around and spun within, your tangled web of love and lies - "The Spider and the Fly."

With that same hand, you pulled me in, you stroked my skin and tantalised, you soothed and smoothed and polished me, till I was bright like moonlit stone and rocking on a silver sea, you reawakened love in me. Then I was back within your net, not wanting to escape – and yet. As I was feeling safe and sure, you pushed me with your other hand and slammed love's door, "I'll call you sometime," then nothing more, just cold, old, silence.

Pull and push, push and shove, if you don't take care, you'll lose my love - just like before. I enclose this very fitting article I found in the newspaper.

YEAR OF THE SPIDER – OR WHY IT'S NEVER BEEN A WORSE TIME TO BE A FLY - Fact file on nature's tiny spin-doctors.

Spiders' feet are coated with waxy hairs, so they don't get stuck to their own webs. They build a non-sticky platform in the centre of the web. Once a fly has been trapped in a web, the spider sprays it with silk. With the insect immobilised, the spider bites any extruding part of the body and injects venom into it. Pound for pound, spider silk is tougher than steel. Synthetic silk made from the same chemicals has been turned into bullet-proof vests and forms the cross hairs on rifle sights.

Sound familiar? It does to me,
Adrienne

No reply, not a word, so I send him another letter with a list of questions I needed answering, but still no reply. So I wrote to him again asking him to send the questions back and his response was as follows.

Dear Adrienne,

Your "questions" are returned as requested. The more I read the two enclosed missives, the more distressed I become. Have you always been right and have I always been wrong?

Sincerely,

Brian

Dear Brian,

Obviously a leopard as set in his ways as you are, cannot possibly change his spots

Well, neither can a leopardess – a paintress – a sculptress – a mistress!

Yours in DISTRESS (or DATDRESS)

Adrienne

Dearest Adrienne,

Please, please, come to Kenolbri this weekend.

I've told Mrs Coombs to order some lamb chops,

Much love,

Brian

That man and his bloody lamb chops. It was the same every weekend. The housekeeper, Mrs Coombs, always knew if Brian and I weren't speaking if the lamb chops were still sitting in the fridge in a neat orderly row when she arrived on Monday morning. If we'd managed to make it through the entire weekend without falling out, which could be as rare as he liked his 'cutlets', she would serve us breakfast in the sunroom then I would escape to my studio in 'Pittarrow' to paint and leave Brian to try to solve the world's energy crisis.

Sometimes, on Sunday, if the weather was nice, we would get the Mercedes out of the garage and go for a drive in the country. I drove nearly all the time these days because Brian's eyesight was rapidly deteriorating. One such Sunday, we drove to Yorkshire to visit Ben at boarding school. The car naturally caused quite a stir as we drove up the drive and a crowd of boys gathered round to look.

"Are you Ben's dad?" one of them asked Brian with curiosity. Luckily, he didn't say granddad!

Ben was waiting for us in his smart blue blazer and we took him and a friend out for tea – well, a McDonald's actually.

"I've never been to a McDonald's in my life," Brian complained stuffily.

"Oh well, there's a first time for everything," I laughed.

"Do they allow you to wear that earring at school," Brian asked Ben in horror, referring to his pierced ear.

"Only at weekends," Ben informed him, his mouth full of Big Mac and chips.

CHAPTER 26

Diamonds on the soles of her trainers

Daughters need their mothers and I certainly needed mine and I didn't know what I was going to do if anything happened to her. But the way things were going, I was going to have to face up to the fact that one day, she would no longer be here to support me and that thought didn't bear thinking about - so I didn't think about it. I just carried on doing what I could for her and making life as pleasurable for her, well, for both of us, as possible. On top of all that and aside from the constant worries about my own health, there was also all the worry of Ben to contend with. Mothers need their daughters, but sons need their fathers and Ben's father was a complete waste of space, at least as far as I was concerned. As for Brian he'd actively encouraged me to send Ben back to Ibiza.

"Ben is old enough now to fend for himself," Brian had reasoned, "After all he's been away at boarding school and he's used to not having you around"

"But he needs me," I cried.

"So do I," said Brian, "And you need to work for this exhibition."

Even though I'd been sure I wasn't doing the right thing, I'd eventually given in and Brian had bought Ben a ticket to Ibiza.

If only you could turn back the clock, go back and start again. But you can't, you just have to live with your mistakes and somehow try to rectify the damage you have done. Some things cannot be rectified of course and HIV is one of them. It's out of my hands, out of my control, and maybe if I hadn't allowed myself to be so controlled by Brian, I wouldn't be in the position I am in now. And yet the very fact that I am the carrier of this virus until the day I die signifies that I am still being controlled, by both of them – a double whammy!

Maybe that's what I should call this new painting I've just started. At the moment I've called it 'The Last Supper' and it's teeming with symbolic images related to this horrible illness – the huge yellow pills which are keeping me alive lying on a long wooden table at which only one person sits - a 'symbolic' me in a Netlon ballet dress, while a sad fairy with a feathered headdress stands on a plinth with her head bowed and her arms crossed over her chest, looking down on the empty chairs. Brian is there of course, but represented as the white rabbit of 'Alice in Wonderland' fame, dressed in a white suit and dangling a stop watch to signify time (as in mine) is running out. His Netlon tie flaps defiantly over his shoulder like a red ensign. I can hear his pompous voice in my head every time I look at it, saying, "You're not going to put a Netlon tie on that are you?"

Too late, I already have. Actually, there is Netlon everywhere, swathes of the bloody stuff draping over the edges of the canvas, meticulously painted in different colours, red, yellow, green and of course black. The colour of the spider's web. A man in a business suit with yet another flapping tie (Brian again) walks on water, while at the water's edge, empty and abandoned, are the two tiny pink crocodile shoes I'd given him in Ibiza. In the background, three men in black tailcoats, the coffin bearers, carry a symbolic me, recumbent on a velvet sofa like Mae West to my death. A solitary oversized autumn leaf, the symbol of death and decay, hangs suspended in the air, crinkled and dry. Alice through the looking glass, yet another symbolic me, sits on a high window ledge looking down over the table, her last supper and the row of empty coloured bowls.

But for all its morbid subject matter, it's an uncharacteristically bright and vibrant painting and I wonder what Brian would have thought about it. Perhaps I will include it in my next exhibition, but who knows when that will be?

The last exhibition I'd had was the one woman show Brian had arranged for me in Belgium. I'd worked so hard to get enough work together for that exhibition, but then so had Brian. He'd arranged everything for me, down to the very last detail; in fact he'd done everything apart from paint the paintings. Although, in some ways, he'd even had a hand in that by helping me choose the subject matter.

When all the work was ready we'd carted the whole collection down to the framers and spent hours choosing the frames and mounts, which Brian had greatly enjoyed and of course he'd paid for everything. As ever, only the best would do, especially in relation to my art. But before the paintings were shipped to the gallery in Antwerp, Brian suddenly decided we should hold a preview at 'Pittarrow' to show anyone who mattered in Blackburn the high standard (in his words) of the work that I'd done since we'd been back together – and more importantly (again in his words) that we were back together again as a couple.

True to form, everything had to be done to his exacting high standards and expense was not a problem. He personally designed the invitations for the long list of carefully selected guests - his selected guests that is, not mine. I was only allowed to invite my family, certain friends that he approved of (in other words not many) and Erik. Brian was very jealous of my close bond with Erik and didn't really want to invite him either, but for once I put my foot down.

Magnificent floral arrangements were ordered from the florist to adorn the rooms and the caterers were called in, along with a butler to greet the guests and waiters and waitresses to serve the food and wine. The whole middle floor of 'Pittarrow', which consisted of four big rooms branching off from a long corridor, were lined with my paintings and Brian summoned a specialist electrician to come and arrange the lighting. We spent days hanging the paintings, which gave Brian the opportunity to get his tape measure out, which he did with great glee. He loved measuring things and couldn't abide it if anything was even slightly out of line. When the paintings were finally hung to his satisfaction, he called in his photographer to take stills of all my work and also arranged for someone to come and make a video. Finally, he insisted on buying me a new outfit for the occasion, which he chose of course, and I was sent off to the hairdresser to have my hair styled and my nails done.

The night of the preview arrived to find me a cowering wreck. I was suddenly feeling uneasy about being the focus of everyone's attention and having my work, not to mention my artistic soul, up for public dissection and criticism. Brian on the other hand was raring to go; he was striding around in a masterly fashion, checking everything was all in order before all the guests arrived. But I was suffering from pre-show nerves and dreading having to socialize with everyone, especially some of Brian's more supposedly 'upper class' friends, who I found to be pompous and overbearing at the best of times - and then of course there was the dreaded Olga to contend with, Brian's older sister. I downed a couple of glasses of wine for Dutch courage, then, in a total panic, snuck off and called Erik on the downstairs phone to make sure he was coming along to support me.

"Why don't you come early," I implored him, "In fact why don't you come right now and we can have a drink or two before everyone gets here. Please hurry darling, I need you," I begged dramatically, "I can't get through this evening without you."

Unfortunately, Brian happened to walk in right at that moment, just in time to overhear my last remark. He said nothing at the time, instead he grabbed my arm and almost shoved me into the entrance hall,

"The press are here," he snapped short temperedly, ushering them in.

We then stood together, arm in arm, smiling, next to one of my paintings to be photographed.

The preview was a great success as it turned out and, thanks to the wine, I managed to do my networking bit, chatting away and socialising, even with the dreaded Olga!

When most of the guests had gone home, apart from Erik and a few of my friends, I looked around for Brian but he was nowhere to be seen. In fact, when I thought about it, I hadn't seen him for quite a while. I grabbed the torch that he always kept by the front door and walked along the dark, tree lined path to 'Kenolbri.' I tried the door but it was locked and there appeared to be no lights on. I banged on the door, no answer. But he had to be there – where else could he be? I stumbled my way back to 'Pittarrow' by the light of the torch and called him on the phone. He answered straight away.

"What are you doing there?" I demanded, "Why have you gone back home?

We've still got guests," I reminded him shortly, feeling a bit put out that he'd gone and left me to it.

"You've still got guests you mean," he replied sulkily. "In fact, why don't you just stay there all night with your 'darling' Erik? You obviously can't do without him."

"Don't be so pathetic," I told him impatiently. "Erik's my best friend. I've known him for years and so have you. Anyway, you know he's gay."

"I heard you earlier on the phone, calling him 'darling' and telling him you couldn't do without him," Brian whinged jealously. "Well, you can have him; have him I say. And what about me? After all the things I've done for you. Not many men would be prepared to put in the amount of effort I have on your behalf. Not many men would put up with your outrageous behaviour …etc. etc."

It was obvious he was off on one, so I slammed the phone down and went to help my friends and of course my 'darling' Erik to finish the wine.

The following week, Brian and I flew to Brussels and checked into the Hilton, two days before the exhibition was due to start, because he wanted to make sure everything was organised correctly and to his satisfaction. As we pulled up outside the gallery in the taxi, my paintings were lit up in the windows and my name was displayed in big letters for all to see.

"I'm so proud of you," Brian beamed, squeezing my hand and I must admit, I felt quite proud of myself.

Representatives from the Belgian newspapers and art magazines were at the opening, which also hosted an impressive guest list. Brian had previously written to his friend, the Right Honourable Barbara Castle, to arrange for the British Ambassador to open the exhibition. Unfortunately he was away on official business so we had to make do with his deputy instead. Waiters in immaculate white gloves flitted amongst the throngs, holding trays aloft laden with Lobster canapés and smoked salmon and caviar, followed by sumptuous cream cakes and profiteroles.

I was far too nervous to eat anything and anyway, I was too busy carrying out my obligatory networking and socialising commitments. It's an activity I dislike, but if you want to get on in the art world, or at least according to Brian, it had to be done.

Despite my reluctance to 'sell myself', the show was a great success and the walls were quickly scattered with red dots, although Brian bought four of my most expensive paintings himself, because he said he couldn't bear to part with them. He even paid the gallery's commission, which, for someone who was renowned for watching the pennies, (even though he had eighty million pounds worth of them), was quite a gesture in itself.

As soon as we got back from Belgium I went straight to Ibiza to see Ben. Brian wasn't at all happy about this, but suggested that instead of coming back to England after Ibiza, I should fly directly to Nice and meet him there; then we would join the yacht for a cruise along the Spanish coast.

I did as he suggested and joined Corinthian in the South of France and we'd been on board for almost three weeks, just the two of us and the crew, but things weren't going at all well. I was too preoccupied about Ben and kept suggesting to the captain that he changed course and set sail to Ibiza. But, needless to say, Brian wouldn't hear of it. He was terrified that, if we went to Ibiza, I'd abandon ship and leave him. The way he'd been behaving, I probably would have done.

So there we were, anchored off the Spanish coast in the most idyllic setting imaginable, with a romantic silvery moon shining down on us from above and a fragrant flower-filled breeze wafting in from the shore: the perfect scenario. But Brian was in one of his moods about something; I can't remember what and had gone down to bed, leaving me alone on the deck, looking at the lights of Cadaques making jagged knives of colour over the moonlit bay. I could see the floodlit church with its blue bell tower dominating the vista of the tiny white village, made famous by Salvador Dali and music from one of the harbour bars where a band was playing. Someone was playing along on the bongos and I could hear the sound of people having a good time and I wished I was with them. In fact, I wished I was anywhere other than where I was right at that moment. Every word, either I or any of the crew had uttered that evening had seemed to annoy him and in the end he'd stomped off to bed leaving me there on my own, spinning slowly round and round in this silver bay on this beautiful boat. Why couldn't he just be happy, like he was before and enjoy it? Why couldn't I?

I finish my drink and go down to the cabin. He is either asleep or pretending to be asleep, so I curl up on my side of the bed and listen to the faint sound of music wafting in from the shore, until I eventually drift off.

The next day the pea souper of silences descends over the entire boat. It's bad enough that he's not speaking to me and I have to endure a very rough crossing on the high seas to Menorca in solitary confinement. Brian hates people who can't sail and although I am trying my very best to be on my dignity, there is nothing dignified about seasickness, I can tell you. He casts me a look of pure contempt as I huddle miserably on deck, feeling wretched, and goes below. It's lonely on deck in the crashing waves when 'one' isn't speaking to 'one.'

Ollie takes pity on me and brings me what we fondly refer to as the smoking blanket, in other words an all weather quilt. She also hands me a big blue bowl to be sick in, a bottle of water, some salty

Twiglets, and the distress rocket I like to have directly to hand, just in case. Every now and then I poke my head out from under the smoking blanket, take a peek at the angry black waves battling with each other for supremacy, all fighting to go in different directions, then I duck back under again. I am definitely not cut out to be a sailor. I hate being trapped on the high seas with my insides swinging back and forth and feeling so sick. Neither do I like the fact that things are out of my control and completely under his.

Eventually, the low, rocky shores of Menorca appear on the horizon and I crawl out from under the blanket looking like a bedraggled dog. The captain puts the sail up and we fly like an arrow along the narrow entrance channel to the harbour. People gather on the quay to watch us speed past. Brian's mood lightens and he smiles at me, so I smile back - with relief more than anything else that we are finally approaching dry land.

That night, keen to disembark, we invite Graham and Ollie out for dinner, but like the weather, Brian's mood takes a sudden turn for the worst again and he starts drinking vodka – Stolichnaya.

"If you're so bloody unhappy," he growls, unexpectedly turning on me,

"Why don't you just pack your fucking bags and go?"

"I never said a word," I answer defensively, taken by surprise.

"You don't bloody need to," he swore, waving a crab claw at me, "Just leave why don't you? Go back to Ibiza and your precious son. Go on; pack your fucking bags and go."

Graham and Ollie hang their heads and look down at their plates in embarrassment.

"Is everything alright sir?" The maitre d rushes over in a panic to see if anything's wrong with the cuisine.

"Well if that's what you want," I stand up scraping my chair back, "Maybe I will then." I throw my shawl dramatically over my shoulder and stalk out of the restaurant.

The next morning Brian is in a mega huff and goes off for a walk on his own. Knowing his bad sense of direction, not to mention his poor eyesight, I knew he would get lost without me, which of course he did. But I didn't bother to go and find him. In fact, I would have abandoned ship right then and there but for two reasons. I didn't have enough money for an airline ticket and I'd left my bag containing my passport in the bar last night and it didn't open again until seven.

When Brian finally found his way back to Corinthian, many hours later, he apologised profusely for his outrageous behaviour, slipped me some money in an envelope so that I could buy a ticket if perchance, "An unfortunate incident such as this should ever arise again," which he swore it wouldn't, and promises to get psychiatric help the minute we get back to England, if I don't leave.

So I stay on – and on, until thankfully it's time to go home

We get back to England and don't speak to each other for a week. Then he sends me an itemised bill.

Dear Adrienne,

Out of curiosity I have examined my accounts going back to August 1995 and have produced the figures shown on the attached sheet. I realise that it is not a King's ransom, but neither is it an insignificant sum. I am sure that you will be absolutely furious that I have taken the trouble to extract these figures but I must defend myself to some extent. The following figures do not include any foreign travel or the large number of visits to restaurants during this period of nine months. For the purpose of the account, I refer to myself as FBM and you as AJS, accordingly,

Yours very sincerely

Brian

Dear Brian,

You are right, I am absolutely furious that, as usual, you have reduced everything to terms of money. As for the itemised account; if I remember rightly it was FBM who chose expensive leather bag for AJS because he objected to her old hippy rucksack and probably fancied young Italian girl in bag shop. Camel coat was also purchased on FBM's insistence so AJS wouldn't 'shame' FBM at Savoy. AJS doesn't wear camel coat very often it has to be said; only on visits to Savoy and when with FBM, as is slightly dated. Peruvian sweater bought as birthday gift for AJS, rather itchy and at the risk of sounding ungrateful, she was rather hoping for a camera like Erik's!

Oil and acrylic paints, two of each colour, every artist's dream and best present FBM could ever give to AJS and she remains to this day eternally grateful.

If FBM casts his memory back, AJS thinks he will find that it was indeed he who invited mother of AJS to join them at Savoy for birthday treat and a great time was had by all.

Designer clothes from Harrods, strictly on FBM's insistence, as were knickers, stockings and suspenders, although there is still some doubt about who got the most pleasure from wandering around the lingerie department, selecting ladies' smalls.

?-?-96 - Not surprising FBM can't remember exact date when this money changed hands, because in drunken rage, told AJS to pack fucking bags and abandon ship. Money was for ticket if it ever happened again. By the way, some further items FBM forgot to mention - tub of anti-wrinkle cream on offer in Barcelona, warm sweater to wear on boat because was fucking freezing, several cartons of camel lights for nervous strain inflicted on AJS by FBM, pair of trainers so AJS could keep up with FBM walking round ancient monuments.

CHAPTER 27

The Factory Gates

It was such a glorious day when I woke up this morning, one of the first days of spring and a day that was just beckoning to be enjoyed. I quickly got dressed then walked down to my mum's and suggested we had a picnic in my garden. My mum's house doesn't have a garden only a tiny back yard, which makes her feel claustrophobic at times, especially on a day like today so she was glad to get out, even if it was only down to mine. I pushed her along the road, which is only a short distance but even that is too much for her these days. I left her watching telly while I nipped down town in the car to buy some picky things from M&S. Then when I got back I put the cushions out on the swinging seat and set the recliner out for my mum.

The day before, we'd had a trip to the garden centre to buy some bedding plants, and while we were there we'd bought a lilac tree in memory of my mum's mum: my grandma Annie, who I can't really remember because she died not long after I was born. The idea was to have a planting ceremony to commemorate her memory and today was the perfect day to do it. I got out my spade and I'd just finished digging the hole, ready to plant the lilac bush, when the phone rang. I let it ring and was in two minds whether to bother answering it or not because my hands were all dirty. But I could see my mum was starting to get agitated thinking it might be my sister, or my even my brother, although chance would be a fine thing as he very rarely rang her, or me for that matter, yet this didn't stop my mum from living in constant hope that he would. Besides, she had a thing about not answering telephones which dated back to the days when our typical teenage antics caused her to live in perpetual fear of an emergency. This time her fears were justified however and it's a good job I picked up the phone as it turned out, because it was Ben and he was in a right state, in fact, he was almost hysterical.

"Calm down, Ben, what on earth's the matter?" I asked him, my heart racing.

My mum looked on, a worried expression on her face.

"I've got something wrong with me," he sobbed down the phone.

"What kind of thing?" I demanded my heart in my mouth.

"I don't know but I'm in agony," he was crying with pain.

He refused to tell me anything more than that, just kept groaning down the phone so I told him to call a doctor, then because that's easier said than done in Spain, to get himself to the local hospital instead. "Go to 'urgencias'," I ordered him, "Now – go on, off you go."

He refused point blank at first, as he hated hospitals and doctors, but eventually, after some cajoling on my part, he finally agreed to go to the local Spanish hospital and we waited nervously by the phone until he called back.

"Well? What did the doctor say?" I demanded.

"It was a woman," Ben spat with disgust, "so I walked out."

"Bloody hell, Ben, for heaven's sake," I swore.

I then had to start calling round various friends in Ibiza to try to find a male doctor who would come to the flat to see him. We found one eventually who was willing to make private house calls, at a huge expense of course, and after examining him, told him that he was suffering from an acute infection and prescribed him a course of strong antibiotics.

This was my chance. I began immediate negotiations using my newly acquired counselling skills, to try to talk him into coming home. In other words, I let him make the decision, and once he had made it, he simply couldn't wait to get on the plane. I got straight on the internet and found him the first available direct flight to England, which was for the following day to somewhere called Manstone in Kent, an airport I had never heard of (but I would find it, nothing surer!)

I was so excited that night I could hardly sleep, even though I knew I would need all my wits about me in order to make the long drive. My mum insisted on coming with me in the car to pick him up. I tried to warn her that the long journey would be too much for her, especially going all that time without her oxygen machine, but she wasn't having it. We set off at six in the morning, just in case, which turned out to be a good job, because it took us nearly ten hours to find the airport. But we were there just in time to meet the plane.

The airport was in the middle of nowhere, deep in desolate countryside, surrounded by endless cabbage fields. Relics of old Jumbo jets loomed out of the mist, put out to pasture like old carthorses. It was only a tiny airport and we were so close to France that when Ben put his mobile on it said, 'Welcome to France.' He was first through the arrivals door, with a big beaming smile on his face and I couldn't believe that he'd actually done it; he was back in England after nearly six years.

The drive took twenty-one hours in total, but I didn't really mind because it was so wonderful to have my son back in the fold. I would have driven to the ends of the earth and back to get him if needs be, which I very nearly did (at least to the end of England) and Ben was also very happy to be home, talking about staying here and doing his driving test and maybe even a course at college. It was nothing short of a miracle.

But two days on and life will never be the same again. My peace, for what it was, has been totally destroyed and so has my mum's. Everything now revolves around Ben and I'm desperately trying to build him up by cooking huge meals for him; fried breakfasts every morning, then lunch, followed by dinner, not to mention the snacks in between and of course the odd McDonalds from the drive-in. He was so thin. It looks as though we'd got him back just in the nick of time.

We went to Halfords to buy some 'L' plates and I let him drive the car around Pleasington cemetery, which sounds a bit of a morbid choice, but which in fact was quite pleasant as all the spring flowers were out and the trees bursting into leaf. Every now and then, we slowed down to look at the gravestones and read the names of some of the deceased.

"Have we not got anyone to visit?" Ben asked me and I suddenly realized I didn't know where my dad was. The only way I'd been able to handle his tragic death from a brain tumour was to pretend that he was still alive somewhere, which I was still doing. Not healthy I know, especially in counselling terms, you have to face up to things in order to be able to move on. But, like dentists often have bad teeth and hairdressers crappy hairstyles, when it came to my own mental health, my counselling skills were non- existent.

We called in at my mum's before we went home and Ben parked the car proudly outside her window and tooted the horn. There was a blue van parked outside with 'Pest Control' written on the side and when we got in, the 'rat man' as we called him, was busy poking his head in the cupboards and scuttling around the skirting boards to check if the trays of poison he'd left the week before had done their dastardly business. Because my poor mum could hardly see anymore, she constantly left a trail of toast crusts and peanuts in her wake and the mice had taken advantage of her semi-blindness and moved in to take up permanent residence. In fact, they'd become really cheeky with it, not even bothering to try to hide their verminous presence from us. I'd been lying on her sofa the week before watching 'Coronation Street' and to my horror, I'd looked down and one had been sitting there on the carpet, raised up on its furry haunches nibbling a peanut, so close I could see its beady little eyes – a bit like Basil - Manuel's pet rat in 'Fawlty Towers'.

The 'rat man' was something of a chatterbox and he and Ben immediately struck up a conversation about what was in the poison and how it worked, which led on to taking drugs. This encouraged 'rat man' to impart his unsavoury descriptions of some of the more sleazy establishments he was forced to visit during the course of his work; the council flats and vermin- infested squats inhabited by drug dealers and junkies, where he couldn't even put poison down because the drug addicts would smoke the pellets out of the tray or inject it in their privates. Ben was fascinated but also suitably horrified.

The course of antibiotics seemed to have done the trick and Ben was feeling and also looking so much better now, although he still complained of being in pain from time to time.

To take his mind (and mine) off his ailments and also because he couldn't wait to get back behind the wheel of the car, we went for another drive around the cemetery and he told me that, when he'd been ill in Ibiza, he'd seen a little angel on his shoulder. I'd like to think it was my dad.

So thanks, Dad.

I was still finding it hard to believe that I finally had my son back, after all this time. He was here in Blackburn, with me and his granny and he was learning to drive. It really was a miracle.

Recounting Ben's revelation about the angel to my mum later, she took on that 'I already knew it, you can't tell me anything' look that she's so good at and informed me that she'd been regularly calling on my dad and also communing with God and asking him to take Ben under his wing. Whatever had happened, it had certainly given him a fright - enough to come back to England. So, it had obviously been a joint venture between God the Heavenly Father and my own heavenly father, working from above (and below) on Ben's behalf. The hands of the Gods - and of my dad, work in very mysterious ways.

The prodigal son is now back in the proverbial fold and that's an experience in itself and an exhausting one at that, I think to myself, as I slave over a hot stove cooking endless dinners for him. I am carrying out my almost forgotten maternal role, but at the same time still trying to practise my 'tough love' approach and also trying my very hardest not to call him 'pet'.

Talking of pets, horror of horrors, we have a resident spider. Ben thinks it's the same one that was here when he left, six years ago and it's been living here ever since, so he won't let me stamp on it. I am not keen on the spider, needless to say. I think it might be the reincarnation of Brian, back to haunt me. But Ben wants to keep it as pet. I don't think Brian would take very kindly to being kept as a pet, but I go along with the idea for Ben's sake.

"What shall we call him?" he asks, putting a sliver of cheese on the floor for him.

"How about 'Long gone'," I mutter under my breath, resisting the urge to get out the can of insect repellant.

"Long John?" luckily Ben mishears me, "He was a pirate mum," he sighs wearily, "I know," he suggests brightly, "We'll call him Lonely."

This causes a huge lump to form in my throat, because that's how Ben must feel, so I quickly adapt to the idea that I now have to share my living quarters with a giant spider, just so that Ben has got a friend and is not a 'Billy no mates.'

"Go on boy, back in your house," he shoos it gently back under the filing cabinet where it resides. I wish it would bloody stay there, it gives me the creeps and it's getting bigger and bolshier by the day, stomping around in broad daylight and scuttling across the carpet.

"Maybe it would be happier living in the garden?" I suggest hopefully. But Ben won't hear of it.

But aside from our hugely differing attitudes over the health and well being of 'Lonely', on the whole, me and the prodigal son are getting along just fine and he's been behaving himself. Well, for most of the time. There have been a couple of setbacks, I have to admit, but then Rome wasn't built in a day I have to keep reminding myself. His dad came to take him snowboarding at the local dry slope. He had a new girlfriend, a lorry driver called Sarah who is the real reason he comes up north and not to see his only son.

The snowboarding didn't last long it has to be said. Dave soon brought him back then he zoomed off with Sarah. She's quite nice as it happens although she insists on her name being pronounced with an 'arh' instead of the more regular 'air', otherwise, up here, they would pronounce it Suruh, like they do at the chip shop.

"Are those fish done yet, Suruh?"

Ben got the local paper and started calling up for jobs and somehow managed to talk someone into giving him one at a warehouse. So joy of joys, the following morning, off he went to work. I got up at seven to make him a fried breakfast, drove him to the industrial estate where the warehouse was situated, then waited nervously by the phone all day, expecting bad news – that he would call and tell me to come and get him because he'd had the sack or something. But no, he loved it, packing brochures for Thompson's holidays, working so fast, he was christened 'formula one.'

Sadly, the job was only temporary, but he immediately found himself another one as an assembler, where, unfortunately for me, he has to start at eight in the morning.

I've just got back from dropping the 'Great British Worker', as my mum calls him, off at the factory gates. It's one of those depressing Industrial Revolution-type factories in Lower Darwen, an old mill possibly, with the bricked in windows and jagged shards of glass lining the walls. My mum wanted to come with me when it was time to pick him up because she lived in Lower Darwen in her youth, and worked in a fuse factory during the war. She was looking forward to a trip down memory lane and seeing the downtrodden hordes clocking off and clattering down the cobbled streets in their clogs and shawls. We set off early for this very purpose and I slowed down as we drove past her old house, and the new housing estate which was where the fuse factory used to be. My mum told stories of sitting on the garden wall with her sisters, watching the bombs lighting up the sky as they blitzed Manchester. We stopped at the old churchyard where my mum's two baby boys, who would have been my older brothers should they have lived, were buried, and also her mother - my grandma Annie. I left her in the car and went to try to find their graves, but the graveyard was so neglected and overgrown it was a hopeless task.

Back in the car we drove alongside the River Ribble which, as my mum recalled, in her days, was glorious untamed countryside, lush with buttercups and wild flowers, but was now a dual carriageway forging its way through a huge industrial estate. We passed the remains of the old paint factory where my granddad had been employed as the chief paint mixer but which was now derelict and on the point of being bulldozed to extinction. My mum remembered with a smile how her and her sisters had walked miles through those once buttercup-filled fields to meet him every day after work, and also the many times he'd determinedly tossed his packet of Capstan full strength over the wall, swearing to give up smoking, only to buy another packet at the newsagents on the corner of their street when they arrived home. Like granddad, like granddaughter then.

We arrived just in time at Ben's workplace to pick him up and pulled up outside the factory gates to wait for the whistle to sound, signifying the end of the long working day. At five o'clock on the dot a big burly man came out, reasonably dressed in a suit and tie and drove off in his car.

"That must be the boss," my mum nodded approvingly.

Another man came out wearing a shabby looking overall. "That's probably the tattler," she pronounced knowledgeably.

I always thought the Tattler was a magazine, but you live and learn.

A woman wearing a woolly hat clicked, as opposed to clocked off in her high heels. "The wages clerk," she said with a nod of one who knows.

An Asian youth sloped out bent under a heavy rucksack, followed by a worn out looking woman wearing a baker boy cap. They disappeared into the swirling grey mist.

No sign of the great British worker. Ah, there he was at last, appearing out of the gloom, swinging his lunch bag and beaming. As soon as he was through the factory gates what must have been the foreman (according to my mum) swung them to and locked them with a huge chain.

"Where are all the hordes?" my mum peered blearily through the car window in disappointment. But the hordes should there have been any, had obviously already clocked off and gone home. No clacking clogs then.

"Well, what did you do today, son?" I asked Ben as he got in the car.

"I made the holders for walking sticks," he beamed proudly. "It were great."

"Were? Don't you mean was?" I corrected him.

So much for a private education.

The prodigal son appears to love it up north and no longer wants to return to Ibiza, so we can now sever all ties, which is a great relief to me, but also means that Blackburn has now become home and I will have to accustom myself to Ben saying 'were' instead of 'was.'

A small price to pay.

CHAPTER 28

The Elephants' Graveyard

Although it seems to all intents and purposes that Ben has settled down and become an honest working man, I live in permanent fear that the bubble will burst and he will want to go back to Ibiza. Brian had wanted me to send Ben back to Ibiza, for the simple and very selfish reason that he wanted me all to himself. I could have stood up to him of course, but I was weak and, as ever, allowed him to control and influence me. Since the day he'd been born, like any mother, all I'd ever wanted for Ben was for him to be happy. I had tended to give in to his demands - and still do in fact. But it hadn't felt right him being in Ibiza on his own and me being here in Blackburn living the life of a millionairess with Brian. Ibiza is not an ideal place for a teenage boy to be left up to his own devices as I should have known. There are too many temptations on that crazy island with its wild party scene, abundance of drugs and full moon festivals, which can go on for days on end.

Ibiza also has many good points of course, it's not all sex and drugs and Manumission. It is an incredibly beautiful island, which, if you can avoid the many temptations and handle the strange energies, can inspire the heart and soul. Ibiza is often known as 'The White Island' or 'The Elephant's Graveyard', because so many creative minds have lived and died there and is supposed to be one of the five centres or fields of magnetic energy in the world, but not being a scientist, I'm not quite sure what that signifies. I do know that many mystics, mediums and old hippies (some of whom still live there) were drawn to the island for its supernatural energies and that Nostradamus apparently wrote that it would be one of the few safe places in the world to live in the event of a nuclear holocaust. I wasn't sure about all that, but one thing I was sure of, I wasn't happy about Ben being there on his own.

During that time I'd spoken to Ben every day on the phone but after these phone calls I always felt very down and dejected, which had annoyed Brian no end, because aside from personally affecting him, it was also interfering with my painting. He told me I worried about Ben too much. It was time to cut the apron strings he said and concentrate on my work. But what he really meant of course was that I tie those apron strings around my waist, cook his lamb chops and concentrate more on him.

I'd flown out to Ibiza regularly to see Ben, much to Brian's disapproval and we'd had endless arguments about it. He'd hated me going to Ibiza and while I was there, he'd phoned me several times a day to check up on me.

"When are you coming back?" he'd ask me gloomily.

"You know when. Next Tuesday. You've arranged for Bob to come and pick me up at the airport."

"I'm missing you."

"I'm missing you too."

"I hate you being there. You've been away for ages."

"Come on Brian, it's only been a week. When I'm in Blackburn I see you every single day and spend every weekend with you."

"Well, I wish you were here right now."

"I can't be in two places at once," I snapped, feeling torn. "I'm only here because I have to be for Ben. I feel like I've abandoned him. Surely you don't resent me for that?"

Silence.

"Do you?"

Silence.

"You do, don't you," I sighed. "Well, I suppose it's hard for you to understand how I feel, never having had children of your own."

Maybe that wasn't the most tactful thing to say, but nevertheless it was true.

"Brian, speak to me for God's sake," I begged him. "Look, I've tried to be everything you want me to be, but the one thing I can't stop being is a mother."

Silence.

"Look, perhaps I am not the right woman for you after all," I told him, losing patience. "I obviously can't fulfil your needs. Your past wives only had to devote themselves to you, but I can't. I'm a mother first and foremost with a son who needs setting back on the right track. I can't split myself in two so don't try to make me feel guilty about it. I'll be back as soon as I can."

Brian could see that I would never settle until the situation was resolved so finally, he came up with a solution. He bought me a cottage on the same street as my mum's, number 21, the idea being that Ben could come back to England to resume his studies; my mum could keep an eye on him if we had to go away, and we could carry on more or less as we were. Brian wasn't very comfortable with children of any age, not having had any of his own, so he simply couldn't face the idea of living with a difficult teenage boy at 'Kenolbri' and I must admit, I couldn't see it working out either. The two of them were totally incompatible and Ben resented me being with anyone who wasn't his dad - especially Brian who in Ben's eyes seemed so much older than me and in his words, was 'a pompous old git' to boot.

The plan was that as soon as the refurbishment of number 21 was finished, we would send for Ben and he would come back to England and study at Blackburn College. Brian and I drove to Ikea and chose the furniture for his room and brought the whole lot back to number 21 in Tom the housekeeper's van. The rest of the furniture for the house we chose together and as usual, only the best would do. The only thing he skimped on were the fitted carpets, insisting on making use of the old carpets from 'Kenolbri', which had been stored in the garage for years. For all his millions, Brian hated to see things go to waste and never threw anything away.

"Look, it's still in perfectly good condition," he beamed at me, as the gardeners unrolled the dusty carpets out on the drive at 'Kenolbri' for inspection. One of the carpets was from the time of his first marriage, and looked like it!

"I don't like the colour very much," I moaned, pulling my face. It was a mouldy green colour and covered in patches of dust, "How many years has it been rolled up in the garage? It's probably crawling with bugs."

"I'll send it off to be cleaned," Brian said, beating it enthusiastically with his hand, unleashing clouds of dust from ages past, "It will be as good as new. Look, it's a lovely colour underneath and very good quality. It will do perfectly well for the stairs and Ben's study."

The carpet from his second marriage was a dusky pink colour and I had to admit it would look quite nice in the lounge at 21. I don't think wife number three had had a choice of carpet and once she was safely off the scene, Brian had stripped 'Kenolbri' bare and redecorated it for the first time according to his own taste - and quite a lot of mine it has to be said. Blue was our favourite colour, so most of the fixtures and fittings at 'Kenolbri' were now in varying shades of blue.

Brian assembled a whole team of workmen to gut number 21 from top to bottom, insisting that everything had to be done to the highest standard of workmanship. To be honest, the tiny cottage didn't really warrant the amount of money he spent on it, especially in the area that it was situated, but Brian couldn't do things by halves. If a job was worth doing, it had to be done properly and because money wasn't an obstacle, only the best would do.

Brian enjoyed transforming 21 and making it into a completely new house. He looked forward to checking on the workmen's progress every day and his daily chats with them, and of course it gave him the opportunity to get his tape measure out. Heaven help the workmen if a wall wasn't straight or if they had laid one tile even slightly out of line.

Brian pressurized the workmen to finish number 21 as quickly as possible so that when Ben finally came home he would have somewhere nice to come home to.

And the miracle had finally happened. Ben was back here with me in Blackburn - be careful for what you wish for because it might come true! No, it was a huge relief off my shoulders and one thing less to worry about. The worst was over, or so I thought.

CHAPTER 29

An Eye for an Eye

With Ben safely back home I start to work again. I spend less time in my studio at 'Pittarrow' and more time working in the conservatory at 21. Brian isn't happy about this but accepts, for the time being at least, that my son has to come first.

I start work on my first sculpture. I find it comes easy to me and I like it. I like it even more than painting in fact and I'm good at it. I think I like it more because unlike a painting, a sculpture goes all the way round instead of just being flat. It joins up again from where it starts and arrives at its own natural conclusion, if that makes any sense. For the moment, the sheer physical labour suits me better than the mental torture of painting. Brian is over the moon and very excited by the quality of work I'm producing. He tells me he prefers me making sculptures because he can be physically involved in the production, in fact, I can't do them without him, because he makes the armatures for me. We go to his laboratory at 'Kenolbri' to use his tools and special cutting machines. Brian can indulge in his favourite pastime: measuring things. He spends hours making the armatures, which he measures to within a fraction of a centimetre, and he loves it. Sculpture reunites us and we are happy again, joined in a common aim - creating art, making monuments.

At the weekends my mum stays at 21 with Ben and I stay at 'Kenolbri' with Brian. Life goes on as it did before, including the obligatory lamb chops on a Saturday night. We have a routine which never varies. On Friday afternoon, I write an order for Mrs Coombs, Brian's loyal and long time housekeeper, and she does our shopping for the weekend and puts it in the fridge. On Friday nights, Bob picks us up in the car and we go out to dinner somewhere nice, but on Saturday nights Brian likes me to cook – the usual: lamb chops, new potatoes and freshly shelled peas if they are in season. We pick the mint from the garden at 'Kenolbri' and Brian sharpens the knife and chops it up to make the mint sauce. He loves doing this and takes great delight in shelling the peas. He tells me it reminds him of when he was a child and that these simple tasks make him feel like we are a proper married couple.

'Kenolbri' and 'Pittarrow' are our secret worlds, worlds in which we can both escape from all our problems. 'Pittarrow' is my place of work, whereas 'Kenolbri' is more of a home, although some have likened it to a museum because it's so crammed with beautiful artefacts. Abstract and impressionist paintings light up the walls, while the darker, more sinister surreal works, such as the original Delvaux and Dali's slightly tongue-in-cheek portrait of Brian, add a touch of mystery and a sense of the unknown. Marble and bronze sculptures by Ralph Brown R.A., Brian's friend and once associate of Henry Moore, people the rooms, their sensuous forms calling out to be touched. A huge bookcase lined with row after row of art books and catalogues of exhibitions wait in their glass case begging to be read. Persian and Chinese rugs add a touch of the Orient while statuettes and antiques mingle in with the more modern lamps and ornaments.

When we dine it is always on the long, polished wooden table, laden with candelabra and laid with shining silver cutlery and delicate bone china dinner services, even if there is only the two of us, which is usually the case. At nights, after dinner, we sit in the lounge by the fire; the fireplace Brian designed himself after being inspired by Salvador Dali's house at Cadaques where he often stayed while he was having his portrait painted by the great maestro. The fireplace is built into the wall like a huge concave egg and amongst the coals there are three bronze casts of Brian's hand reaching out from the flames. Sometimes we lay the cushions from the settee on the Persian rug in front of the fire and give each other a massage, the room in darkness apart from the flickering flames and the special ceiling lights which illuminate the paintings so they appear to be lit from within like tropical fish tanks: aquariums of brightly coloured dreams.

In the entrance hall, at the foot of the blue carpeted staircase, there is a life size bronze sculpture of a girl in an armchair with her leg resting over the arm of the chair. On our way up to bed Brian sometimes pats her bottom or puts one of his socks on her foot.

Because the time we spend alone at 'Kenolbri' is so very special to us, we fill the house with more and more things of beauty, things we have chosen together. Brian loves flowers and so do I, so when I express a desire to make a marble sculpture based on the evocative and often erotic form of orchid petals, off we go to the annual Orchid fair in Southport with one of the gardeners. We drive back in a convoy, the back seat of the Mercedes crammed with exotic blooms, the gardener's van following behind also crammed to the hilt. We place the orchids all around the house until it resembles a tropical garden, lush and vibrant with colour, then we take countless photographs from every angle and make rough drawings and designs for a sculpture. We go out through the French doors of our bedroom and lay on the roof of the sunroom, peering down through the domes of glass, gazing into the fish-eye view of a Rousseau like jungle with the sculptures peeking out from the tropical leaves, surrounded by these strange, exotic blooms.

Living in that house, for the weekends at least, among those wondrous works of art and beautiful things, Brian and I inhabit a magical world: an oasis of love, a place that is ours and ours alone, with no interference from the outside world. There we can make love or fight (as we often did) to our hearts' content. We have everything it seems, the two luxurious houses all to ourselves; the magnificent gardens where we can pick armfuls of daffodils or fragrant sweet peas, as many as we could carry. Everything was done for us, the fridge stocked with food, the logs chopped, the silver polished, the laundry washed and ironed. Mrs Coombs even ironed my white cotton nightdresses for me, the layers of frills and lace perfectly pressed, and then hung in the wardrobe like bridal gowns.

There were the magnificent gardens to stroll in, fresh vegetables always to hand, a well stocked bar and a cellar full of wine. And of course we had each other. What more could we ask? We even had the glorious sunsets over the Fylde coast in the evenings; weather permitting of course. But no matter how ordered and harmonious our secret world, there were some things that even Brian couldn't control, that seemed forever intent on spoiling our peace. The bats that flew outside the dining room window every night at a certain hour, swooping and diving, their black wings silhouetted by the light; one persistently annoying bird that made an ugly squawking sound in the mornings waking us up with its raucous, unstoppable alarm call, and of course, Brian's interfering sister, the dreaded Olga. But life can never be perfect I suppose, although that didn't stop Brian from expecting it to be. And if it wasn't, sometimes it was me who paid the price.

We drive down to the Cotswolds in the Mercedes to visit Ralph Brown (R.A.) the sculptor, and his wife Carrie, who is also an accomplished sculptor in her own right. Ralph introduces us to his foundry, where we proudly present my first clay to be made into a plaster. Brian has designed a special, ingenious box to transport it, which stops it from drying out. We spend the weekend at the Browns' magnificent country house and sleep in a big four-poster bed; then drive back up to Blackburn to wait with anticipation for the plaster to be finished. When it's ready, Brian has it delivered by special courier to 'Pittarrow' and we un-wrap it together with excitement. I then discover the joys of carving, riffling and sanding and I am as happy as the traditional sand boy himself – whoever or whatever he may have been.

But Brian is desperate for us to go to Corinthian again, and manages to convince me that I need a break. So we fly out to Italy to meet the Browns who are going to join us on Corinthian for the first week.

We have a great time with Ralph and Carrie, visiting all the marble studios, sailing along the coast of Italy, eating freshly cooked pasta and drinking lots of bottles of red wine. They leave after a week and we are alone on the boat again.

I am drawing in my sketchpad. Brian is watching me, fascinated and asks me if I'll teach him how to draw using light and shade, so I demonstrate how to draw an eye. I give him a pencil and he follows my directions, step by step, and after a while, two huge eyes stare up at us from the white page.

"There you go, an eye for an eye," I joke.

We stayed on board all day lying on the deck holding hands and watching the passing coastline, sometimes dozing off, lulled by the gentle waves. Every now and then Ollie would appear from down below and ask us if we wanted a cold drink or later if we fancied some 'afternoon tea'.

We ate dinner that night under the stars and after the crew had cleared away our plates and we were sipping our liqueurs, feeling romantic Brian ordered the captain to put Frank Sinatra on the stereo. He then disappeared down below and came back wearing his short, black silk kimono. He picks up a chair and starts dancing around to the music. He waltzes the chair around the deck, looking at me meaningfully. He smooches closer to the chair and pretends to sing in its ear. He strokes its leg.

He leads the chair back to the table and thanks it for the pleasure with a sweeping bow.

"Come down to the swimming platform with me," he orders, reaching for my hand, "I want to ask you something."

"Can't you ask me here?" I moan, not wanting to move. The sea's a bit choppy and it's dark down there. But frightened of breaking his good mood, I reluctantly gather the smoking blanket around me and shuffle along behind him down to the swimming platform. He leans on the rail in his short black kimono, chewing noisily on his Nicorette gum.

"Stand here beside me," he taps the rail in an authoritative manner. The boat is rocking around and I don't fancy tripping on the smoking blanket and ending up in the sea, so I ignore his command and kneel at his feet like a faithful squaw.

"Well, that ruins my plans," he hisses down at me.

"What plans?" I enquire. Had he been contemplating asking for my hand in matrimony? I think not. More like contemplating pushing me over the side by the look that had come over his face.

"Oh forget it," he snarls.

"Sorry, but I don't like taking orders," I announce curtly and rather foolishly under the circumstances as it would have only taken one short, sharp shove and that would have been the end of me, woman overboard. "That's just the way I am," I continue stubbornly, "And you will never change me."

"Change you?" he scoffed, chewing angrily on his gum. "Why on earth would I want to change you? I couldn't be bloody bothered," he points his nose moonward and curls his mouth into an upper class sneer.

"Fine then," I say, getting unsteadily to my feet, "That's absolutely fine by me."

I gather up the smoking blanket like a robe; toss one corner haughtily over my shoulder, then glide as regally as the moving boat will allow me back to the safety of the wheelhouse.

He stays leaning on the rail for a while, contemplating the moon, then struts past me like a sergeant major on his long, white legs, muttering something about not giving a tuppenny damn and me being an appendage, and goes down to bed.

The following evening we walk slowly along the harbour like a pair of doddery old pensioners, still cross with each other from the night before.

"Do you really consider me to be an appendage?" I ask him.

"An appendage?" he repeats. "That's hardly an expression I would use."

"Well, you called me one last night," I remind him.

"I most certainly did not," he snorts. "You must have misheard me, I would remember if I had."

"You did," I insist, "Just before you stomped off to bed."

"My head is in perfectly good working order," he snapped, "It is you who must be wrong."

He suddenly decides he's hungry, so we stop at a fish restaurant in the harbour and he goes off to the brightly illuminated aquarium with the waiter to select a lobster. I'm a bit off my food at the moment and the sight of the lobster kicking its fluorescent spindly legs as it goes off to be scalded to death, does nothing to whet my appetite. To tell the truth, I'm becoming sick of sitting at restaurants for hours on end watching Brian eat. I've watched him plough his way through three meals a day for two weeks now and it's not always a pretty sight. When he orders a steak for example, cooked 'blue' - the flesh barely scalded on the outside - he doesn't swallow the meat, but just chews it for a bit, sucks out the juice and then puts it on the side of his plate. I'm not a vegetarian by any means, but the sight of those chewed up lumps of bloodless meat and grey bits of rubbery gristle, turn my stomach. I try not to look.

I find that I'm trying not to look at a lot of things: the strange spots that have appeared on his back and legs and the flaky white thrush on the side of his nose and chin. He had informed me, almost proudly, that he is suffering from a fungal infection in his fingernails, which despite repeated prescriptions from the doctor, he simply can't get rid of. And as if all that wasn't bad enough, to add insult to injury, today while we'd been sunbathing on deck, he'd started shaving his corns.

"Do you mind," I'd objected, "The wind is blowing in my direction."

He'd paid me no heed whatsoever and carried on shaving away regardless. It was his boat after all and he could do as he pleased, as he quite often pointed out.

"The captain won't like his deck being messed up," I'd persisted.

"The captain does as he's damn well told," he'd snapped, changing feet and attacking the hard skin on the bunion of his big toe.

"Don't we all," I'd muttered miserably.

The lobster eventually arrives on a huge silver platter and Brian puts his mind to addressing the complicated business of extracting its innards, as I look on, feeling decidedly squeamish.

"I wonder how John and Lulabelle are," I ask him in an attempt to take my mind off the proceedings.

"The trick cyclists," Brian scoffs, poking inside a lobster claw with a torturous instrument that resembled a long crochet hook. He fishes out a long sliver of rubbery, orange flesh and sucks it up like a string of spaghetti.

"I haven't much faith in psychiatrists if those two are anything to go by," I tell him scathingly.

"Rubbish!" Brian jumps to the defence of his nephew, which is unusual as he's usually the first to criticise him. "John is an expert in his field, but I don't know about Lesley. She never says a word, and if she does, nobody can bloody well understand her. Psychiatry can sometimes work in your favour you know, as I found out with wife number two. Have I ever told you this story?"

"Probably," I muttered disrespectfully under my breath.

"I had to trick her into going to see a psychiatrist while we were going through the divorce," he smirked nastily, dipping his shaky, white fingers into the fingerbowl and rubbing them with the lemon.

"Is that why you call them trick cyclists?" I asked sarcastically.

"The psychiatrist was the best in London of course," he carefully wiped his hands on the linen napkin and continued, "And on his advice, I also checked myself into the clinic for the weekend, where after consulting with me at great length, he declared that there was nothing whatsoever wrong with me."

"I told my ex-wife that it would help our situation enormously if she would also agree to be interviewed, so in she went, the stupid woman, and the psychiatrist pronounced her to be a complete hysteric. Needless to say, his report greatly helped to reduce the divorce settlement," Brian smirked to himself with pride and ordered another bottle of wine.

When we get back to Corinthian later that evening I was feeling vaguely incensed on the part of wife number two, who, in all fairness, hadn't been that bad once I'd got to know her a bit better. I was reluctant to let the subject drop.

"Don't you think that was a bit unfair," I insisted, "That bloody psychiatrist pronouncing her to be a hysteric when she'd only gone in to help you?"

"*An* hysteric," Brian corrected me, "A term that can only be used in relation to a woman. A man cannot be termed an hysteric."

"I don't believe that," I argued petulantly. "The word probably derives from hysterectomies, although we feminists would say HIS terectomy and HIS terical not HERS." I tried to make a joke of it, "And what's more that all women's problems start with the word men, such as menstrual, menopause, mental etc."

Brian was not amused, either that or he didn't get it.

"Pass me the Oxford dictionary," he demanded smugly.

> *Hysteria – A syndrome formally regarded as a disease peculiar to women whose symptoms include shallow, volatile emotions, overdramatic behaviour, susceptibility to suggestion and amnesia.*

It was written there in black and white, so I couldn't argue with him or with the Oxford dictionary. Instead what did I do? I acted true to form of course and as an over emotional, volatile and at that particular moment in time 'hysterical', or at least verging on the hysterical, woman, it was me this time who stomped off down to bed in a huff.

We seem to be arguing more and more. At dinner, while we wait to be served, Brian restlessly strokes the empty plate before him with his long, shaky fingers and taps the table impatiently. He is extremely pissed off with me. I am not acting accordingly; not obeying his demands and this simply will not do. He readjusts the salt and pepper pots, refolds the creases on the napkins; rearranges the cutlery. Everything has to be perfectly straight and in its place, including me. I straighten my back and hunch it again, then just to be annoying I lift the salt pot, hover it around in the air, then put it back somewhere else, to see how long he can stand it before he puts it back in its rightful place. Childish, I know.

We visit the Picasso museum, but even that doesn't seem to mend the rift. Walking back to the marina, we pass a dingy old shop in a back street, displaying a selection of weird carnival masks in the window. Brian disappears inside and begins trying on the evil looking masks with their curved horns and long phallic noses. He stands admiring himself in the mirror, tilting his head from side to side, preening like a cockerel. I turn my back on him and stare impatiently out of the door at the glaring sunshine. He taps me on the shoulder and I turn round to face him. For a moment I am completely sun blind, then my blood runs cold and I have to clutch hold of the counter for support, as I am confronted by a red devil's face with curly gold horns and a sinister sneer.

"Are you alright señora?" the assistant asks me, concerned.

"Wrap it up," Brian tells her. "I'm going to take it home and wear it with a curly red wig and long painted fingernails."

Back on Corinthian he can't wait to unwrap the devil mask and put it on.

"I'm going to wear it to answer the door at 'Kenolbri' to frighten people away," he informs me, his voice muffled behind the mask, "Especially Olga."

"Well you're frightening me now," I shudder, "Take it off."

He laughs, a strange eerie sound, pleased with himself that it's having such an effect on me.

"Please take it off," I implore him. "It's making me feel ill."

But he refuses, so I go out on deck for a cigarette. He creeps up behind me and starts making weird grunting noises in my ear. I push past him and go back down below. He follows close on my heels and sits down right beside me. I refuse to talk to him so we sit there in silence, with him still wearing the mask. The Captain passes by on his way to check the anchor and gives us both a funny look.

Eventually, to my relief, Brian takes the mask off and props it carefully on the seat next to us, where it continues to stare at me with its evil, eyeless gaze. Brian sits there smirking to himself, breathing down his nose and chomping on his Nicorette gum, enjoying the fact that he's freaking me out.

Ollie comes up from the crew room to see if we want anything before she retires for the night. Brian passes her his camera and asks her to take our photograph. He puts the mask back on and grabbing a bunch of red tulips out of the cut glass vase, hands them to me. We stand side by side as Ollie takes our picture with me tightly clutching hold of my bridal bouquet of wilting tulips and looking terrified. The red devil and his bride!

I think I'd better go and put on my cross.

The next morning Brian shuffles up to breakfast wearing his shorts and a loose-fitting, long-sleeved shirt. He looks concerned and preoccupied.

"Good Morning," I offer by way of recompense for the night before, even though it wasn't strictly my fault.

"Good Morning," he replies gruffly then rolling up one of his shirt sleeves says, "I woke up and found these." His arm was covered with bruises the like of which I had never seen before.

"My God," I exclaimed, "What happened? Did you fall out of bed or something?"

"Not as far as I remember," he shook his head, "In fact I slept very well, but I have them on my other arm too."

I helped him slide off his shirt and to my horror he was covered in them.

"Let's ask Ollie," I suggested, concerned, "She has a First Aid Certificate and quite a bit of medical knowledge so she might know what has caused them."

Ollie didn't know, she had no idea, or if she did she didn't say. Instead she got her camera out and took some more photos, but this time for medical reference so Brian could show his doctor when we got home. There was a medical term for this condition as I found out later, Thrombocytopenia (low platelet count) consistent with people with a suppressed immune system, such as someone with undiagnosed HIV. But I didn't know that at the time.

I was just concerned about Brian. "Maybe you banged into the sliding doors yesterday without noticing," I offered as an explanation. "You know how easy it is to lose your balance when the sea's a bit rough."

It hadn't been rough actually, it had been as calm as anything, but I was trying to stop him worrying. Although he didn't seem to be worried as he posed for the camera, even though I knew he must be. He posed this way and that way, flexing his bruised muscles like a boxer.

"Bruiser Brian," I tried to make light of it too, but secretly I was worried sick. Bruising like that was simply not normal.

We return to England and after a few days, Brian's bruises fade and the traumas of the boat and our hostilities towards each other are quickly forgotten. The red devil mask resides in a cupboard in the utility room and does not reappear, at least in my presence, until many years later.

Then I am inspired to do a painting of him wearing it, slouched in a dentist's chair with his red Netlon tie undone, clutching a wilting tulip in his unmistakable long, white, veined hand.

But for now we both get back to work and to being in love and life carries on as before.

How much time we wasted with our silly feuds and arguments; If only we had known back then that our time was rapidly running out, maybe we wouldn't have tormented each other to such an extent.

CHAPTER 30

Hoo doo voo doo and fucking bones

I know you shouldn't dwell too much on the past, but sometimes it acts as an escape from the present and in my case it was hard not to as I had my 'condition' as a daily reminder. HIV is like the proverbial elephant in the room. Its ominous presence can always be felt even though it is never spoken about and like an elephant, HIV never forgets and never forgets to remind me that it is always there, just waiting for me to let down my guard. Although since the prodigal son had been back in the fold, I hadn't had much time to think about myself or my 'condition.' Everything these days tended to revolve around him, and as long as my health was holding out, which at the moment, touch wood, it seemed to be doing, there were some days when I almost forgot about my predicament. Then there were other days when I had to disguise how ill I was feeling for his sake, or when the thought of him finding out about me and discovering my shameful secret completely traumatised me. I did everything in my power to prevent this from happening by making sure I kept my medication hidden and not letting him know when I was sneaking off for my various hospital appointments. In this my mum, my main ally, always covered for me and between us we were doing a pretty good job of keeping my 'shameful' condition to ourselves.

I'd managed to complete my counselling course at Blackburn College by this time and had been accepted at the University of Central Lancashire on the Graduate Diploma in Professional Counselling Skills, starting in September which I was really looking forward to. I was still caring for my mum whose health was deteriorating daily, but like me she continued to put on a brave face, both to Ben and to the outside world. It goes without saying that she was always there for me, for us both in fact, no matter how bad she was feeling herself.

That morning, I hadn't been round for coffee as usual, as Ben and I had got up late and I was still trying to get myself together. The phone was ringing away but I was busy cooking breakfast so I shouted over my shoulder for Ben to get it.

"Can't you get it, mum?" he moaned, "I'm right in the middle of watching something on telly."

"No I can't," I rattled the frying pan bad temperedly, "Because I'm right in the middle of cooking your bloody sausages."

I heard him shuffle off lethargically in his baggy jeans to pick up the phone then all at once my back stiffened and my stomach churned with nerves when I heard the concerned tone of his voice.

"I'll send my mum right away," I could hear him saying, "Don't move."

"Is it your Granny?" I asked him in a panic, "What's happened?"

"She said she's fallen over and can't get up off the floor," Ben could hardly get the words out fast enough, "Be quick, mum."

"Tell her I'm on my way," I kicked off my slippers and stuck my feet in my boots and without stopping to zip them up, left Ben to stir the sausages and charged straight down to my mum's. I found her lying on the floor in front of the telly with the telephone still clutched in her hand. Her leg was twisted under her at an awkward angle and she was groaning in agony.

"What happened?" I frantically looked around for the remote to try to turn the telly down so I could hear her.

"I was waiting for you to come for coffee and I must have fallen asleep in the chair and when I woke up I fancied a grape, so I stood up to go to the kitchen and my leg just gave way under me and I toppled over, luckily right here by the telephone."

"We'd better get you seen to right away in case you've broken anything," I tried to get her into a more comfortable position, "I'll call an ambulance."

"You'll do no such thing," my mum looked horrified and clutched tightly on to the phone, refusing to give it to me.

"Give me that phone," I tried to wrestle it from her.

"I don't need a bloody ambulance," she insisted crossly. "They'll only keep me in hospital and then I'll never get out of there."

"Don't be daft, you have to let someone look at you, you might have broken your hip or something," I finally managed to grab the phone off her and dialled 999 asked for an ambulance and gave them our address.

While we were waiting for it to come, I called Ben and told him what was happening. He wanted to come with us but I told him to wait at home till I got back. When the ambulance finally arrived, I went with my mum to A&E where she had to wait hours on a stretcher, first for an X-ray then for a bone specialist to come and see her.

My mum is the worst patient in the world. "Get me out of here," she kept screaming at the top of her voice and pushing the poor nurses away.

"Sorry," I was forced to apologise on her behalf, "She's not normally as rude as this." She was sometimes actually, but I had to placate them somehow. Lately, she'd been even more impatient with people than usual I'd noted, especially at the hairdressers when I'd been taking her to get her hair set. In fact, we'd had to change hairdressers several times because of it and were fast running out of new salons to try.

On this occasion, however, all my mum's outraged protestations fell on deaf medical ears and, as she'd correctly predicted, they insisted on keeping her in for a few days because her blood pressure was sky high. Once they'd sorted her out a bed, which was in a mixed ward, much to her disgust, I left her to go home to give Ben a lift to work, promising I'd be back as soon as I could.

Ben came back with me at visiting time after he'd finished work, but even the fact that her beloved grandson had braved the gauntlet of a hospital visit strictly in her honour did nothing to appease her. Ben's dad, who happened to be up north visiting his lorry driver girlfriend, had arranged to take him out to the cinema that evening, so we had to leave before the end of visiting time, which didn't help the situation. I drove Ben back home and dropped him at the door, then went down to my mum's empty house in order to escape a face-to-face confrontation with his dad, as apparently, according to Ben, he couldn't stand to be in the same room as me. But no offence taken on my part, as the feeling was entirely mutual.

While I was down at my mum's house, after I'd tidied up a bit and in an attempt to pass the time until I could safely go home without bumping in to my dreaded ex, I started routing through some old photograph albums I found in the drawer and I came across a snapshot of me and Brian together with Ben. There we were the three of us smiling happily for the camera in San Moritz on Ben's eighteenth birthday.

Ben had started to take an interest in snowboarding. Anything to encourage him in a healthy pursuit at the time, I'd ferried him and car loads of his friends to ski centres hither and thither across the land. I'd frozen my pants off watching him whizzing down the slopes, with a certain amount of motherly pride coursing through my veins. Sometimes Brian would come along with us and one particular freezing cold November evening, we'd driven the boys up to Pendle Hill then left them to do their thing on the slopes while we sat by the log fire in the pub next door, enjoying a hot toddy.

"I have a proposition for both of you," Brian suddenly announces. "I've been considering it for quite some time. Why don't the three of us go to San Moritz," he suggests, beaming with enthusiasm, further fuelled by the hot toddy, "We could take him after Christmas for his 18th birthday."

"That would be absolutely wonderful," I beam back at him excitedly, squeezing his hand.

"But don't say anything to my family," he pleads, "They might be upset. I've never taken my two nephews skiing, or any of my family to San Moritz for that matter, although I have been there many times myself and I would love to take you – well, take you both."

It was decided then and shortly after Christmas, as promised, the three of us fly to Switzerland and stay at the Kulm hotel in San Moritz. Brian and I have a luxurious suite with long French windows opening on to a wide balcony with white wrought iron railings, where we can sit out and look down over the frozen lake and beyond to the picturesque snow-covered mountains. Ben has his own room, also luxurious but far away in another part of the hotel, probably at Brian's specific request. Although Brian has been good enough to arrange this trip to San Moritz ostensibly for Ben's birthday, I am under no illusions that his main motive is to get round me by getting Ben on his side. A way to a man's heart may well be through his stomach, but a way to a woman's heart, or should I say a mother's, is definitely through her son. Brian knew only too well by now that unless my son was included in the package, there would be no future for him and me. So not a man to do things by halves, before we'd left he'd bought Ben a magnificent new snowboard, plus all the paraphernalia that goes with it, as well as a smart suit so he could accompany us to dinner, as dining at the Kulm hotel was all very posh and black tie.

In the evenings, at the appointed hour, Ben would join us in the resplendent dining room wearing the requisite suit and collar and tie, but with his tee shirt hidden under his shirt, then as soon as he'd finished eating, he'd excuse himself and nip off to the gents where he'd whip off his tie and jacket, put his baggy jeans back on and go off down to the pub to join his friends, fellow snowboarders he'd met on the slopes. Every morning at the crack of dawn he couldn't wait to be off snowboarding and we wouldn't see him all day until dinner, which suited Brian right down to the ground.

In the meantime, with Ben out of the way, Brian and I enjoy a romantic time on our own, walking hand in hand in the fairytale surroundings, crunching over the sparkling white snow in our snow boots and wandering along the weaving paths in between the snow-laden fir trees. We take sleigh rides cuddled up together under the furry blankets with the sleigh bells jingling in our ears, harmonizing to snow-themed songs.

Sometimes we'd sit on the sun loungers sipping hot chocolate and watching the ice skaters twirling around, carving perfect figures of eight on the sparkling ice to lively waltzes by Strauss. Or we'd walk through the picture postcard town and gaze in wonder at the magnificent snow sculptures on exhibition in the square. It was a truly magical time and for a while, we were idyllically happy. But like all good things, predictably, it was about to come to an end. It was the night of Ben's 18th birthday and Brian had booked a celebration dinner in the restaurant. We had all dressed up to the nines for the occasion; I was wearing one of my long designer gowns from Harrods and a sequinned jacket and Ben looked very dashing and grown up in his black suit with a white shirt and a silk tie. It all seemed to be going so well at first; the two of them had somehow managed to bond over the last few days and to all intents and purposes were getting along like a house on fire. The service in the restaurant, much to Brian's approval, was excellent; the headwaiter sufficiently subservient and fawning all over us, tending to our each and every need.

"He's what I would call a real head waiter," Brian sang his praises. "I wonder if he wants to come back to 'Kenolbri' with us and be my manservant."

"Why don't you ask him?" I suggested, although I found him a bit too creepy for my liking. Playing the part, I politely excused myself to go to the ladies to powder my nose, at which point Brian scraped his chair back and performed that ridiculous bunny dipping practice, which involves half sitting and half standing when a 'lady' leaves the table. He did it again when I came back and as he didn't normally indulge in this sort of outmoded gentlemanly behaviour, I presumed it was for the creepy headwaiter's benefit rather than mine.

After we'd finished our main meal and Ben had blown out the eighteen candles on his birthday cake, we sang happy birthday, then off he went to meet his mates with a wad of birthday money tucked in his pocket compliments of Brian. I thanked Brian profusely for giving Ben such a lovely birthday and we were holding hands and looking fondly into each other's eyes, giving off the appearance to the world that we were very much in love, which we were of course. But I'd failed to take into account that we'd downed two bottles of excellent Italian wine during the course of the meal and the effects were starting to tell on Brian.

With his normal reserve in 'polite' company freed somewhat by the intake of alcohol, he took out his pen and started to make a quick sketch of me on the back of the menu with his spiky hand.

"I am one hundred percent confident," he bragged, his pen flying across the paper, "That had I wanted to, I would have been a great artist. Greater even than Picasso."

"I have no doubt," I agreed compliantly. I'd learnt from past experience, that it was always better to agree with Brian, especially when he'd had a drink.

He signed the sketch, which actually was quite a good likeness of me, with a flourish and ceremoniously handed it to me.

"I'd better hang onto this then," I told him, putting it carefully in my bag, "It might be valuable one day."

We left the table and the fawning head waiter behind and strolled arm in arm along the long carpeted corridor to the piano bar, to partake of our usual after dinner Grand Marniers. But as soon as the waiter had shown us to our seats, Brian started to complain about the pianist.

"Bloody awful racket, why doesn't he shut up. I can't hear myself think," he barked in a loud, pompous voice.

"I quite like it," I disagreed, humming along, which of course further added to his annoyance

"If I had taken up the piano," Brian declared, "I would have been the very best. I would have played like a maestro."

"Yes, I'm sure you would," I nodded obediently.

"I would also have been a wonderful singer. I was the head chorister in the choir you know?" he bragged.

"Yes, I know, you have mentioned it before - Pavarotti," I mumbled under my breath.

"Ben seemed very happy tonight," Brian remarked, thankfully not hearing me.

"And so he should. You gave him a wonderful birthday," I patted his hand fondly, "One he'll always remember, and so will I."

"I think I would have made a brilliant father don't you?" he asked me.

"Yes, Brian," I agreed, not quite convinced, as he was way too self-centred to make a good dad. Anyway by this time I was getting slightly bored with listening to him sing his own praises.

"But I wouldn't have wanted children with any of those women I had the misfortune to be married to," he shuddered with distaste.

"No Brian," I agreed distractedly listening to the music.

"Yes Brian, no Brian," he mimicked me, getting ratty.

Oh dear, I thought to myself, here we go.

I lit a cigarette.

"Pwhooo, pwhooo," he pursed his lips and started to imitate the way I smoke, so I muttered something to myself about him being drunk.

"I do beg your pardon?" he uttered, putting on his posh voice.

"Do you have to speak with that ridiculous accent?" I asked him crossly, "You sound like a laird."

"A LARD?" he repeated in horror, "It is pronounced Laird, L-A-Y-E-R-D," he spelt it out. "Lard is something you cook sausages in."

"Chop my tongue out," I laughed disrespectfully, "I'm so sorry my LAYERED."

We sat in stony silence for a few minutes and Brian tapped his long, white fingers impatiently on the table.

"I have so many degrees," he declared loudly, "And I have won so many awards, there is really nowhere else for me to go now, apart from to win the Nobel Prize of course, which I surely will with my next invention."

"What will your next invention do exactly?" I asked with genuine interest.

I had a vague idea, but he was always very cagey when the subject was broached, especially in front of other people.

"It will stop global warming," he declared confidently, "And therefore solve the world's energy crisis."

"That would be wonderful," I enthused, "But how will it actually do that?" I asked curiously.

"By taking salt out of the water," he looked at me like I was an idiot. "By preventing drought and providing water for the poor people of the world, especially in Africa. Men, women and children will no longer die of thirst and will be able to maintain themselves by growing their own vegetables and running small businesses to avoid poverty."

I was genuinely impressed. I wasn't used to Brian being concerned about poor people in any shape or form, let alone poverty issues concerning the third world. He seemed to have a genuine dislike of the 'under classes' as he called them and wouldn't even let me drive him through what he described as the working class areas of Blackburn, saying they depressed him too much. Maybe I'd had him all wrong I was quickly forced to reconsider, but then again, he'd also refused to watch the film, "The Full Monty" for the very same reasons, declaring it was far too working class for the likes of him, so maybe not. In any event, to find him suddenly concerned about the poor people of the world was a complete shock to me.

"It must be wonderful to have the powers to be able do that," I told him admiringly. "Powers?" he mimicked me sarcastically, "You mean power don't you? What have 'powers' got to do with anything? Powers," he sneered, "Bloody hoodoo, voodoo and fucking bones."

"You remind me of a man," I chuckled to myself, recalling a verse my dad used to recite to us as children that could go on forever and ever. I repeated it to Brian.

You remind me of a man

What man?

The man with the power

What power?

The power of hoodoo

Hoodoo?

You do

Do what?

Remind me of a man.

"God, it's impossible to have an intelligent conversation with you," Brian bellowed at the top of his voice. "Anyway, never mind, you won't have to talk to me for much longer. You'll soon be back in England," he added menacingly, "With your Prince of Hearts."

"My Prince of Hearts?" I repeated, totally baffled.

"Yes, your Prince of fucking hearts. The Grand old Prince of Benidorm," he added to further confuse me.

Who did he mean exactly, I wondered, by my Prince of Hearts? I didn't have one as far as I knew, apart from him that is. Surely he didn't mean my ex-husband did he? Brian was still jealous of him and was always asking me if I would ever go back with him. Fat chance of that! So if it wasn't him, who did he mean? Was he referring to Ben perhaps? But Ben was here with us.

"I have absolutely no idea who you are talking about," I told him truthfully.

"Yes you do, you know full well," he snapped. "Your precious Erik of course, the Prince of Benidorm with his crystal bloody ball and his hoodoo, voodoo, and fucking bones."

I burst out laughing, it was so ridiculous it was impossible not to.

"I really don't see why you're so jealous of Erik," I tried to be serious. "You know that he's gay."

"That didn't stop you from telling me once that you adored the man and that he was the most intelligent person you had ever met."

"It's true, I do adore him," I admitted, "And he is intelligent. He's a font of knowledge. He knows everything. If I ever need to know anything, I only have to ask Erik."

Well that was it, Brian blew his top! The pianist had unfortunately chosen that precise moment to close his piano lid and go off for his break, so Brian's furious accusations resounded throughout the bar. I could see the waiters out of the corner of my eye, looking on with interest, but I tried to remain aloof and not let myself be dragged into his pathetic dispute. Finally, frustrated by my lack of response, he stood up, signalled for the waiter, snarled at the pianist who was taking his seat back at the piano, signed the bill and stormed out.

I reluctantly followed after him and we walked in silence along the seemingly endless miles of plushly carpeted corridor to our suite, where after opening the door, he pushed past me and stomped directly to the bedroom. He immediately started to get undressed, struggling with his pale blue pyjamas and fumbling with the buttons, still mumbling to himself about hoodoo, voodoo and fucking bones.

The following morning, after a sleepless night on my part, I was on my dignity and told him that I was going to have my breakfast downstairs with Ben to spare him from having to endure yet another 'unintelligent' conversation with me.

"Stupid woman," he shouted after me, tucking into his runny boiled eggs, a trail of yellow egg yoke slowly making its way down his dimpled chin.

"Pompous ignorant shit," I shouted back at him as I slammed the door.

When I came back to get my coat and snow boots, he asked me sullenly what I intended to do for the rest of the day.

"I'm going out, away from you," I told him angrily. "I'm going to try cross- country skiing if you must know."

"Well you'll need some money," he tried to thrust a wad of notes in my hand.

"Keep it," I shoved it aside, "I don't want your filthy money."

"You really are a very stupid woman. What are you going to do all day without any money?" he yelled at me.

I grabbed my coat and snow boots, going back for my woolly hat, then slammed the door on him and went off to enrol on my first class of cross-country skiing.

It was a totally joyous experience as it turned out and far less terrifying than being up on the high slopes. I enjoyed myself immensely, skiing along the gentle inclines, gliding through the chocolate box scenery through the sparkling snow covered pine trees, humming waltzes out loud to myself

Every now and then I would pass the odd fellow cross-country skier on the opposite track; the serious athletic types with tight pants and headgear or the more refined looking women adorned in long, expensive looking, not to mention controversial fur coats, and we'd nod to each other in a polite and gentile fashion as we glided by on our merry way.

When my lesson was over and I'd used up my allotted time on the tracks, I reluctantly handed back my skis to find Brian waiting for me at the reception desk. He was obviously still in a bad mood and refusing to speak to me.

"That was great," I smiled at him brightly, feeling uplifted and energised by all the exercise and fresh air. "Let's stop it now shall we and make friends?"

No response.

"Come on," I tried to take his hand, "Why don't we kiss and make up?"

He pushed past me and stomped off ahead, his shoulders hunched sulkily, trying to keep his footing on the slithery surface.

"Stubborn old bugger," I muttered to myself, following his hunched back.

We passed by the picturesque Alpine houses, their slanting roofs covered with an icing of thick white snow and strung with necklaces of crystal icicles shimmering in the sun.

"Look Brian," I shouted breathlessly, "Have you got your camera with you? Look at those icicles, aren't they beautiful?"

But he continued to ignore me.

"Oh, fall over why don't you," I cursed evilly in my head as we surmounted the steep, icy paths that led back to the hotel. "Slip up you pompous bastard."

And guess what. He did! So I've obviously got powers too.

Hoodoo, voodoo and fucking bones!

But thankfully, he didn't actually break any!

After that, I couldn't do right for doing wrong. He'd caught a cold, my fault of course, and insisted on keeping the radiators turned up full blast in the room and when I opened the French windows to go out on to the balcony to get some fresh air he accused me of trying to freeze him to death. He went for a nap so I shut the adjoining door between the bedroom and the sitting room so that I wouldn't disturb him and when he woke up he went mad saying that I had deprived him of oxygen and given him a headache. Before we went to bed I sat on the balcony to have a last cigarette with my coat over my nightie and he accused me of ignoring him and shutting him out. I opened the curtains to admire the view of the full moon over the lake and he moaned at me saying he couldn't sleep for the light. In the morning I turned the radio on to try to lighten the atmosphere and he turned it off, saying it was a bloody awful racket. And things only went from bad to worse.

On our last night in San Moritz we were having coffee after dinner in the bar and Brian suddenly started talking (for some reason best known to him self) about bondage.

"I believe," he leered at me, "That tying the wrists and ankles lightly with silk scarves can be very sensuous."

"I would hate that," I shuddered. "I don't like the feeling of being trapped."

"Some women, or so I've heard," he went on to inform me, "Like to be beaten, and enjoy having their bottoms smacked with a hairbrush."

"Well, don't get any ideas," I told him promptly. "I'm not into physical punishment."

But perhaps he is? Maybe that's what he wants me to do, take his pale blue pyjama bottoms down and give him six of the best, and the way I'm feeling tonight, it would be a pleasure.

Bend over Mercer!

In the car on the way back to the airport, Ben, who had also caught a bad chill on the slopes, was coughing heavily, much to Brian's annoyance. I think he was fed up with both of us actually and was making it very clear that I was still in his bad books. On the plane he deliberately chose a seat across the aisle from me and didn't say a word for the duration of the flight. When we arrived back in England,

Bob was waiting for us at the airport with the car and Ben and I were dropped off at number 21 without so much as a goodbye.

A few days later some photographs were shoved through the letterbox at number 21 with a terse note telling me I could keep the negatives, which I supposed held some deep inner message, such as the 'Lard' of the Manor has dismissed the maid and she is back in Mill Hill on the Floss, where she belongs.

But of course I hadn't been dismissed for long. The faxes started arriving by the ream and as quickly as they came, I faxed him directly back.

25- 1- 98

Dear Adrienne,

I hope to write to you in a few days on the subject of the rubber mould for the new plaster.

Neither the doctor nor his antibiotics can cure my cold. I have now had the cold for almost three weeks.

I sincerely hope that you and Ben are keeping well. With kind regards,

Brian.

25 -1- 98

Dear Brian,

I have made two new clay models.

Should I leave them on the table at Pittarrow for you to look at?

You can tell me whether I'm barking up the wrong tree or just barking mad!

Adrienne

25-1-98

Dear Adrienne,

If you can leave the two models on the table in my office at Pittarrow I can study them on Saturday morning and then send you a fax containing my comments. I shall leave your mother's glass trifle dish on the Pittarrow table,

Brian

In between faxes I quickly whizzed the two clay models down to Pittarrow and dutifully collected my mum's trifle dish.

25 -1 -98

Dear Brian,

The two models are already there. I have left a spray because they are drying out.

Adrienne

25-1 -98

Dear Adrienne,

I have looked at the two models at great length but would prefer to discuss them face to face rather than in a fax.

Perhaps we could meet at Pittarrow tomorrow?

Brian

25 –1 -98

Dear Brian,

Thank you for taking time to look at the models. I would love to come to Pittarrow tomorrow as you suggested but I don't know how you will react to me face to face. I felt from the cool remarks in your fax that you weren't too impressed with them.

Adrienne

25-1 -98

Dear Adrienne,

I was very pleased that you asked me to take a critical look at the two models. Difficult as it may be, we have to separate the two issues of our relationship and your work and the only way to make any progress is for us to meet at Pittarrow. If we don't, we have an impasse, a place from which there is no outlet. Please send a fax as soon as possible within next half hour if you can because I'm going out to dinner,

Regards

Brian

25- 1- 98

Dear Brian,

Perhaps we should just keep it to a working relationship. Please arrange a time at your convenience. Hope you enjoy your dinner,

Regards,

Adrienne

25 - 1 – 98

Dear Adrienne,

Your plaster of the clay we delivered to Pangolins arrived at Pittarrow two minutes ago. The plaster was in the box I had made. I think that it is sealed somehow. No, I was not trying to look. If you can come down I would love to see it – in fact I can hardly wait. Well, I can't wait. Please phone me,

Regards – breathless regards,

Brian

I'd gone straight down to Pittarrow of course and Brian never made it to his dinner.

Hoo doo voo doo and fucking bones. I slid the photo of that never to be forgotten trip to San Moritz back in the album and shut the drawer. Then I put my mind back to the situation in hand and my mum's poor old bones which, I hoped with all my voo doo powers, were not broken.

CHAPTER 31

The Twilight Zone

My mum never really recovered after she'd hurt her leg that time. She was in and out of hospital and I became accustomed to the ambulance pulling up outside the house with a wail of sirens, often in the middle of the night, and following behind in my car to A&E. Then waiting and hoping she would survive, hoping and waiting – so much waiting around. Sometimes she was only in for a few days; sometimes it was a few weeks. I got to know all the nurses on intensive care and on the various wards on first name terms. I must have walked miles of corridors, day and night, with my shoulders drooping and a heavy heart - and always alone.

When they did let my mum out it was almost worse in a way because I daren't let her out of my sight for very long in case anything happened. She had become so ill by this time that she really needed to be cared for full time professionally, in a nursing home, but that option, at least as far as I was concerned, didn't bear thinking about. She kept trying to convince me that she wanted to go – she would have lots of company in there she told me and she could play bridge. Who was she trying to kid? She was never the most sociable person in the world, especially these days and couldn't even hold a card in her hand without shaking, let alone see one.

At first it wasn't too bad, I could just about manage, but gradually between caring for her and trying to keep my errant son on the rails, it got to the point where they were taking over my life and my own health was starting to suffer. I wanted to bring her to my house to live, but she couldn't manage the stairs (we'd had a stair lift put in at her house.) So I went first thing in the morning to make her a cup of tea and a piece of toast which I took upstairs to her and then I helped her get up. I went backwards and forwards during the day, taking Ben to work and then picking him up, not to mention cooking for him, then putting my mum to bed at night. It was hard work and I was getting worn out. I'd had to give up my teaching job but somehow I still managed to keep on with my counselling studies and began my university course. Trying to study at a much deeper level was hard going at first, and I found all that digging and delving into my own problems, which was part of the personal development side of the course and one of the most important aspects for any prospective counsellor, extremely traumatic at times. I had to face up to my own demons, one of which was the impending and inevitable loss of my mum and the other unthinkable quandary of disclosing to my son that I was HIV positive. I hadn't yet told my fellow students on the course about my status, I wanted first to see how they would react to me as a 'normal' person without my HIV baggage. Anyway, I had enough to deal with coping with my mum and my son, both of whom in their own ways were living in their own separate worlds.

It finally got to the point where I was so exhausted, I too became sick. I was so ill in fact that I was on the verge of pneumonia and as we all know, that's what sees people in my condition off, it's not actually the condition itself. That just lays dormant, waiting for its chance to pounce. My sister came over from Holland to look after us, staying at my mum's house to see to her so that I could have a rest, but in the middle of the night my mum had a seizure and was rushed into hospital. After that, even though they allowed her to come home again, her health rapidly declined and then we had to accept the inevitable; she had to go into a nursing home.

She was more than ready to go she told me and even joked that she wished Harold Shipman would call round and put her out of her misery. I didn't find that at all funny, in fact I was hurt to think she could even consider leaving me, but I was being totally selfish and I knew the real truth was she didn't want to continue being a burden to me. She was really suffering now and her life had become a total misery. She was virtually blind and couldn't even see the television anymore, or me.

I went to M&S and bought her some new pyjamas and a pink fluffy bed jacket. Then with a heavy heart I packed her case. She sat in her wheelchair with her new cosy slippers on her tiny feet, her bright blue eyes still shining in my direction even though she could hardly see me, pretending she was excited about going as we waited for the ambulance to come and take her to the nursing home, but in reality not knowing if she would ever make it back again through her own front door. It was heartbreaking for me, for both of us, but those words were left unsaid. There was no other choice, we both knew that and I knew her heart was breaking too, but she would never let it show. She loved me too much.

We then entered the twilight zone of the 'old folks home'; the smells, the shouts, the confusion, the sometimes cruelty. The sister on my mum's ward, a West Indian woman with a huge chip on her shoulder, turned out to be a bully of the worst degree and from day one she made my poor mum's life a misery. I nicknamed her nurse Ratchet from 'One flew over the cuckoo's nest', and she seemed intent on making things hard for my mum, although I don't know why. Maybe she was just like that with all the old people, but it was hard to comprehend why someone would want to be so cruel to someone as vulnerable as my mum, who because she couldn't see anymore was confused and disorientated by her new and often hostile surroundings. I spent as much time as I could with her and often tended to the other old people in the next rooms who were often left unattended lying on the floor in pools of urine or calling out in a panic because they didn't know where they were. Even though I repeatedly asked the staff to help my mum at mealtimes because she couldn't see, I would find her sitting hunched over her tray with food all over the place, on the floor, on her bed, on her new pyjamas. Because I couldn't trust them to look after her I spent more and more time there, staying with her till she went to sleep and then going back early in the morning. My mum begged me to get her out of there, saying she would rather die in a ditch and it would break my heart when the time came to leave her to their tender mercies and walk out of the door. It was a nightmare, a total nightmare and it was tearing me in two. All I wanted was to put her in the car and bring her home with me but felt I couldn't go against medical advice, but now how I wish I had done. Instead, I set about finding another nursing home and after visiting several equally depressing places I'd finally found one, a really nice one that didn't smell of urine and where the nurses and the staff seemed really kind. But when I went back to tell my mum, I found her in a terrible state. She was hardly able to breathe and was obviously seriously ill and in need of attention, but nurse Ratchet refused to call the doctor, insisting that my mum was just being difficult because she was finding it hard to settle in. After a head to head battle with her, she finally agreed to let me call our family doctor myself from her office and when he arrived, he was horrified and had called an ambulance and had my mum rushed straight to hospital to intensive care.

I stayed with her all that night and in the morning, her condition had stabilised somewhat, but the specialist told me she was still seriously ill and not to get my hopes up. I had the feeling as I walked dejectedly to my car to go home to get some rest that she would probably never come out of there.

When I got home, I just sat in my car and cried. I couldn't face going inside and telling Ben. I've coped with many things in my life but this had to be one of the most heartbreaking, watching my mum's slow and painful decline. She is amazing though, somehow she keeps on reviving. I used to say like George Best but he's not with us anymore - although neither is my mum in some ways, even though she is and I'm missing her already.

This scenario of waiting for the inevitable was all too familiar to me and brought all those painful memories of Brian flooding back and that dreadful, dreadful time, with me having to be the strong one, the dependable one. But I wasn't strong anymore and I felt then, as I did now, so very alone.

CHAPTER 32

THE SUMMER OF 1998

Brian found a lump under his ribcage. His doctor told him it was probably a hernia caused by over exercising on the new gym equipment he'd recently installed at 'Kenolbri' and nothing much to worry about, so we went on our annual summer cruise to Italy on Corinthian as planned and John and Lesley came out to join us for the first two weeks.

For some reason, and I could never really get him to explain why, Brian had decided to fire the captain and all the crew of Corinthian and replace them with an entirely new crew. I was most upset about this, because I really liked Graham and Ollie and all the old crew and felt that Corinthian wouldn't be the same without them, which of course it wasn't. I took an instant dislike to the new captain, who as far as I could see was a jumped up, pompous, arrogant twit and from day one there was a strange and uncomfortable atmosphere on the boat, in fact for the duration of that whole trip. Brian didn't take to the new captain either, but was too stubborn to admit it; anyway it was too late to do anything about it now. As the new captain's wife, who would have taken on the role of cook, was unable to join us because her mother was seriously ill with cancer, Brian had to employ a chef from an agency and hire another cabin girl, a silly young thing, who was only interested in making eyes at the captain and the rest of the male crew.

As I'd feared, it just wasn't the same without Ollie's cheerful smile, eccentric sense of humour and wonderful cooking. Neither did I feel we were in such safe hands as we'd been with Graham at the helm, with his expert handling of 'Corinthian.' Brian was eventually forced to admit that he might have been a bit hasty in his decision to replace them and began to wish that he hadn't.

We commenced that fateful voyage by sailing along the coast of Italy, stopping off at Capri so we could visit the famous 'Blue Grotto', a place I'd always wanted to see since I'd seen it in an old romantic movie. The captain anchored Corinthian alongside the cave's entrance, but there was a queue of long wooden boats crammed full of tourists waiting to go in, so we decided we would sail around the island and come back when it had quietened down a bit.

When we arrived back later that afternoon, all the tourist boats had gone and it was deserted, apart from a group of noisy Italian children swimming in and out of the cave's entrance and a solitary old man in a rowing boat, who said he would take us in for a guided tour at a much inflated price. Brian agreed, after some haggling over the fare and we climbed nervously down into the dilapidated wooden rowing boat wearing our orange lifejackets. John and Lesley, who were both good swimmers, swam along behind us. The old boatman, whose weathered back was wrinkled and cracked like a piece of tanned leather, proudly rowed us through the narrow entrance into the cave, babbling away over his shoulder to us in rapid Italian. At first glance I was bitterly disappointed, as it appeared to be nothing more than a dark, black hole, but once our eyes had become accustomed to the gloom, we could make out a patch of luminous blue water, which seemed to be lit from within by some mystical source.

"Where are all the stalagmites and stalactites?" I turned round and asked Brian who was sitting behind me, the echo of my voice sounding thin and reedy, "It's nothing like in the film, is it?"

The old boatman rowed us slowly away from the eerie blue light and we were suddenly enveloped by the oppressive blackness. It was spookily silent apart from the irregular drops of condensation that dripped from the dank curved walls and the rounded ceiling, plip-plopping into the black water and falling on our heads like the first drops of a rainstorm.

The old boatman rested his oars on the side of the boat allowing us to drift slowly along the black tunnel-like chasm and it felt as though we were taking part in a scene out of Phantom of the Opera and I was overcome by a sense of ghostly unease. Towards the entrance of the cave, the mystical blue orb of light glanced across the surface of the water like a laser beam, but where we were, seemingly floating adrift in the echoing chambers of the cave's cavernous heart, it was as black as the darkest of nights with not even the slightest chink of light - as dark as a coffin, as dark as death. I shuddered and turned my head to look at Brian, but he was an indistinguishable shape, a dark form that I could sense rather than see. The old boatman who had been quiet now for quite some time, suddenly stood up, causing the boat to rock dangerously and stretching his arms heavenwards began to serenade us in broken English, his voice echoing around the cave and bouncing back at us.

I could hear the shrill laughter of the children merging with his impassioned rendition as they splashed around near the cave's entrance and I could see their dark shapes perched on the ledges, diving in and out of the water like shiny seals. Within the luminous blue laser beam of light I could just about make out the bobbing heads of John and Lesley, swimming around in a circle; then stopping to form a silhouette kiss.

"I think I'd like to go back now," I turned round and whispered to Brian, suddenly feeling claustrophobic and suffering from a premonition of doom. But before Brian had chance to say anything, the old boatman had taken up his oars and begun to row us round again, obviously determined to make the most of his last passengers and probably anticipating a huge tip after seeing the size of Corinthian.

"We'd like to go back now," Brian ordered sternly, tapping him on his weathered shoulder, but the old boatman steadfastly ignored him and decided instead to finish his song.

As he was reaching his passionate and unstoppable climax, another unsettling and disturbing sound began to emerge; a strange, high-pitched whistling noise, causing me to grit my teeth and put my hands over my ears. Then seemingly from out of nowhere, a sudden gust of wind started to howl through the narrow entrance of the cave, whipping the still water into a frenzy of pounding waves. The boat started to rock perilously as the waves slapped angrily against our hands, which were clutching tightly onto the sides to stop ourselves from falling out.

"What's happening?" I shouted over my shoulder to Brian, fear gripping me. But he didn't answer, or if he did, I couldn't hear him for the howling and whistling of the wind. I could sense his dark shape however sitting behind me like a stone statue, rigid with fright.

The water level inside the cave began to rapidly rise at an alarming rate, closing the exit of the cave's mouth and cutting off any semblance of natural light, leaving only the faint ghostly tinge of the circular blue patch of water.

"What the hell's going on?" I screamed to Brian, in a complete panic. It was almost impossible to see now, but I could hear the sound of the children screaming, their terrified cries mingling with the screeching and whistling echoes of the wind. I peered through the darkness desperately looking for John and Lesley, hoping that they had managed to get out before the exit to the cave had been closed off, but it was impossible to see. Then my eyes focused on the bedraggled head of Lesley, who had managed to swim over to us and was now clutching onto the side of the boat, sobbing hysterically. John's head suddenly popped up out of the churning waters next to hers and he tried to calm her down, but with no success. He shouted at her and told her to pull herself together, at which point she became even more hysterical, so he slapped her twice round the face and she suddenly went quiet. I could just about make out the outline of her ghostly face, tinged an eerie shade of blue by the reflection of the water, and her white, bony knuckles clutching tightly onto the side of the rocking boat.

The waves began to crash even more forcefully against the curved innards of the dank cave and the ledges were now completely covered by water. The old boatman was mumbling away to himself in Italian, the folds of his bent back glistening darkly in the half-light as he rowed us towards the cave's entrance, with John and Lesley clutching onto the keel end of the rickety wooden boat being towed along like flotsam. But it was impossible to get out. By this time it was like a force ten gale in there, as though the wind was also trapped and howling around in frenetic circles, trying to find its way back out.

One by one, seizing the moment, the seal-like children managed to dive under the churning waves and make their escape, leaving us trapped there in the black inferno, the old wooden boat bobbing up and down like a cork tossed on an angry sea. Lesley was sobbing uncontrollably now, clutching on to the rocking boat for all her worth. With frantic words of encouragement John finally managed to prise away her clutching hands and take them in his, then together they dived under a wave and disappeared, sucked out by the force of the water to the other side and into the daylight. That just left Brian and I and the old boatman, trapped inside the cave.

My mouth was completely dry with fear by this time, so dry that I couldn't even scream. I turned my head and looked back at Brian for support, but he just sat there silently, his back rigid and his chest puffed out like a penguin illuminated by the dull orange glow his lifejacket. The old boatman motioned to us wildly in sign language that we would have to lie flat on our backs on the floor of the boat and pointed to the roof of the cave's entrance, making throat cutting gestures. We waited nervously for a gap to appear in the waves, but if anything they seemed to be getting higher by the minute and more frequent. Then all at once the old boatman must have decided the time had come. But there was no singing from him this time, instead he uttered a quick prayer, made the sign of the cross, and flinging back his arm, pushed Brian and I, toppling like dominoes, flat on our backs. Then grabbing hold of the slimy seaweed-encrusted chain nailed to the wall, seized his moment and hoisted us out with his gnarled old hands. We popped out of the other side with the force of a champagne cork to the ensuing cheers from the children crouched on the rocks and the relieved faces of John and Lesley, who were by now safely back on Corinthian. They were leaning over the railings and looking out for us with the Captain and rest of the crew. Never have I been so glad to see anything as I was to see Corinthian that day and even the sullen face of the captain was almost a pleasure to behold. Brian and I were helped back on board, shaking like leaves, and it was only after several large whiskies that I could I breathe again.

This terrifying event, which apparently was not uncommon, had been caused by the swell of a large cruise ship passing by. The locals, of course, were well aware of the danger of passing vessels and for that reason tourist boats never entered the cave at certain times of day. If the new captain had only known his stuff, he would never have allowed us to go into the cave at that particular time, but he obviously didn't know his stuff. This became more and more apparent as the cruise went on. It was as if the entire voyage was cursed from the word go. Everything seemed to go wrong, even the weather. Strong winds would blow up out of nowhere; rumbling black clouds would form threateningly overhead in the sulphurous sky and flashes of fork lightning would splice them in two, lighting up the horizon with a strange yellow light. We would be forced to anchor off in locations which were not on the itinerary; dark, eerie bays, surrounded by forbidding black rocks, with Corinthian swinging round and round on her anchor chain in dizzying and disorientating circles. Even the south coast of Italy, well known for its staggering rugged beauty, seemed threatening somehow: the people swarthy and unfriendly. And as for the crew, they were resentful and unhelpful towards us – mutinous even.

We left Naples after only one night and, heading out to sea, came upon a group of islands called the Tontines. We anchored off in the bay and the captain reluctantly ferried us ashore in the tender. The island was riddled with tunnels and in order to reach the main town we had to risk life and limb, flattening ourselves against the tunnel walls as motorbikes and cars roared past, missing us by fractions of an inch and nearly taking us with them. We soon hurried back to the safety of

Corinthian, but the atmosphere on board seemed just as threatening, with the captain in a sullen mood and none of the other crew members around, or at least available.

I awoke very early the next morning while it was still dark, to feel the boat already in motion, the engines forging ahead at a rate of knots. I threw on Brian's towelling dressing gown, which was behind the bathroom door and rushed upstairs to find the captain at the wheel and the boat way out to sea.

"Where are we going?" I asked him, still half asleep, "We weren't supposed to be leaving until after breakfast?"

"We're heading back to Naples," he informed me brusquely.

"But Dr Mercer wanted to sail around the islands," I told him. "The itinerary was decided yesterday, I heard him discussing it with you."

But he didn't even answer me. He just carried on looking out to sea with his expressionless, dead eyes.

"Dr Mercer won't be at all happy about this," I told him angrily and went back down below to the master cabin to tell Brian.

By the time Brian got himself dressed and came up on deck to confront the new captain, we were already approaching the harbour at Naples. I thought Brian would go berserk, but he didn't say a word. Something else seemed to be troubling him and I think he may have been worrying about his health. There were times when he had no energy whatsoever, when he found it hard to even walk. But then there were other times when he seemed perfectly fit and could easily outpace me walking round ancient monuments. So I wasn't too concerned.

Brian and I, desperate to get off the boat for a while, took the train into Rome where we visited all the famous tourist sights: the Coliseum, the Pantheon, The Spanish Steps and of course St Peter's Square and the Vatican. Although all this sightseeing was exhausting, it was also extremely exhilarating. The thrill of seeing all these famous landmarks and buildings of extraordinary architectural beauty, spurred us ever onwards and we walked the ancient city until our feet would walk no more. We strolled around numerous dimly lit churches and joined on to conducted tours. We gazed in awe at the marble sculptures and threw coins in the Trevi fountain – two each, which, according to the legend, means a forthcoming marriage. Then we boarded the train back to the marina, exhausted but happy. The day after, John and Lesley flew back to England, leaving us alone with the mutinous crew.

On the last day of the cruise, Brian and I decided we would like to have to a last sail on Corinthian, so we asked the captain to take us on a short trip round the headland into the next bay. The sea was very rough at the entrance to the marina and it took us quite a while to get out, but once we did, we sailed around the headland and anchored off in the next bay. It turned out to be an ugly location; an eyesore in fact, surrounded by huge oil tanks and industrial warehouses, so Brian told the captain that we wanted to go back. But that was easier said than done as the captain, somehow or other, had managed to get the anchor stuck perilously close to an oil pipe on the seabed. He'd obviously not bothered to check the sea charts on the satnav. As the crew frantically tried to dislodge the reluctant anchor, Corinthian rocked to and fro on the swell, her huge mast swinging back and forth nearly touching the water as her belly crashed from side to side against the waves. Brian and I sat gripping tightly onto the white leather seats, being swung high into the air and then flung down again, as if we were on some terrifying ride on the fair, our stomachs heaving and churning. Down below we could hear the sound of all the new china we'd bought at Thomas Goode's and Harrods, crashing to the floor as the locker doors flew open, and smell the sickly mix of my broken perfume bottles and Brian's aftershaves as they shattered into pieces of jagged glass in the bathroom sinks. It was a fitting end to a cruise that was filled with nothing but bad omens. But that was nothing in comparison to what happened next.

The worst was definitely yet to come.

CHAPTER 33

Swan Song

The day after we'd got back to Blackburn after that doomed voyage, Brian went to see his doctor about the lump under his ribcage, which seemed to have got bigger while we were away. He was sent directly to a clinic in Manchester the next day for tests.

I didn't go with him. He didn't want me to, but I had a horrible black feeling all day and I think I knew. He didn't really have to tell me, I already knew what he was going to say when I picked up the phone. The moment I'd dreaded since the day I'd first fallen in love with him, all those years ago, had finally arrived. The day I would find out I was going to lose him forever. I knew it would happen one day of course, by the very fact that he was so much older than me, but that didn't make it any easier when it did. And anyway that might not necessarily have been the case. I could have been the first to go, which in some ways, in view of the way events transpired, may have been a much easier option; at least for me. But it is not for any of us to decide these things. It is, as ever, in the hands of the Gods.

It was September the twenty-third, 1998, my forty-ninth birthday. While I'd waited for Brian to phone me at number 21, I'd busied myself with household chores, which wasn't like me at all. I usually spent my time painting or sculpting and only resorted to domestic matters when it was absolutely necessary. But I needed to lose myself in some kind of mindless physical labour, so I'd cleaned everything in the house. It was as though I was trying to scrub the terrible truth away; bleach it out, get rid of it down the waste disposal. The waste – time wasted. We'd wasted so much time Brian and I, but we'd been trying to make up for it and I'm sure we would have done, if only fate or the fickle hands of the Gods had not decided to intervene.

The phone call had finally come later that afternoon. He'd called me from the clinic as soon as he'd got the results. It turned out that the lump was not a hernia at all, it was his enlarged liver and tragically, the specialist had informed him, it was too late to do anything about it.

I was furious. Why hadn't his stupid doctors spotted it before now? So much for private bloody medicine I raged. I tried so hard not to cry while he was telling me. I was determined I wouldn't break down for his sake. I was going to be the strong one, the optimistic one. Where there's life there's hope I told him. Don't give up.

But when I saw him later at 'Kenolbri' we both broke down and clung onto each other in despair. What on earth were we going to do? What on earth was I going to do? But most importantly of all, what was he going to do, how was he going to be able to cope with the fact that he was going to die.

And so soon.

The next day, we threw a few bags in the back of the Mercedes, put the roof down and sped up to the Lakes. It seemed like the right thing to do, to get away from everyone and everything. He only wanted to be with me he told me, to take in the terrible news, to absorb it together. We'd spoken once of what it would be like to only have a short time left to live – where we would go, what would we do etc. Well, now we knew what it felt like, or at least he did and in a way so did I, because for me, living without him would be a certain death in itself.

I drove the Mercedes up the motorway, my hair blowing in the warm September breeze like a film star and in a way, it felt as if we were both actors in a movie, playing a part. This wasn't really happening; it couldn't be, not to Brian. He always seemed indestructible, God-like even, not an ordinary mortal at all.

He sat silently beside me, huddled in his seat as we sped along. I tried to be bright and cheerful, as if we were just going off on one of our adventures together to try to take his mind off it, although I knew it was an impossible task. But somehow he managed to play along in this most tragic game of pretence and even mustered a smile now and then.

We checked into a beautiful old hotel overlooking Lake Windermere. The porter carried our bags into the elevator and I took Brian's arm, as he seemed to be having trouble walking. Standing shoulder to shoulder inside the small confined space, we stared at our grey, shocked faces reflected back at us by the mirrored walls as the ancient lift juddered its way up to the second floor. I felt Brian's shoulder suddenly start to shake and knock against mine and at first I thought it was caused by the jerky movements of the rickety old lift, but it wasn't that at all, it was him. He was shaking from head to toe and his teeth were chattering loud enough to hear. The porter looked at him with concern.

"Is the gentleman all right, madam?" he asked me.

I noticed that he didn't say 'your husband.' We must not have looked like a married couple that day, if in fact we ever did. I don't know what we did look like, to tell the truth; traumatised probably, and a bit mad, as we were both still in total shock.

As soon as we got into our room, Brian collapsed on the double bed without even taking his shoes off, which wasn't like him at all. The porter was fussing with our bags but I ignored him and covered Brian up as best I could with the old-fashioned eiderdown, folding it over him so that the top of his head poked out like the tip of a sausage in a sausage roll. He pulled the eiderdown under his chin and tried to smile at me. His face was dark red, the colour of old port wine.

"Shall I call the hotel doctor madam?" the porter asked, concerned.

"No, there's really no need," Brian tried to sit up, "I'll just take a short nap and I'll be as right as rain."

"Brian," I begged him, after the porter had pocketed his tip and backed out, quietly closing the door behind him, "Please let me call a doctor."

"I don't need a bloody doctor," Brian swore. "I've had quite enough of hospitals and doctors thank you very much. I just want to be on my own with you."

327

He smiled weakly over the cover at me, his face full of love and trust, content that he finally had me all to himself at last. That's all he'd ever really wanted if the truth be known, for it to be just the two of us. He didn't like other people, never had.

"I'll have a nap for half an hour," he closed his eyes, "You can wake me up in time for dinner."

But it wasn't half an hour it was much longer than that, although I did try to rouse him at one point, to no avail. He slept on and on until dusk started to fill the room with long, threatening shadows. I turned on the small reading light and sat in the armchair watching over him as he slept, like the Lady of the Lamp.

Out of the low sash window I could see the ghostly forms of two white swans, slowly gliding past on the misty lake. Every now and then I would stand up and check his breathing to make sure he was still alive, as you would with a newborn baby. Then all of a sudden, making me jump, he woke up with a start and said that he would come down to dinner with me.

"Why don't we call room service instead," I suggested, "We can have a picnic in bed." I was forgetting that eating in bed was an anathema to Brian. He'd once told me that he'd never eaten so much as a piece of toast in bed.

We went downstairs to the dining room, but he could hardly walk. He kept banging into things; walls, tables, other diners - the waitress. Everyone must have thought he was drunk and looked at me with pity.

Brian ordered the Lemon Sole but he couldn't eat it. He told me as he pushed it wearily around his plate that he'd lost interest in everything now, even his latest invention. He said that his only remaining interest was in me and in my work and he made me promise that I would never stop painting or sculpting. I promised him that I wouldn't.

He didn't want a dessert and neither did he want any coffee but insisted that I ordered one; then he said he was feeling tired and wanted to go back upstairs. I wanted to go with him but he insisted that I stay and finish my coffee. I watched him stagger out of the dining room, banging into everything as he went, with an ache in my heart.

After he'd gone, I gave up all pretence of putting on a brave face and broke down and cried. People stared at me but I didn't care. I couldn't help it. I broke my heart. I suppose everyone thought that we'd had a row because he was drunk and that he'd gone off in a huff. If only they knew.

How can anyone deal with the knowledge that they only have a short time left to live, especially someone like Brian, with so much still to do in life, so much to accomplish.

"I don't want it to be the end," I sobbed to myself. "I want it to be the beginning again." We'd wasted so much of our lives, Brian and I, with other people and our stupid, pathetic arguments. We'd sworn to each other after the last one that we would never let it happen again. Life is too short we'd told each other, only we didn't know then exactly how short. We were determined that we'd make up for lost time, but now it seemed that that was not to be.

It was unbearably hot in our room. The double bed was in an alcove next to an old fashioned radiator. I tried to turn it down but the knob wouldn't budge so I called reception and they said they would send someone up. Brian was burning with fever by this time and the sweat was pouring off him. I managed to get him into the pale blue pyjamas he always wore to sleep in and he was like a big rag doll in my hands. He would have let me do anything I'd wanted, just as long as it didn't involve calling the doctor, or anyone else for that matter.

I tried to move the bed closer to the window but it was too heavy. Brian made a weak attempt to roll himself out and stand up to help me, but the effort was too much for him and he quickly lay down again, exhausted. Somehow, I managed to shove the bed across the room with my knees with Brian lying on it, until it was half in the alcove and half in the sitting room. He looked up at me sheepishly from upside down and tried to smile, his face dripping with perspiration. He could never have slept with the bed like that under normal circumstances. Everything always had to be in its rightful place and in line. He wouldn't even get into bed unless the sheet had been turned down for him. I used to complain about things like that and accuse him of being spoilt, but not anymore.

Throughout the long, endless night, I tried to bring his fever down by cooling his forehead, his wrists and the back of his knees with wet towels, like I used to do with Ben when he was a baby. I rolled his pale blue pyjamas bottoms up and dripped wet towels down his legs and all over the bed and he didn't even complain. He just lay there smiling helplessly and let me.

"Nurse Seed," he joked.

During the night as I lay there beside him our pillows kept falling onto the floor and I had to keep getting out of bed to put them back under his head. Needless to say I couldn't sleep. I could feel the fever raging in his body, passing into mine.

I eventually gave up trying and carefully got out of bed, without disturbing him and took out my notebook to try and write down the million thoughts that were whizzing through my mind.

Hours passed to find me still sitting in the high-backed blue armchair by the open sash window, looking at the early morning sun now sparkling on the lake and wondering how many days Brian and I had left to sleep in each other's arms and wake up together to greet a new day. It was so peaceful watching the gently lapping ripples of water softly caressing the rushes fringing the lakeside, so much more peaceful than being by the pounding, crashing and yet exhilarating sea. I couldn't have borne that right now; the energy, the life force of the ocean wouldn't have fitted with these circumstances. I needed the peace of nature, not the force. I needed the stillness. I needed to prepare.

The two majestic white swans, their feathers tinged with gold by the early morning sun are gliding around in a slow circle on the mirrored surface of the cut glass water and there's a jet ski painted with fluorescent stripes tied to the small pontoon. Both of these images make me feel unbearably sad. The two swans because a swan has only one partner; a partner for life and that is how it should have been for Brian and me - and it was really I suppose. We may have been separated at times, but we were never really apart, at least not in our hearts. The jet ski conjured up the happy vision of Brian roaring past Corinthian wearing his bright orange lifejacket and holding a huge, blue and white-striped umbrella over his head so that I could take a photograph of him Who on earth would I be able to do crazy, surreal things with, other than him? We were so alike Brian and I, in many ways; perhaps too alike.

When Brian awoke his fever seemed to have abated somewhat, but he declined breakfast, so I just ordered some tea and toast from room service. I thought we should pack up and go home; but Brian was adamant that he didn't want to, and there was no point arguing with him, so we decided to move to another hotel instead. I tried to help him pack his bag, but he was determined to do it himself, even though he was dizzy and unsteady on his feet. He was always a very stubborn man.

While the receptionist was preparing our bill, we ordered a coffee in the conservatory. I gathered up the pile of Sunday papers that were lying around and placed them in front of him. He loved the Sunday papers, especially the Times, but he fell asleep as soon as he'd opened the first page. He lay there slouched on the bamboo sofa, the pages of the newspaper gently rising and falling with his every ragged breath, his mouth open wide, snoring loudly. The French windows were open as it was a beautiful September day, and the hot weather had brought all the wasps out. There were swarms of the pesky things buzzing around the conservatory, banging into the glass, circling Brian's head. I was frightened one would fly into his open mouth, so I stood guard over him like a warrior, batting them away with a rolled up newspaper.

A wedding party started to arrive, the men resplendent in grey morning suits adorned with flowered buttonholes and carrying dashing top hats under their arms; the women elegantly dressed in pastel coloured coats with matching hats. As they grouped together in an animated huddle at the bar, they stared at us with open curiosity, especially the children, amused presumably by Brian's snores and the sight of me with my rolled up newspaper. I glared back at them, challengingly, daring anyone to laugh at him.

I imagined the wedding that Brian and I would have had if things had only been different; where the reception would have been held, who we would have invited etc. No one probably knowing him! But it was no good thinking of such things now. That could never be. Brian and I no longer had a future, we only had a past.

Brian woke himself up with a loud snore and, embarrassed, quickly stood up and shakily made his way to Reception to pay the bill. The doorman drove the Mercedes to the front door and handed me the keys.

"Are you sure the gentleman is alright madam?" he mouthed aside to me as I climbed into the driving seat.

Of course he wasn't alright – nothing was right, but that wasn't going to stop us from enjoying this time together. We sped off through the gates and up the steep hill, leaving Lake Windermere and the rooftops of the hotel crouching at its shore peeking through the tree tops. We would never go back there. Anything we did from now on would never be repeated and for that reason I wanted every experience to be one of beauty and meaning for both of us as these memories would be the last we would ever have.

I drove slowly through the winding country lanes with the top down and it was like driving through an enchanted forest. Low, September sun slanted through the trees and shone through the leaves, illuminating the autumn colours: red, yellow and gold. It was unbelievably peaceful with nothing but the soft hum of the car's engine and occasionally, the odd musical trill of a bird breaking into song. We seemed to be the only car on the road and it felt like this magical scenario was in place only for us to discover. We mounted the steep inclines then slowly descended through the trees, to circle the mirrored edges of gently lapping lakes, with clusters of shiny-feathered ducks bobbing on the glistening water and stately white swans basking in the autumn sun. Brian was deep in thought for most of the time and didn't say much, but he kept reaching for my hand and squeezing it. I was so glad that we had that magical autumn day together, because only the dark days were left to come.

We had our own private suite in the next hotel, which was situated in a small house in the grounds, away from the main hotel and hidden by tall pine trees and enormous hedges. The rooms were very chintzy and flowery, rather like being in the parlour or front room of a very posh aunt, and not our style at all! But what did a bit of chintz matter as long as we were together.

Brian said he was suddenly feeling hungry so I ordered some soup from room service, which he managed to eat; then afterwards he lay down on the bed and had a short nap. When he woke up I took him out for another drive, but the scenery here was more rugged and bleak, the jagged hills covered with heather and interspersed with patches of craggy grey rock. We watched the sun go down and disappear between the darkening peaks and then drove slowly back. He'd stopped shaking by this time and seemed to be feeling a bit better, although he was still very tired.

But that night, back in our chintzy suite, just before we went to bed, he suddenly complained he was suffering from terrible stomach cramps, but before he had time to rush to the bathroom, bright yellow diarrhoea started to spurt out of his body like struck oil. He was absolutely mortified because it had gone all over his pyjamas, and began to fret that in our haste to get away he'd only brought two pairs with him.

"Don't worry," I quickly consoled him, "It doesn't matter. I'll wash them for you." Then to save his pride, I tried to make light of the situation by telling him I was used to it after dealing with Ben's nappies when he was a baby. Perhaps not the right analogy, but I didn't know what else to say.

I washed the soiled pyjama bottoms out in the sink and put them on the radiator to dry; then found him the only remaining clean pair. He was shaking so badly I had to help him put them on. Brian hung his head in shame and crawled back into bed, still fretting about the fact that now he didn't have a spare pair. Honestly, that man and his bloody pyjamas. He had a crisis if he didn't have more than one spare pair of everything. What's more, they always had to be identical and always the same make. Like the rows and rows of pale blue shirts in his dressing room at home, perfectly ironed and pressed by Mrs Coombs and hung in formation in a stiff orderly line like a regiment of starched ghosts. Brian nearly always chose to wear blue, apart from when he was on the boat, or more recently at the weekends when he'd started to wear beige and stone colours to please me. Not that I didn't like blue. It was my favourite colour too, but it made a change to see him dressed in something different, something a bit more modern. But I didn't think I would ever be able to look at the colour blue ever again without thinking of him.

Brian crawled into the big double bed under the padded flowered eiderdown, but even though it was hot in the room and he was covered up, he started to shiver and shake uncontrollably and complain once again of stomach pains, of pains everywhere. I think he thought that this was it, his time had come. And so did I, but he still refused to let me call anyone and became very distressed if I even mentioned it. I didn't want to upset him further or go against his wishes when he was so distressed. But in the end, risking his wrath, I had to call the doctor and I also called John and Lesley.

The doctor seemed to take forever to get there, during which time I paced the floor and called my mum for some moral support from the sanctuary of the bathroom so that Brian couldn't hear me. When I finally heard a car pull up outside, I rushed to open the door to find it was a woman doctor. As she was examining Brian and taking his temperature, she lost the thermometer down his pyjama bottoms. I had to retrieve it for her and that made him laugh. She told him that she thought he had a secondary infection on top of being allergic to the Radio Iodine they'd pumped into him at the clinic for the tests. She prescribed a course of strong antibiotics and said that we should go straight home the following day so that he could see his own doctor.

I didn't sleep a wink again that night. Brian was breathing like a train in my ear and groaning in agony with a pain in his shoulder. There was more diarrhoea on the sheets, but he was too ill to notice or even care by this time. I cleaned it up as best I could and kept trying to make him sip from a glass of water, because I was sure by now that he would be badly dehydrated.

Sometime in the night, he suddenly woke up and said that he'd been dreaming about cornflakes.

"I'll phone room service right away and order some," I told him grabbing the phone at the side of the bed.

"But it's three o'clock in the morning," he said aghast, looking at his watch.

I ordered them anyway and they arrived on a lace covered tray with a silver milk jug and like a famished child Brian ate every last cornflake, even the ones that had got stuck to the side of the bowl.

The next morning it was all I could do to persuade him to get back in the car and we set off back home with heavy hearts, this time with the roof up because it was raining. I think he would have let me drive him to the end of the earth and back rather than go home, but go home we must.

We drove back down the motorway in silence.

"They'll be round me like flies," was the only thing he said.

"I'll protect you," I promised, "I'll stand by you till the very end."

And I meant it.

As soon as we got through the door of 'Kenolbri' I immediately set about trying to find another doctor – anyone but his own doctor who seemed to have done absolutely nothing for him and had let his condition go undiagnosed to the point where it was now untreatable. Through a mutual friend who was a nurse at the private BUPA hospital just down the road, we managed to get a really nice Welsh doctor called, unsurprisingly, Dr Jones, who was a specialist in these conditions. But by the time he arrived at 'Kenolbri' later that evening, Brian was in a terrible state. He was really short of breath to the point where he was panting at the slightest exertion. In fact he could hardly move and his voice was becoming slurred and his mind seemed to be extremely fuddled. Dr Jones examined him in the sunroom and when he'd finished, he advised me that Brian had to go into Hospital immediately.

"It's all a bad dream, isn't it?" Dr Jones patted Brian on the shoulder, "You don't really know where you are old chap, do you?"

Brian didn't even respond. I could just imagine what he would have said to Dr Jones or to anyone else who spoke to him in that manner under normal circumstances. He'd have banished them from 'Kenolbri', from the Kingdom even. But these weren't normal circumstances. Anything but!

It was arranged that Brian would go in to hospital first thing the next morning.

That night, neither of us could sleep. Brian couldn't get comfortable for the pain in his shoulder and he was groaning out loud. He got up many times to go to the bathroom and once he didn't make it in time. I could hear him stumbling around in the dark trying to change his pyjamas. I didn't want to embarrass him further by coming in to help him and he wouldn't let me put the light on. I could hear him opening and shutting cupboard doors.

"I'm lost, Adrienne," he cried pitifully. "Where am I?"

Hearing him say that nearly broke my heart, but I hid my feelings and helped him find some clean pyjamas and led him by the hand through the dark, back to bed.

It was a long, long night. The only thing I could do was to hold his hand and try my best to soothe him. I daren't sleep myself, just in case.

Early in the morning, Brian was dozing fitfully at my side, so I got up and went downstairs to make a cup of tea, wanting the dawn to break and the overwhelming blackness to go. I sat in the sunroom, feeling so sad, sitting in this room where we had first watched the sunrise together so many years ago. We'd sat up all night then, making love and listening to Bartok and we didn't want the night to end, unlike now.

I was only twenty-one then and we'd had the whole future in front of us. Now we would only have a few months if we are lucky. It was all coming to an end too soon.

I write him a letter to read before he goes into hospital, in case he never comes out. It's only a short letter although I could have written pages and pages. For once I kept it brief. I found that I could say all I needed to say in just these few lines.

Monday 25 September 1998

Dear Brian,

I want you to know that I will be with you at this time and through it all, no matter what it involves or how bad it gets. You can count on me one hundred percent and trust in me. I will not let anyone do anything to you that you do not want and I will not leave you on your own. I promise. Nothing and no one has been as important to me in my life as you. Please don't leave me,

I love you,

Adrienne x

About seven o'clock I heard a car coming down the drive. It was Anne, Brian's secretary. She started crying when I told her what had happened. Then Mrs Coombs the housekeeper arrived and she cried too. Then the three of us quickly pulled ourselves together, and in the spirit of women being strong in the face of adversity, we all did our bit to get him ready for hospital. Brian was panicking of course about not having enough pyjamas and about his accident the previous night, so I explained the situation to Mrs Coombs as tactfully as I could.

"Tell him not to worry," she told me, "I've worked in nursing homes. I'm used to it."

I carried the bag that I'd packed for him the night before downstairs, and Anne drove us to the hospital. We checked him in and sat with him for a while, then when he wanted us to leave, we did. I told him I would come back as soon as he wanted me to. I was only a phone call away.

When I came back later that afternoon he was all wired up to drips and bottles. Dr Jones told me that the only thing we could do now was to make him as comfortable and as happy as possible. He didn't say in the short time that he has left. He didn't need to. Brian held my hand tightly and smiled at me and said that he was so glad I was there and that my being there made him feel happy.

So that's my job then. I will try my best not to be sad or to cry in front of him, no matter how hard that may be. I will do everything in my power to make the last time he has on earth as pleasurable as possible, to the very best of my ability. I owe him that at the very least.

After a few days a miracle seemed to have taken place because when I got to the hospital and opened the door to his room Brian was sitting in a chair in his dressing gown waiting for me.

"Doctor Jones said you can take me home," he beamed excitedly. "I just have to wait for him to sign some papers."

When Brian came out of hospital he seemed to be a lot better and we even felt optimistic and determined that we could fight this thing together. We'd heard other stories of people surviving terminal illnesses against all the odds and there was always the possibility of a liver transplant or alternative cancer treatments. Money wasn't an obstacle in Brian's case, so I found out all the information I could and we even considered going to Mexico where a certain doctor was having amazing results with patients who were considered to be at death's door. With the help of Anne, his secretary, Brian gathered together all of his medical notes and sent them off to a specialist cancer hospital in America. It was only when they were returned with a note saying that he couldn't be treated there, that the truth really dawned. There was no hope. Brian was going to die and there was nothing in this world, not even with all his millions, that we could do about it.

It was then that Brian really started to decline. He cried all the time and I couldn't console him. Once again with the help of his secretary, he set about shredding all his letters and papers and he advised me to do the same. Luckily for me, I didn't.

October 2nd Friday night

It all seems to be happening too quickly. Every day Brian gets worse and more and more depressed - and so do I. Things keep making me sad, silly things - like he doesn't bother to plump the cushions up anymore or stand them to attention in a neat orderly line. I find I'm straightening them up for him and plumping the living daylights out of them because I know that's how he likes them to be. I used to tease him by telling him that if he wanted orderly cushions he shouldn't choose silk ones because they were always slithering out of his grasp – a bit like me. But not anymore. If I was to describe myself as one of his cushions now, I'd be a bolster; a barricade, a sand bag even, to stop the rising flood of the river of his desolate tears. It's a never ending river that stems from deep in the heart of him, breaking free of the dams that he'd forged and engineered and set into place over the years to hold back his pain. He cries about everything; his long dead brother, his failed marriages, the fact that we never got married, but most of all the fact that he will soon be leaving me. Such a long and yet painfully short goodbye. Every minute, every second that we spend together now is a goodbye of sorts.

A nurse came to 'Kenolbri' today to arrange for his care in the future.

"I'm his carer," I wanted to shout at her, "He doesn't want anyone else."

But we have no choice anymore. There will come a time when I can't do certain things, the necessary medical interventions which will ease his pain, like give him morphine injections if he should need them. I am there only to ease his heart and his mind, to ward off the fear, to pave the way. To love him.

"What do you want the nurses to call you?" she asked him, "Mr Mercer? Brian?"

"I don't mind," he said, tiredly. But I knew that he did.

"He wants them to call him Dr Mercer," I told her, "That's how he's used to being addressed."

Brian gave me a grateful smile.

He's swelling up. It started with his feet and ankles and now it's his stomach. It's as tight as a drum, unnaturally tight. When I hold him it's like holding someone else, or as though something is trying to come between us and is forcing us apart. And something is of course; his oncoming death.

He was so pleased with himself today. He thought he'd put weight on. He still weighs himself every day, as he always has. Even on the boat we used to take the scales onto the quay so that he could get a correct reading. Today, Dr Jones told him it was only fluid retention, so I think he'll stop weighing himself now.

Dr Jones warned Brian that he would have a very difficult time ahead of him and so would I. He told him that he would probably feel very angry and that he would also feel pain.

"So this condition, this tiredness won't improve?" Brian asked him hopelessly.

"No. No I'm afraid it won't," Doctor Jones sighed. He knew the signs only too well and must have been through it in his role as a doctor a thousand times before.

Brian slumped down in his seat in defeat. It was no good pretending anymore. We both knew now that there wasn't any hope. It had been said out loud.

Dr Jones stayed for a long time chatting and talking about other things. What a nice man he is. Brian is very lucky to have him for his doctor, although Dr Jones keeps telling me that Brian is the lucky one to have me with him at a time like this, and I suppose he is. Who will I have to look after me when he's gone? But that's a selfish thought. No time for those now.

I have taken control. I put him to bed and I turn the sheet down for him, perfectly aligned and not a crease in sight, just as he likes it. We'd once had a stupid argument, because feeling romantic one morning, I'd brought him breakfast in bed and he'd gone mad.

"Beds are to sleep in and to make love in," he'd barked at me, "Not to eat in."

How silly it seems now. But I think this deep-rooted aversion of his may have been caused by his association of eating in bed with illness. His worst fear, he told me, was that that he'd end up confined to bed downstairs like his father before him, in this same house. I have promised him that I won't let that happen. So every night, even though it's hard for him, and for me, I help him upstairs to bed. I slide his arms and legs into his pale blue pyjamas and he goes into the bathroom to brush his hair and clean his teeth. Sometimes I brush his hair for him and he watches me through the mirror as I gently sweep his once black fringe back into a silver quiff and try not to notice the widening partings or the shiny pink patches of baldness.

We get into bed; in an unspoken agreement we've swapped sides so that I am nearer to the phone and to the door. I turn off the light then hold his hand and tell him a story about something - anything that comes to mind. When he finally drops off, I lay very still in bed so I that I won't disturb him. I lay there watching over him in the dark; I'm watching over the man I love. The man I have always loved and always will. He is sleeping and I am on guard.

October 3rd

Saturday morning 6.30 am.

I simply can't bear it. The thought that Brian will soon be gone is breaking my heart. Everything is going to remind me of him, everything. They say that a person never really dies as long as they live on in your memory. In that case he will always be with me because I will never forget him, how could I? It can't be any other way and I wouldn't want it to be. He's been too big a part of my life. Even writing the date at the top of this page is something that he trained me to do. I never used to put dates on anything and it used to drive him mad. We wasted so much time bickering over silly things, but I'll even miss that. Love and hate. You can't hate someone unless you love them - or so they say, but there wasn't a 'they' as far as we were concerned; only an 'us.' We were two on our own and soon there will only be one. I will never find anyone to replace him and I wouldn't even try. He will still be with me in everything I do and see, forever present in a thousand memories that span over so many years. How I wish I could have been with him through every one of them. Even though we weren't always together, he was always in my thoughts as he told me I was always in his. All I ever really wanted to do with my life was create some great work of art that would really bowl him over. He was my judge and my jury and I couldn't get away with anything less than the best with him. He'll still continue to be my judge and jury in spirit and one day I'll do it, I promise myself as I have promised him. Every time I paint a picture or create a sculpture, he'll be with me. He'll be in my hands and in my mind, my spiritual inspiration. Every time I see a beautiful sunset, or the moon on the water; skim a smooth white pebble over a still lake, or put up an umbrella, look at a jet ski, or even a half-drunk cup of cold tea, I will think of him. He'll be there in all the things he bought me; my lovely silver car, my cosy cottage number 21, even my glasses, or should I say spectacles. The designer clothes from Harrods hanging in my wardrobe, which I'll probably never wear again and the rows of shoes with their obligatory wooden shoe trees. And every time I am on a plane and it's coming in to land, I will imagine that he is there at my side, holding my hand, as he always used to do. Every time I say pound I will stop myself and say 'pounds' because I will hear him in my head telling me to. He'll be over my shoulder correcting my spelling mistakes and frowning on me from above if I don't use the Queen's English. So many, many things, but most importantly of all, he'll be with me as an artist. I will carry on and complete all the projects that we planned together. I'll do it and he'll be so proud of me – you'll see.

Brian wants everything to stay the same. I order the food as usual from Mrs Coombs to buy in for us at the weekends. The lamb chops are a bit too much for him now, so we order Dover Soles instead.

"And shall we have some raspberries for dessert?" he asks, as he always has.

"Two cartons of raspberries and a carton of double cream," I write down.

We won't eat them of course, but I'll serve them anyway and I'll grill the Dover Soles just how he likes them in butter with a dash of lemon. I'll set the long, polished wooden table with the shining silver cutlery, straighten the napkins and light the dining room fire and the huge white candles. That used to be his job but even that's beyond him now. He refuses to give in however and I admire him for that.

Saturdays and Sundays no one is allowed to visit. He wants it to be just the two of us. He asked me to bring my latest clay to work on in the sunroom, so that he could watch me. I used to be funny about working in front of him, preferring to work alone, at least until I'd reached a point where I felt I needed his advice or I could withstand his criticism. But all that no longer matters. He lies there on the white sofa with his long legs hanging over the edge. Sometimes he falls asleep and when he opens his eyes, I am still working away, almost demented with clay in my hair, on my face and all over the white carpet. But he just smiles at me.

We have a routine. When I arrive for the weekend Anne and Tom leave and Brian heaves a big sigh of relief and says, "Thank God we're alone at last."

I pour myself a gin and tonic and just a tonic water for him. We clink glasses and Brian pretends that his tonic water has a large gin in it. Then we sit together holding hands in the darkening sunroom, watching the sunset streak the sky pink and purple and the lights twinkle into life on the hill. The whole weekend lies before us, with no one else to intervene, apart from the 'Kenolbri' ghosts. It's quite frightening for me sometimes being alone in this big old house with a dying man, with no staff and no friendly neighbours close at hand. What if something should happen? Dr Jones said it could at anytime. He said I might just hear a bump one day or one night and that would be that. Dr Jones warned me that either way it will be a terrible shock. Death always is, he said and patted me on the shoulder and told me that I was very brave. I don't feel very brave though.

Sometimes, when I've got Brian to sleep, I come downstairs so I won't disturb him and it's so quiet and spooky here on my own. I would prefer a nurse to be here to help me but Brian doesn't want one until it's absolutely necessary. He insists that he only wants me. It's a big responsibility for me but if that's what he wants, then that's how it has to be. He has no patience with anyone else. He doesn't want me to answer the door and he won't speak to anyone on the phone. If it rings he gestures me to tell them to go away. Well actually, he tells me to tell them all to fuck off. So I make excuses for him, "He's having a nap, he's very tired or he'll call you later," but he never does. I'm sure they all think that it's me not letting them speak to him. Olga keeps trying to come round but Brian tells me to tell her to fuck off too.

"Don't be like that," I try to convince him, "She's your only sister, your flesh and blood."

She comes anyway and always manages to time it to arrive when Dr Jones comes. She brings tins of homemade cakes and mince pies but Dr Jones ends up eating them all. I try to keep the peace and get Brian and Olga to talk about their childhood, or anything apart from sickness and dying. I'm sure Dr Jones thinks I'm a bit batty the way I go on, although he's probably used to people acting strangely at times like these. Olga keeps telling me how good I am, and how they couldn't manage without me. She doesn't seem quite as bad as everyone says she is but Brian is terrified of her and tells me he always has been, from being a small boy. He still calls her 'Olga from the Volga' but only when she can't hear him.

Because Brian is so easily disturbed at nights, I've brought my mum's camp bed to 'Kenolbri' for me to sleep on and one of Ben's brightly coloured quilts, but I stay in the big bed with him until he's drifted off. Although he's always so very tired, he finds it hard to sleep, especially at night in the oppressive blackness of the bedroom with the heavy drapes shut tight, but he won't let me open them or keep the lamp on. So I lay there holding his hand and telling him stories in the dark to take his mind off the fact that it might be tonight, it might be tomorrow. Then I carefully release my hand from his and slither out of his arms and lower myself onto the camp bed at his side. It's not very comfortable but I don't really sleep anyway, just in case.

As I lie there in the dark, I think about a lot of different things. This bedroom; all the nights we'd slept and made love in the king-sized bed. The time I made him cut all the big orange bows off the curtains because I thought they were too fancy and he couldn't even remember which wife had put them there. The fact that he wanted me to leave bits of myself all around the room, so that he always felt I was here, even when I wasn't. The two miniature crocodile shoes I'd bought him in Ibiza when we first got back together again, standing side by side in pride of place on the fireplace. My Harrods nighties hanging in the wardrobe like flimsy white ghosts, ethereal reminders of the honeymoon we will never have.

I don't know how Brian is coping. Every day during the week he has endless appointments with lawyers and accountants and it wears him out. It exhausts him. That's why the weekends are so special for him with just the two of us. Sometimes he tries to talk to me about money and the contents of his Will.

"You know you have been a beneficiary of my Will for some time," he told me tonight, his eyes filling with tears and he started to cry. I tried to change the subject but he persisted.

"I've left you a legacy that will tide you over until the Trust comes through, for bacon butties and the like," he tried to joke, drying his eyes, "And I'm in the process of drafting out the details of an Arts Trust," he thrust a piece of paper at me which had my name on it and asked me to read it. "This is so you will never have to ask anyone for anything in relation to your work. It is very important for me that you carry on with your art. In fact it's the only thing that really matters to me now. Promise me that you will."

I promised him.

"I will never let you down Adrienne."

"I know you won't," I told him.

"I've never let you down in the past and I don't intend to in the future."

The mention of the future set him off crying again, so I put the paper pertaining to the Arts Trust back on his desk and then rooted through the stack of videos piled up on the coffee table trying to find a suitable film that would take his mind off financial matters and thinking about the rapidly approaching time when he would no longer be here with me. But we didn't really watch it. We just sat there holding hands in the two armchairs, side by side in front of the huge television screen, thinking our separate thoughts.

"I wonder how much longer now," I was thinking to myself. And I'm sure he was too.

Today Brian was rushed back into hospital because he kept being sick. I wasn't with him at the time; I was at my mum's sorting out some paperwork for her. When I got there he was sitting in the bedside chair propped up by pillows surrounded by accountants and lawyers thrusting papers at him to sign and two women I'd never seen before were waiting in the corridor by the door ready to be called in as witnesses. I asked Brian if he wanted me to wait outside until they'd all finished, but he said no, insisting that I stay in the room with him. I sat on the bed while Keith Martin kept me talking, in order to distract me no doubt from hearing what was going on. Not that I had the slightest interest. My only concern was for Brian. He was hunched over the table looking weary, signing paper after paper with a shaky hand, while his lawyer and his accountant hovered over him like a pair of gannets. The two women were eventually called in to act as witnesses and then everyone breezed out, satisfied judging by the relieved looks on their faces that Brian had signed everything he needed to sign before he popped off. They made me feel sick, the lot of them. All they cared about was Brian's money and what he was going to do with it after he died. No one really cared about him as far as I could see, apart from me, and it made me feel incredibly sad to think that Brian had probably had to live with that all his life; sycophantic hangers on, only pretending to care about him because he had so much money.

I helped him crawl back into bed and passed him a glass of cold water. He was absolutely exhausted and said he felt dehydrated and his mouth was dry from all that talking. But I think it was from all the tears he'd shed. He was crying again now, big tears rolling down his cheeks and he was clutching my arm and begging me to take him home.

"I'll talk to Dr Jones and see what I can do," I promised him, pulling the chair up to the bed and resting my head on the pillow next to his. I held his trembling hands between mine and tried to stop them from shaking. Dr Jones popped his head round the door and smiled at me. "That's nice," he said and carried on doing his rounds.

I stayed at Brian's side until the nurse told me I had to leave. I spoke to Dr Jones on the way out about the possibility of Brian coming home and he said we'd have to see how he was the next day.

Brian seemed to have somehow rallied himself round during the night, probably in an attempt to convince Dr Jones to allow him to come home and he was a lot brighter the next morning and sitting in the bedside chair when I arrived to visit him and very excited about an idea he'd had for my next sculpture. The idea was based on the design of the peculiar shaped cardboard bottles they'd given him to pee in.

"Look," he said excitedly placing two of them together, "It's like a Henry Moore. Imagine that a hundred times bigger and in marble."

He got so carried away moving the bottles around in different positions, his tubes and drips got all tangled up, which set the alarms off. The nurse came rushing in to see what was wrong and I suppose it must have looked a bit odd to find Brian all tied up in knots and me on the floor at his feet, lining up the pee bottles.

"We need some more of these," he told the nurse, pointing to the bottles.

The nurse unravelled him making tutting noises and then made him get back in bed. Later, as I was leaving, she handed me a carrier bag full of cardboard pee bottles, looking at me as if I was stark staring mad.

The nurse told me that Brian could come home this afternoon when I called the hospital, just in time for my weekend shift. When I arrived at 'Kenolbri', I found Keith Martin, his long time business associate who had been working with him on his latest invention, along with the dreaded Olga. They had installed a single bed downstairs in the sitting room, the very thing that Brian dreaded the most. In order to make room for it, they'd moved one of our two armchairs and positioned the bed right in front of the television. The bed was very narrow and high and it had a mattress you could pump up with air, Keith told me, to stop Brian from getting bedsores and Olga had covered it with a dingy camel coloured blanket she'd been out and bought especially. To my horror, they'd also got him a walking stick and a zimmer-frame.

Brian, on their insistence, tried the zimmer-frame out for size when they brought him back from the hospital in the ambulance, still wearing his pyjamas and dressing gown, and for the first time he looked like a very old, sick man. When Dr Jones arrived a few minutes later, he advised Brian to throw the zimmer-frame away and not to bother with it as it was obviously distressing him.

Brian hated the bed. Olga made him lie down on it to test the mattress but he was restless and kept trying to get off, making angry, impatient gestures with his hands and looking round for me, calling out my name. He seemed very drugged up and not at all like his usual self.

Brain asked me what time it was and when I said it was seven o'clock, he insisted that I make our customary 'gin and tonics' which I did, but as soon as I passed him his glass, Olga snatched it from out of his shaking hand and poured the tonic water into a baby cup she'd bought for him, with a spill proof spout. I was furious. What was she trying to do to him? I grabbed the baby cup back off him and poured the tonic water back into the glass, risking her disapproval for the first time. Brian's self-respect was all that he had left now.

When they'd all finally gone, Brian suggested that we watch a film. He liked watching films these days, something he could never be bothered with before. He'd always had more important things to do with his time, he used to say, than to watch films, like getting on with his invention to solve the world's energy crisis for example. But now he had an energy crisis all of his own caused by his failing liver; which no inventor, nor invention and tragically no medical intervention could possibly resolve. Watching movies had now become an escape for him, one of the few things that could take his mind off his tragic situation. So I put 'Titanic' on as he hadn't seen it yet and also because it was a very long film (Brian would have hated me using the word movie). We usually sat side by side in the two armchairs close to the television screen with all the lights turned off so we could pretend we were at the cinema. But now one chair had been removed and the single bed was towering there in its place. These new seating arrangements were upsetting and disorientating him, making him restless and unable to settle. He tried getting up on the bed, but he couldn't hold my hand from that elevated vantage point, so we swapped places. But obviously that didn't work either and anyway it just didn't feel right. All this messing around was making it hard for Brian to concentrate on the plot, so in the end we gave up and went upstairs to bed, long before the end of the film and I told him a story instead.

The next morning he woke up and he was bright yellow, even the whites of his eyes. I was horrified because I knew what that meant. His liver was finally packing in; giving up on him, drying up like a pumice stone. I was nervous about how he would react when he saw himself in the bathroom mirror when he went to have a shave and take his customary morning shower.

"Why don't you stay in bed for a bit longer," I tried to discourage him from getting up, "It's still early." But I was only trying to delay the inevitable and anyway, Brian was a man of habit and not one to stay in bed all day, no matter how tired he was feeling. I followed him into the bathroom, dreading him witnessing the image that he was about to confront, he would also know what his dreadful yellow pallor signified.

I stood behind him as he sat down at his dressing table and took out his electric razor. Our two bleak faces stared back at us reflected in the magnifying mirror, mine as pale as the white of an egg and Brian's as yellow as the yoke. He must have noticed the disparity in our complexions, but he didn't comment on it. Instead he stood up and asked me to help him in to the shower and then to get dressed. He wanted to put his weekend clothes on as usual, so I helped him root through the wardrobe to find them. Then we went downstairs and I made breakfast. He wanted boiled eggs with soldiers and fresh orange juice. Needless to say I couldn't eat my eggs, couldn't even look at them.

The effort of getting up and dressed had worn him out, so after breakfast he lay down on the white sofa in the sunroom. I worked on my latest clay sculpture which was called 'The Couple' and was based on the two of us, while Brian watched. It was almost finished now and we'd arranged for Bob his driver to pick it up the next morning and drive it down to the foundry in the Cotswolds with some more of my finished work. Bob would then pick up the first two of the cast bronzes made from my previous clays and plasters, which were finally ready, and drive them back to 'Kenolbri.' Ralph Brown had explained the tragic situation to the foundry so they had rushed them through so that Brian could see them before he died.

I'd spoken to Bob myself and explained the urgency of the situation and somehow I'd managed to talk Brian into letting him come in for a cup of tea with us when he got back. Bob was thrilled to bits about this because he always thought very highly of Brian and was flattered that Brian would see him when he wouldn't see anyone else. I told him to try to keep the conversation light and Bob gave me his word that he would. He said that he would be at 'Kenolbri' at six thirty the next morning and would be back in Blackburn with the bronzes by the early afternoon.

"I'll have the kettle on," I'd promised him.

That afternoon Olga phoned and insisted on coming round to 'Kenolbri' with Jane and her two sons before they went to watch Blackburn Rovers play. Brian, as usual, wasn't in the mood for visitors, especially Olga, and told me to put them off. But Olga wouldn't listen, so I moved all the sculpture equipment out of the way and assured Brian that I wouldn't let them stay for very long.

Olga barged straight into the kitchen while I was making tea for them all and started banging around in the cupboards and poking her nose in the fridge, where to her annoyance she saw the Dover Soles that Mrs Coombs had got in for us that morning fresh from the market.

"Ridiculous waste of money," she snapped bossily, "It's too much for him. He can't eat them."

"I know," I agreed patiently, trying not to lose my cool with her, "But he wants me to cook them anyway."

"Such a waste," she tutted loudly, "And he shouldn't be up and dressed. He should be in bed."

It was almost as though she was trying to make him more of an invalid than he already was.

That night I cooked the Dover soles for Brian regardless of his overbearing sister's disapproval. I lit the candles and put a match to the fire, then we ceremoniously took our places at the big table and I served the two Soles with the accompanying vegetables. Brian made a vague attempt at trying to eat, then wearily put down his knife and fork, hung his head and started to cry. It all came pouring out then, all his regrets; all his dashed hopes. He told me that his biggest regret of all was that we'd never got married. Then words failed him and he couldn't speak for crying. He asked me to get him a piece of paper so I went to the bar and got him a notepad and a pen. He quickly wrote something down then passed it to me with shaking hands.

"I have always loved you Adrienne," it said in his spidery handwriting.

I will always treasure that note.

Dr Jones had insisted that we had a nurse to stay with us at 'Kenolbri' that weekend. He was a huge man called Eric strangely enough and nothing like my infamous friend Erik of hoo doo voo doo and fucking bones fame, who Brian had always been so jealous of. In fact, he was the direct opposite of 'my' Erik in that he was very quiet and unobtrusive - to the point where I'd almost forgotten that he was there. He'd stayed out of our way and sat in the breakfast room most of the time reading the paper while I'd cooked the dinner.

We abandoned the soles and left them lying almost untouched on the plates, Olga had been right on that score at least! We went into the darkened lounge to sit in front of the 'Dali' fire. The flames were flickering brightly and licking the fingers of the bronze casts of Brian's hands, reaching out from the flames as though from the very fires of hell. His own hands, wasted and thin with the sickly tinge of chicken flesh, were clutching on to me like yellow claws. I was frightened; filled with a sense of foreboding, as though his fingers were the fingers of death itself trying to drag me down with him. I quickly tried to dispel this terrifying image from my mind and I was glad that there was someone else with us in the house that night.

I stood up and walked over to the television to put a video on, I don't even know which one it was and it didn't matter anyhow because neither of us could concentrate. Brian said that he would like to go upstairs to bed, so we climbed the stairs together, arm in arm, for what turned out to be the very last time. I think Brian knew somehow that this would be his last journey, because he kept stopping on the way up to stare at each painting, one by one; my painting of 'The Spider and the Fly' in pride of place in the entrance hall then the huge abstracts painted by other well known artists and the surreal images which had fired his imagination and his nightly dreams for nearly half a century. Perhaps he knew that he would never see them again.

I helped him put his pale blue pyjamas on and brushed his hair for him, then I turned back the sheet, also for the very last time, although I didn't know it then, and I sat at the side of the bed holding his hand. We talked for ages about all kinds of things, but he had a strange look in his eyes that night, a look I'd never seen before. It was a hard, bitter look; almost resentful, as if he begrudged the fact that I would carry on living without him and, although I didn't want to think such thoughts and quickly tried to banish them from my mind, I got the feeling that if he could, he would take me with him. His eyes had turned cold and hard, like two black marbles and it was as though he was harbouring some inner knowledge: that he knew something that I didn't.

Before I turned out the light, he reached up and put his trembling hands on my shoulders and tried to pull me towards him to kiss him goodnight. Maybe it was that strange, foreign look in his eyes, or maybe it was the weeping sore that he had on the side of his mouth, the one he'd had for weeks that simply wouldn't heal, that made me draw back. But I didn't kiss him that night.

Weakly, he rested his head back wearily on the pillows and fell asleep, almost instantly. I knew that I had to go downstairs in a couple of hours to let Bob in so I turned off the light and lay down on the camp bed, fully dressed, staring up at the ceiling in the dark. Not long after, it could have only been ten minutes or so, Brian suddenly sat bolt upright.

"I feel like death, I feel like death," he was screaming, trying to get out of bed.

I quickly put the light on and he stumbled into the bathroom, tripping over the camp bed in his haste. I rang the bell and yelled downstairs for Eric. He came flying upstairs and between us we managed to get Brian back on to the bed, but he was rolling around in agony clutching himself. His stomach had blown up like a tight balloon that was about to burst and he was a vivid yellow colour.

"I feel like death, I feel like death," he kept repeating over and over again.

I grabbed the phone and called Dr Jones who told me he would come as fast as he could and then I called Olga. I covered Brian up with my brightly coloured quilt then lay on the bed by his side, holding his hand and trying to calm him.

As soon as Dr Jones arrived he gave Brian an injection and by the time Olga came, not long after, he was already semi-conscious. Olga immediately took over. "I think we will all need some coffee," she ordered me, "And while you're downstairs find me a pen and paper."

I staggered back upstairs with the laden tray of rattling cups and saucers and we all stood around the bed drinking the coffee, like some ridiculous mad hatters' tea party, watching Brian lying there, breathing peacefully now, under my brightly coloured quilt.

Dr Jones told me that for the moment there was nothing more he could do, so he left, saying that he would be back in a couple of hours and I should ring him immediately if there was any change.

Olga pulled a chair up to the side of the bed and started busily writing things down on the notepaper I'd brought her. She was muttering out loud and from what I could make out, she was making a list of who she was going to call and sorting out the arrangements for the undertakers. I couldn't believe it. Brian wasn't even dead yet. There was still hope as far as I was concerned. Maybe he would suddenly rally round like he had before I was wishing with all my heart, although I knew I was fooling myself.

Olga suddenly stood up. She'd remembered that she'd left a light on in her house and her alarm clock set for seven am, although what that had to do with it I'll never know. She put the notes in her handbag and left, saying that she would be back in the morning.

I was glad she was gone. I sat on her vacant chair next to Brian and held his limp, yellow hand in mine, tracing his blue-black veins with my finger. Please don't die, I begged him, don't leave me.

As he was sleeping so peacefully I felt I could safely leave him for a while, so I called Eric to come and watch over him and went downstairs for a much needed cigarette. I sat in Brian's favourite chair in the sunroom and wrapped myself in the 'comfort blanket' as we'd jokingly called it, that I'd bought for him from Asda, and that's when it happened.

"Our Father, which art in heaven, hallowed be thy name," I suddenly blurted out, although I wasn't usually a one for formal prayers, and I'll swear Brian flew over my right shoulder.

"You'd better come Adrienne," Eric shouted from the top of the stairs, "I think he's gone."

But I already knew that.

I ran up the stairs, two at a time and shoved Olga's empty chair aside and stared at Brian in shock. He was dead. I couldn't believe it and all I could think of was the sore on the side of his lip had gone, drained away, like his life. It had simply disappeared and so had he, or so I thought. The future had yet to prove that he hadn't left me at all and in fact, he never would. But I wasn't to know that then.

I phoned Dr Jones, Olga and Keith Martin in that order. They all trouped through the front door of 'Kenolbri' and matters were then out of my control. Brian was no longer there to give orders. They could do what they wanted with him - and with me.

Olga immediately started foraging through the cupboards and drawers, deciding what he should wear to be cremated in. She yanked my coloured quilt off his lifeless body and replaced it with her camel coloured blanket. I seemed to have lost the capability to speak and was powerless to prevent her. All I could think of was that Brian would hate being under her control and that in some perverted way she was enjoying the fact that he no longer had a choice in what he should wear or what happened to him. This may seem like a cruel and possibly biased judgement about Brian's sister's character on my part, but nevertheless, that was the impression she was giving me and there were no tears or signs of grief to prove otherwise. People deal with grief in peculiar ways, and maybe this was her way of coping with it, by being bossy and efficient. She barged past me and selected a shirt from the line of pale blue ghosts flapping their sleeves in the breeze from the open window in his dressing room and then grabbed a pair of shoes off his shoe rack. Not his famous black crocodile shoes of course, as I would have suggested should she have asked me. Needless to say she didn't.

I felt redundant and as though I was in her way, so I went back downstairs to the sunroom and sat in Brian's chair, huddled up in the 'comfort blanket' and broke my heart.

Within a very short space of time, and it can't have been more than fifteen minutes, the front doorbell rang and it was the undertakers to take Brian's body away. I was not prepared for that. I thought I would have had time to be on my own with him, to say my last goodbyes in private. But no; he was whisked out of the front door and then he was gone, and I was well and truly alone.

Keith and Olga sat together in the breakfast room at the round table making plans and sorting out arrangements that I was no longer included in, a fact that they both made very obvious. I interrupted their conversation to inform them that Bob was due any time now to collect my clays and to bring back the two bronzes that Brian would now never see.

"You mustn't mention to Bob that Brian is dead," Olga lifted her blue rinsed perm and barked at me, "Otherwise it will be all over Blackburn in no time."

"But I'll have to tell him," I cried, "Anyway, he'll know by my face, and besides he should know then he won't have to drive so fast, trying to bring the bronzes back in time for Brian to see them."

"Well, there's no point in that now, is there," she snapped coldly.

When Bob knocked on the door as punctual and as reliable as ever, I did as I'd been ordered and didn't say a word. I silently helped him to load the wet clays into the boot of his car and kept my head down so he couldn't see my traumatised face. Bob promised me that he would drive like the wind to have them back as soon as he could, adding that he was really looking forward to having a cup of tea with us. I rushed back into the house and quickly slammed the door so he wouldn't see me cry. He must have thought I was very rude.

As the dawn slowly broke over the beautiful garden that Brian would never, ever see again, Olga demanded that I hand over my house keys to her and we all left, closing the door of 'Kenolbri' behind us. I didn't know then that I would never be allowed back into the house to collect all my personal possessions, otherwise I never would have left. The only thing I'd taken with me were the two tiny crocodile shoes from the mantelpiece in the bedroom, which I'd slipped into my pocket as a final memento.

Brian was brought back to 'Kenolbri' in his coffin to lie in state in the front room, but I was not allowed to see him or to be present at the family service. Olga forbade it, even though Jane, John and Lesley thought it was only right that I should be there and insisted that Brian would have wanted it. I ordered a wreath to be delivered to 'Kenolbri' to which I attached the two miniature crocodile shoes and a poem he'd given me shortly before he'd died. I phoned the house and spoke to Anne, Brian's secretary, to ask if my wreath could be left in the room with him overnight. But I never found out if Olga honoured my request. Probably not.

Brian's funeral was a very traumatic experience for me. The church was packed to the doors and many local dignitaries were in attendance, including Jack Straw. I was not permitted to sit with the family or to accompany Brian's coffin to the altar along with the 'grieving' family. Instead I was allocated a seat three rows back with the gardeners and the staff. There was no mention of me in Keith Martin's obituary to Brian, not a word, although he talked about his grieving family and how they'd cared for him and been at his side throughout his illness. The only reference to me, somewhat obliquely, was that Brian had supported the Arts throughout his life and several artists. I suppose he was inferring that I was merely one of the artists Brian had supported and his comment was obviously designed to put me in my place. It hurt me so much, especially as Keith Martin knew how much Brian and I had meant to each other. But I knew what my place was. It was with Brian and always had been.

Since that day, they have all treated me as though I was never a part of Brian's life. But I was of course and this story, which by no means is over, will surely prove it.

CHAPTER 34

"If your only tool is a hammer treat everything as if it were a nail"

Brian Mercer deceased

That should really have been the end of the story and gradually, I suppose, under normal circumstances I would have been able to put my grief at losing Brian behind me and get on with my life as best I could. But another saga was about to begin, which would turn out to have the most shocking and devastating consequences. About a month after Brian's death I received a letter from his accountant, who along with Keith Martin was now one of the Executors of Brian's Estate. The letter was to inform me that Brian had left me a legacy which would be paid to me shortly after probate in six months' time and that I should come down to his office to find out the details. This was no surprise to me as Brian and I had talked about what would happen to me after he'd died and he'd promised me that he would continue to look after me and finance my art career, so I was curious to find out what he'd written in his Will in relation to the Arts Trust. But I was in for a bit of a shock. Brian's accountant, in a formal tone of voice, read me the legacy about the 'bacon buttie' money as Brian had jokingly called it and then started to put his papers away.

"Is that it?" I asked him in surprise.

"Yes," he declared, folding his arms, "That's it."

"But what about the reading of the Will and the Arts Trust?"

"Dr Mercer made a discretionary Will," he informed me, "So there will be no formal reading as such."

"And the Arts Trust?" I questioned.

"There is no Arts Trust," he told me bluntly.

"But there must be," I exclaimed. "Brian promised me and anyway, I saw the draft he made just before he died. He showed it to me. You must have seen it too as he had an appointment with you to finalise the details on the Tuesday after he died and my name was definitely on it."

"I know nothing about it I'm afraid," he insisted and subsequently dismissed me.

I left his office in shock. What was going on? Brian had never broken a promise to me in his life, but we weren't talking about Brian's life anymore, we were talking about his death, and what happens after a person has died does not necessarily correspond with their expressed 'wishes', as I was starting to find out.

I sat on a bench outside the office and phoned my mum on my mobile. Like everyone else she had naturally presumed that Brian would look after me financially after his death as he had during his life and so did I, but if what his accountant was saying was true, he had left me in a bit of a mess.

Apart from the large marble he'd commissioned me to make on his behalf for 'Kenolbri', he'd also promised to pay for all of my other marbles and bronzes that were already in production. Then there was the snowboarding teacher's course in America for Ben that Brian had already paid the deposit for. That alone would take care of the 'bacon buttie' money and then what was I going to do? Luckily, I still had some time to run on a Deed of Covenant that Brian had made with me when he'd insisted that I gave up teaching in order to concentrate full time on my art.

I couldn't sleep at all that night. My mind was going round and round in circles. What was Brian playing at? Had he died before he'd had chance to arrange things properly, or was he simply trying to control me from the grave as he had in life? Knowing his character, maybe he hadn't wanted to make things too easy for me. I tried to convince myself that there was a secret clause hidden in his Will that his accountant wasn't telling me about. Then I remembered the strange look in his eyes on the night that he died and how during those last few traumatic days of his life, before he'd passed away, he'd grown increasingly resentful about the fact that he was going to die and that I would continue to live without him. And there was something else in that look, something I couldn't quite put my finger on. Almost as if he knew he was going to take me with him, or at least that I would never be able to forget him. But maybe I was imagining it all, I thought to myself. Grief does funny things to people.

Brian's family, it seemed, had also turned against me, and had obviously been harbouring a deep resentment towards me all along, for all they had pretended not to. Painful images kept jumping into my mind: the horrendous way they'd treated me after his death, Keith Martin's obituary at the funeral with not a single mention of me. For some reason they were all trying to pretend that I was nothing more to Brian than an artist he had helped from time to time. But I knew I had been so much more than that and I had Brian's love letters and written vows of financial commitment in regard to supporting me as an artist to prove it. So the next morning I wrote to Brian's accountant enclosing copies of some of those letters. Thus began the sending and receiving of correspondence between us, which was to go on for years and is still going on to this day.

It soon became obvious from their rather superior and snotty replies to my letters that I was going to have a fight on my hands in order to prove my case; however they did agree to finance my trip to Italy to complete the marble Brian had commissioned for 'Kenolbri.' Aside from that, although they assured me they were very concerned to make sure that they fulfilled Brian's wishes as far as they possibly could, they would need to consider the other matters I'd mentioned in further detail.

This didn't sound too hopeful to me, especially after their staunch denial of the existence of any kind of Arts Trust. But if they wanted a fight, they had one. There was no way I was going to back down on this. It was too important to me and there was so much at stake – like my whole future for instance. Besides, I had promised Brian on his death bed that I would continue with my art and like him, at least before he died, I always keep my promises.

I go to Italy as planned and work on Brian's huge marble sculpture 'The Bricks' which he'd commissioned for the sunroom at 'Kenolbri'. In accordance with Brian's wishes, his friend, the sculptor Ralph Brown, joins me at Studio Sem in Pietra Santa to offer me the benefit of his expert advice, as I have never worked with marble up until now. It proves to be very hard but totally exhilarating and inspiring work and something I had always wanted and dreamed I would do, going back to the days when I was a young art student. Every morning we get up at the crack of dawn and go to the studio to work together alongside the technicians on the big slab of marble.

I soon discover that sculptors are a very different breed to painters and also that the Italians, especially in their work ethic, are very different to the Spanish. Sculptors arise at first light and then work their fingers to the bone in noisy studios equivalent to building sites, drilling, sandblasting, carving, scraping, honing, whittling and riffling, until hard pads of skin form on their fingers and their nostril hairs clog with dust. They suffer from fallen arches, repetitive strain injuries, torn ligaments and various, sometimes fatal, lung diseases.

At twelve o'clock on the dot the whistle blows and they all down tools and go off for lunch, where they eat huge plates of pasta, still shrouded from head to toe in white marble dust. And here is where the Italians differ from the Spanish. Instead of taking a siesta, they clock back on at three where it's the same thing all over again until darkness falls; then it's off to bed. A sculptor's life is not an easy one as I soon discover. Apart from the hard physical labour, there is also the complicated business of trying to secure funding in order to produce the often mammoth works of art they will spend a good portion of their lives trying to complete; therefore sculptors are permanently on the lookout for sponsorship in the form of a rich benefactor: a bank, a sympathetic arts council, a wealthy industrialist or a rich Arab.

After a few days of gruelling labour, I was beginning to wonder if I was physically up to the task to be quite frank. In retrospect, painting certainly seemed to be the easier option. But I had promised Brian on his deathbed that I would become a famous sculptress, so I flexed my new sculptress's muscles and carved and whittled on.

After Ralph had gone back to England I stayed on in Pietra Santa until the 'Bricks' were almost completed, determined that they would be as close as possible to Brian's original design. But Italy for me was too full of painful memories of him, and brought back with a vengeance all the grief and loss I was still trying to suppress. The truth was I felt totally bereft without him and being there on my own didn't help.

At nights I eat dinner on my own in some local restaurant and then, as the rest of the population of Pietra Santa seem to do, I go to bed early. During these solitary dinners I write in my notebook to try to pass the time. When you have no one to talk to writing is a form of conversation, even if it's only with yourself. It gives you something to do, apart from staring at the empty seat opposite you. Hopefully, it makes the other diners, the cosy couples or the noisy family groups, think that you are eating alone by choice.

I scribble away as if I'm madly inspired, or I'm busy writing a thesis on Italian art, or even a travel brochure, when in fact I'm really writing about being alone; about sitting alone, eating alone, facing the rest of your life alone and saddest of all, drinking alone.

When there is no one with you to share that bottle of excellent red wine, you are in trouble. You end up drinking it all by yourself, for several reasons - it's there, someone has to, it gives you something to do with your hands, you've paid for it, it numbs the pain of being alone, it tastes good and you don't intend to leave a single drop for the surly Italian waiter. Italian waiters, I'd noticed, are not particularly sympathetic to women dining alone. Perhaps they thought we wouldn't tip very much or maybe they considered women eating on their own to be sad, pathetic beings that nobody wanted to be with. You feel the need to explain your pitiful situation to them and point out that that's not the case and tell them why you are alone.

"Could I have a table for one please, because a few months ago, the love of my life suddenly dropped dead on me. It was liver cancer, terminal don't you know. No, there was no chance of a transplant even though he had considerable amounts of money. Yes, he had been a drinker in his younger days, sometimes a bottle of whisky a day. That's a lot I know, but he had his reasons. He was trying to solve the world's energy crisis you see. Well someone has to and I'm sure he would have done if his liver hadn't packed up on him like that. Livers do, don't they, they dry up like pumice stones then you turn yellow.

Anyway, that's why I'm here in Italy, the land of love and romance all on my own, eating by myself, sleeping by myself and drinking by myself. They say, don't they, that you start off alone and you end up alone and that life is only practice for dying. You're closing did you say? You want me to pay the bill. Do you accept credit cards by any chance?"

I return to England and send the Executors a list of my expenses. They dutifully send me a cheque for the said expenses then I am summoned to the office for a meeting. At the meeting, Keith Martin informs me that apart from not continuing to pay my personal expenses, neither would they pay for any bronzes or marbles, apart from the ones that were already in production.

"But how will I be able to carry on sculpting after that?" I asked in horror. "It's an expensive business and I can't afford to fund it by myself."

I was finding it hard to understand their attitude when Brian had left so much money in his Estate. Apart from what was already in the coffers, Corinthian had recently been sold for over two million pounds, but only after they'd all enjoyed a final cruise on her at Brian's expense, without inviting me of course. Then to add insult to injury, as I was about to leave the office, Brian's accountant shouted after me.

"Oh, by the way, have you heard the wonderful news about the sale of the Delvaux?" He handed me a photocopy of a press release from Christies.

Surrealist Art Highlights December Sale of Twentieth Century Art at Christie's in London - The highlight of the sale was 'Le miroir' executed in 1936 by Paul Delvaux. The work had been expected to realize between £700,000 and £1,000,000 but competitive bidding drove the final price much higher to a magnificent £3,191,500 – a world record price for the artist at auction.

Brian would have been thrilled no doubt. But I made no comment. Anyway, what was I supposed to say? Even with all that added money in the Trust Fund they were still refusing to comply with Brian's wishes in regard to me. Brian had also clearly stated in the draft of the Arts Trust that I'd witnessed, that apart from helping me, he also wanted to help other figurative artists, especially sculptors. But no matter how many times I asked the Executors about the Arts Trust, they still denied that any such thing existed. It was obvious that I would have to prove otherwise.

My niece came up from Berkshire to spend the weekend with me at number 21 so that I could help her with her art exam. Brian had always thought very highly of her and had been very impressed by her artwork, she was of a surrealist mind and an admirer of Dali like her auntie, so I saw nothing amiss about making an appointment with Brian's secretary Anne, who was still working at 'Kenolbri' although I'm not sure in what role, to take her to see the Dali portrait and to borrow some art books to help her with her exams. Brian had made it very clear to me before he died, that he wanted me to continue to make use of his extended library and to keep going to 'Kenolbri' which he had left in his Will to his own niece Jane. He had discussed this with me at great length before he died and I was adamant that I didn't want to live in 'Kenolbri' as it would have been too painful for me without him and also because it was his old family home, it should by rights be left to a member of his family. He chose Jane over John to inherit the house as she had two children who would be the future heirs so the house would stay in the family. He also thought they could benefit from a larger home as opposed to the more modest house they had in Cheshire, although they had yet to take up residency.

I hadn't been back to 'Kenolbri' since the day of Brian's funeral so it was a very strange feeling to enter the house again and not to find him there. The house felt cold and lifeless without his presence. A framed photograph him of when he was much younger and the one that he always used for newspaper articles, was the only new addition and it seemed to dominate the room, as Brian always could. But apart from that, nothing had been changed or moved. All the paintings were still in their rightful place, including mine. I thought the family might have got rid of them after he'd died, but Brian had apparently written in his Will that nothing in the house could be moved for eighty years. The only exceptions were the Dali, that was later to go to the Royal Society, and the Delvaux which he'd instructed to be sold at Christies.

Anne seemed very uncomfortable with me being there and followed me around, watching over me as I took photographs of my niece standing next to my paintings and Ralph Brown's sculptures, and of course the Dali portrait. Then I opened the huge bookcase and we chose some art books to borrow.

"I'm afraid I can't let you take any books from the premises," Anne told me nervously.

"I only want to borrow them," I said in disbelief. "Anyway, a lot of these books are actually mine," I pointed out. "Brian bought them for me."

"Well," she said hesitantly, "I suppose if you sign for them and promise to return them."

What was she, a bloody librarian all of a sudden?

"I would like to take my niece to 'Pittarrow' now, if that's alright with you," I requested coldly, "To show her the rest of my paintings and I also need to collect some of my painting equipment."

I hadn't been permitted to use my studio at 'Pittarrow' since Brian's death, even though most of my stuff was still there, not to mention my entire collection of paintings which were still adorning the rooms and lining the corridors. I'd begged the Executors repeatedly to let me continue working there, because the space I had at number 21 was totally inadequate, but they'd refused, saying that, according to Brian's instructions "Pittarrow" was to be sold.

Anne reluctantly collected the key from Brian's old safe and then led us along the tree-lined path that connected the two houses like some kind of warder, jangling the keys officiously in her hand. She tapped in the security number of the burglar alarm, shielding it with her other hand so I couldn't see. As if I didn't know it. It was engraved on my heart. But then again, they'd probably had it changed by now so that I couldn't sneak back in.

Once back inside those familiar walls, I ached with sadness and memories of Brian flooded my mind; him sitting at the boardroom table with the photographs of my work spread before him like a pack of brightly coloured tarot cards; pacing up and down with his tape measure ensuring my paintings were hung correctly; making the plaster for my first clay with a specialist especially flown up from London to demonstrate the complicated and lengthy process. The nights we used to sleep there to escape from the 'Kenolbri' ghosts. Now he was a ghost hovering over my shoulder, following us around the house, with Anne close on our heels, as I gave my niece a guided tour of my paintings which were still hanging in all the rooms and corridors.

The studio was just as I had left it, the walls daubed with slashes of paint we'd used as colour trials and lines of poetry Brian had scrawled in big letters to inspire me, as well as silly things he knew would make me laugh. A faded newspaper cutting with the heading "Art Unites Odd Couple" that he'd stuck to the wall with bluetac because he said it made him think of us. My squashed tubes of oil paint on my work table alongside a paint encrusted palette and an empty ashtray. Anne stood right behind me, watching me like a hawk as I retrieved some of my personal papers from the desk drawers. It was highly embarrassing and her suspicious attitude, coupled with the rush of both sad and happy memories, made it so that I couldn't wait to leave.

As soon as I got home I wrote to the Executors and told them how upset I was about both the fact that I had been treated like some kind of stranger and also that I was forbidden to use my studio even though all of my stuff was still there. A few days later I got a letter back apologising for the apparent difficulties I'd suffered while visiting 'Kenolbri' and 'Pittarrow' but it might have been easier, they said, had I given them a ring in advance, as Anne did not have the authority to allow items to be removed from the premises. Furthermore, the four books I still had in my possession should be returned as promised and they'd also been alarmed to hear that I had been taking photographs of the contents of 'Kenolbri' apparently for the use of my niece and it seemed to them that this raised something of a security issue since they were not really clear as to who was going to see the photos and for what purpose.

I immediately wrote back to them pointing out that I already had hundreds of photographs of myself and my family at 'Kenolbri' most of them taken by Brian himself and that, apart from the Dali and Ralph Brown's work, most of the photographs had been taken in front of my own paintings. Had I, or any of my family wanted to take anything from 'Kenolbri,' I coldly pointed out, there would have been ample opportunity during the four years I had been living there. Brian would not be able to rest, I told them, if he knew the things that had been happening since he'd died. I was the only person in this world who had truly loved him, I reminded them and he had loved me, so why was it I asked them, that from the moment he died and was no longer in control, they all seemed hell bent on trying to make out that I'd never existed in his life.

No matter how hard I try to get on with my life and put this whole nasty business out of my mind, everything goes round and round my head at nights and I am tormented by thoughts and memories of Brian. Sometimes I curse him for not sorting things out properly before he died and I am convinced that it was all a plot to keep on controlling me from the grave. Other times I think that he just didn't get time to do it, he believed he still had a few months left to live and he had so many other matters concerning his Estate to sort out, including the copyright and patent for his last invention. Then I remembered how bad-tempered he'd become during those last few weeks; ordering me to tell everyone to 'fuck off', in particular the people from the hospital who'd kept calling to enquire about the pledge he'd made to donate a few million pounds to cancer research.

"You can tell them ALL to fuck off," he'd told me, "They didn't cure me so why should I help them?"

But Brian had started drafting out the Arts Trust. I'd seen it with my own eyes and my name was definitely on it. He'd also discussed it at great length with Ralph Brown and myself, a clause he wanted to add to enable sculptors to borrow money to finance large bronzes and marbles which could be paid back to the Trust when the work was sold. The Executors had even driven down to the Cotswolds a few months after Brian's death and we'd all had a meeting with Ralph Brown at his house to discuss the matter. They'd agreed at the time to put Brian's plan into action, so why didn't they seem inclined to do anything about it now? I knew I had to continue fighting with them, for Brian's sake as well as my own, even though the constant battles were taking their toll on me.

The meetings with the Executors became more and more traumatic for me and I would often end up in tears. Brian's accountant would look on sheepishly and say things like, 'Well, you'll just have to come down a peg or two Adrienne', and if I started crying, as I often did, Keith would look at me in disgust and make snide comments about neurotic women.

I couldn't understand why they were being like that with me especially when they appeared to be so keen to help everyone else.

They'd resolved the issue of 'Kenolbri' which had been causing a bit of family rift, by giving it to Brian's nephew and letting his niece have 'Pittarrow' instead, which was clearly going against Brian's expressed wishes, but they didn't seem to be taking any notice of those anyway, at least in regard to me. I only found out about 'Pittarrow' when one of the gardeners brought my stuff round to number 21 in a van, along with a pile of my drawings he'd recovered from the skip, which Brian's niece had thrown out while she'd been in the process of renovating the house. The gardener had stayed chatting with me for a while, telling me all about what had happened after Brian's funeral and how his ashes had been kept in a cake tin on the shelf and Mrs Coombs had nearly thrown them away. He said there were now only two gardeners employed at 'Kenolbri' to tend those huge gardens, so the place was now rapidly starting to fall into disrepair. He'd shaken his head sorrowfully, adding that Dr Mercer would turn over in his grave if he could see what was going on. The Executors were being very difficult he told me and he feared that the power Brian had given them in his Will had gone to their heads. But I didn't need him to tell me that. Amongst my sculpture equipment which had been delivered, which didn't amount to much considering previously I'd had Brian's entire workroom at my disposal, there were a few tools, a bunch of steel wire and a few metal clasps. There was also a huge bag of heavy grey nails obviously thrown in as an afterthought. Or maybe that was Brian sending me a subliminal message, as one of his favourite expressions in times of battling with legal disputes and law suits was, "If your only tool is a hammer, treat everything as if it were a nail."

As the Executors had made it very clear that I couldn't expect any more financial help from them in regard to my art, I thought I'd better set about trying to fund any future sculptures myself as quickly as possible. As chance would have it I saw an advert in The Art Review for a foundry in Birmingham advertising for new sculptors, so I sent off some photographs of my work. The owner of the foundry was particularly interested in the two bronzes that had arrived too late for

Brian to see them and said that he would like to exhibit them in his gallery, so I drove them down to Birmingham in the back of the car.

A few weeks later I got a phone call informing me that the two bronzes had been stolen and what's more the gallery did not have the adequate insurance policy to cover the cost of replacing them. The police investigation concerning the robbery came up with nothing, so in an effort to locate the stolen bronzes myself I contacted the local newspaper, deliberately keeping the information about my relationship with Brian to a minimum, my main priority being to find my stolen work.

LANCASHIRE EVENING TELEGRAPH Thursday, October 21 1999

CRIME: Reward offered as cruel thieves rob an artist of her poignant memories.

Sculpture theft heartbreak

A distraught artist is appealing for help after two treasured bronzes, which were created for a dying man, were stolen. Adrienne Seed created the unusual sculptures for Dr Brian Mercer, the founder of Netlon, as he was coming to the end of his fight against cancer. Dr Mercer, of Meins Road, Blackburn, was an art collector who encouraged Adrienne to take up sculpture. Adrienne worked on the pieces next to Dr Mercer's bedside as he became more and more ill and even worked round the clock to try to finish them before he died. On the night he died Adrienne was with him and sent his driver to pick up the finished sculptures. But by the time he returned Dr Mercer had died without ever seeing the finished pieces. Now she is devastated that the statues have been stolen from a foundry in Birmingham and is offering £500 reward for their safe return.

Adrienne, of Blackburn, said; "When we found out Dr Mercer had terminal cancer I started making the sculptures especially for him and I was so upset that he never got to see the finished work. After his death I decided to exhibit the bronzes and they went to a foundry in

Birmingham to wait to be moved to an exhibition in Bath. While they were there the foundry was broken into and they and other artworks were stolen. I just hope somebody recognises them and has seen them somewhere so I may have a chance of getting them back."

I received an incensed letter the day after from the Executors saying they had noted the article which appeared in the Evening Telegraph on Thursday 21st of October and since there were frequent references to Brian in the article, they would have much preferred it if I had told them that the article was going to appear in advance rather than their just becoming aware of it when it was pointed out by others and not do anything like this again without prior reference to them. They went on to say that since the dictating of their letter, they had since received mine of 28th of October and now may need to reconsider their position in view of the tone of my letter. That's because I'd written to them yet again about setting up the Arts Trust. As a Libran I can be a bit of a pest if I feel the scales of justice are unbalanced and can't rest until I set matters to rights and in this case the scales were definitely balanced in their favour. I had to set them straight, but it seemed like I was facing an impossible task.

In the end I realised that I was going to get nowhere without resorting to legal action and by this time, I was totally convinced that I was fighting for Brian's sake as well as my own. I contacted a lawyer in Manchester and he told me that I had a very good case, so I started the proceedings. The first thing my lawyers did was to get hold of a copy of Brian's Will then they sent a letter to the Executors to inform them of my intentions. I went to Italy to finish the sculpture.

CHAPTER 35

The Proceedings

IN THE HIGH COURT OF JUSTICE CHANCERY DIVISION
MANCHESTER DISTRICT REGISTRY

IN THE ESTATE OF FRANK BRIAN MERCER deceased

BETWEEN

ADRIENNE JENNIFER SEED

Claimant

-and-

Oh dear! I had no idea I was taking on so many people, there was a whole posse of them; the accountant, the work associate, the dreaded sister, the old gardener, the housekeeper, the secretary, the younger gardener, a man I had never heard of with a hyphenated name and some distant god-daughter. These people were all apparently beneficiaries of Brian's Will, but where was I? Brian had told me I'd been a beneficiary of his Will for years, so why wasn't my name on the list? It later transpired that I had been taken off the list of beneficiaries for some reason shortly before Brian's death and was to be added back on after he'd died. Why I do not know, but for the time being there was no mention of me, which my lawyer found highly suspicious. That was the first shock but there were many others to follow. The first and the most shocking revelation of all, which was to completely rock my world and pull the rug from under my feet, appeared as part of the witness statement of one of the Executors.

"In paragraph 6," the statement read,

"Ms Seed goes on to state that she was Dr Mercer's common law wife for many years and particularly in the 4 years or so before Dr Mercer's death. This is a distortion of the relationship which existed between Dr Mercer and Ms Seed. Even during the period after Dr Mercer returned from Bermuda he and the Claimant were apart for long periods. This is apparent from the large number of letters and faxes that passed between Dr Mercer and the Claimant some of which are exhibited in "AJS6". Furthermore the relationship was not an exclusive one. I know from going through Dr Mercer's private correspondence after his death that he had a relationship with a Russian lady called Lara in 1996. Much of the correspondence was of a personal nature and has not all been retained by the executors. During this relationship Dr Mercer spent considerable sums on clothing, travel and hotels for Lara as he did for Ms Seed."

A Russian woman called Lara? I was in total shock. How was that possible? Brian and I had been together constantly during the last four years of his life. The only time that we'd been apart was the Christmas I'd spent with Ben when Brian had gone on a fishing trip, and one time when he took an old friend of his and his son out to Corinthian on an allegedly all male trip. My lawyers response to this statement was to question why this correspondence had not been retained, what had become of the items disposed of and why had they not been kept? For my part I simply couldn't believe it; if Brian had been unfaithful to me to that extent surely I would have known. What were the Executors playing at and what had they to gain by bringing it up if it was true. I had to get to the bottom of it and find out if there was indeed any truth in these allegations so I emailed the old captain of Corinthian and asked if he knew anything about a Russian girl called Lara. He emailed me back straight away.

Dear Adrienne,

We would be pleased to help you. Of course we remember Lara. We were cruising with his doctor friend and his son (long forgotten the names but would recognise them. We used to called them Pratt and son of Pratt. We were in Portofino and S.O.P. was up at the castle on the hill and made acquaintance with two girls. Later, early evening, the girls were walking by the back of the boat and S.O.P. invited them on board for a drink. I remember that they asked for champagne. This was a problem as I think there was only one bottle on board and that was not chilled. I remember FBM congratulating Ollie on not serving champagne and being amused by the request. They stayed for an hour or so, accepted an invitation to dinner with all of the crew, went off somewhere and then we all met for dinner ashore. There was some nonsense later and I think FBM was back late. Stories in the morning all very 6th form. The girls said they were doctors on holiday. General consensus of all on board was that that was a story.

Lara did seem to have a digestive problem, which involved taking some pills and vodka but I think most Russians are like that. She certainly didn't spend a night on board. We never saw her again. He told us that he went off to see her sometime later and I heard that he took her on a fishing trip (apparently not a success) one Christmas.

Best wishes G and O

I still found it hard to believe, so I wrote to Ralph Brown's wife Carrie. If anyone would know the details, she would, as Brian counted the Browns as two of his closest friends. She wrote back -

25, August 2000

Dear Adrienne,

You ask me what I know about the 'Lara' episode in Brian's life. He confided in us at the time, but he didn't want you to hear of it for fear of appearing to be two-timing you. It seems that a couple of pretty Russian girls were admiring the luxury yachts in Portofino and were invited on board for drinks. They stayed the night needless to say and *a good time was had by all, particularly Brian who said that 'Lara' couldn't leave him alone and was a terrific sexual performer. He showed us photos of her gazing adoringly at him – she was a very pretty blonde – aged 23 I think he said.*

For a man nearly 70 this was heady stuff and he fell for it!

It seemed to us at the time that she and her friend were out to find foreign husbands – preferably rich ones (hence Portofino) as a way out of the misery of Moscow in the mid-nineties. You can't blame them I suppose.

It then became a tiresome saga – I can't quite remember the sequence of events. I know he took her on a fishing trip once where she was demanding, neurotic and seemed to have an eating disorder.

She begged to visit his home, she said she had medical problems and needed to have an operation, which she couldn't have in Russia, plus it would have to be at a private foreign hospital at vast expense. She was in Moscow illegally without papers because she was registered in the provinces.

She started phoning him almost nightly pleading that she couldn't live without him and their separation was making her ill and could he meet her in Paris. Brian told us all this of course and he was finding it increasingly tiresome. He discussed with us his fears that she might be a mafia plant and that if he went to Paris to sort her out he might be kidnapped by Russian gangsters (Paris was full of them, as now) He talked about getting Pinkertons to check her out, but I don't know whether he ever did this.

In the end he realised that she had been on the make and he felt rather foolish. He never mentioned the episode again to us. I think he was embarrassed and chose to forget it. This was understandable under the circumstances and there was no reason to mention it to you after Brian's death as it would only have been hurtful to you and served no purpose. It was all rather ridiculous really and hardly to be taken seriously.

I hope you're not too upset. Call by and see us next time you visit the foundry,

All the best,

Love,

Caroline

Further shocks were revealed in one of the Witness Statements –

"During at least one of those periods, in 1996, FBM turned his romantic attentions elsewhere, and devoted a great deal of time to a Russian girl called Lara. I know, of course, that AJS and FBM had been close for many years before 1995, but this was principally, if not exclusively, between his marriages. As I understood it from him, he was drawn to her by his admiration for her artistic work as a painter, and he bought examples of her work from time to time. A space was made available to AJS at "Pittarrow" so that she could paint and later do her sculpture there. I do not think that space could properly be described as an artist's studio."

They were all banging the same drum, telling the same lies, evading the truth, but why I wanted to know? However, the Executors in their role of carrying out Brian's wishes in regard to me had to admit the following.

"Para 7: FBM made it clear to us before he died that he wanted us as his Executors, to continue the exercise that he had started, namely providing AJS's career as a sculptress with direct and indirect financial support to a stage where she was financially self-supporting,,,, We believe that we have faithfully fulfilled FBM'S wishes, and in the exercise of the discretion given to us by the Will have provided and continue to provide AJS with all the direct and indirect financial support that she could reasonably require. We entirely accept that FBM had a great desire to assist AJS to become a successful artist."

The Litigation dragged on and on, culminating in a day of Mediation in Manchester from which the only people who benefited were the lawyers. The team of lawyers representing matters pertaining to Brian's Estate came up from London, at great expense no doubt, and my sister flew over from Holland to support me. The Mediator was a young whiz kid who seemed to take an instant dislike to me and did not appear to be sympathetic to artists in general, or of matters relating to art. The day dragged on with the two opposing sides in diffcrent rooms. Plates of smoked salmon sandwiches and coffee were served at regular intervals as the mediator went from room to room, trying to resolve the dispute. At one point we were all summoned to assemble in another huge boardroom where the two sides confronted each other across a long wooden table, face to face. It was ridiculous and as far as I was concerned all an unnecessary expense. There I was, a humble artist, sitting amidst some of the finest legal minds in the country, battling for my rights and for Brian's wishes to be carried out. At one point, the wily lawyer from the other side confronted me directly.

"But Adrienne, be honest," he smirked, "If you had money you would stop working. I know I certainly would, I'd be off to the West Indies."

"Artists never stop working," I'd retorted, "Whether they have any money or not. The point is I can't carry on sculpting as Brian wished without financial help from the Executors of his Estate."

But it was hopeless. At ten o'clock that night the mediation was adjourned and my sister and I went home, tired and dejected.

I eventually settled out of court on the advice of my lawyer who terrified me by saying that I could lose everything, including number 21, if I lost the case. I couldn't do that to Ben so I gave in. If I'd only hung on for another few months my case could have been presented in a completely new light in view of my drastically changed circumstances in regard to my health.

And drastic had certainly been the word.

CHAPTER 36

Shocking Loss

My mum was in the new wing at Queen's Park Hospital. It was brand spanking new and bright and spacious, sterile almost, like a futuristic space station. She had her own room, with its own bathroom, but as she couldn't even see where she was anymore, let alone get out of bed to go to the loo, it was a bit of a waste of time really. My sister who had had to return to Holland due to work commitments managed to take some more time off and between us we spent day and night at our dying mother's side. My sister was brilliant, she even slept there for three nights in a row in a chair by her bed to give me chance to catch up on some sleep and then we swapped over and I slept in the chair. Well, I didn't really sleep. My mum kept knocking her oxygen mask off so I had to keep getting up to put it back on again.

I would sit there through those long, uncomfortable nights and gaze sorrowfully at her semi-conscious form as she lay on that narrow hospital bed, wishing I could just take her home with me and let her at least pass away in familiar surroundings. She appeared to be disappearing before my very eyes, wasting away, shrinking, her flesh loose on her bones, her body curled in a permanent question mark of pain; her sightless eyes wildly searching for me. I held her bent, arthritic hand and talked about anything, our happy days involved with the theatre in Ibiza, her part in 'Annie' where her one and only line as the housekeeper had been, "Soap? No, bubbles I think." She loved all that theatrical stuff and I'd only really got involved with it all for her sake. Sometimes between the morphine shots when she was more alert, she would ask me to take her to the beach, a visualisation technique we'd used when she'd first started being ill and couldn't get to sleep.

"We are lying on the sun beds on Bora Bora beach," I would start off, "It's a beautiful sunny day, but not too hot and the warm breeze is caressing our feet," my mum would wiggle her toes appreciatively. "The palm frond umbrella is wafting in the breeze over our heads and the warm sun is dappling our legs. We can hear the sea gently lapping on the shore and hear the sound of children splashing in the turquoise water." She would drift back off to sleep with a contented expression on her face.

Throughout those last days and nights she became more and more confused and kept talking away to herself, rambled mumblings, sometimes rubbish, sometimes making perfect sense. Every now and then she would pass me an imaginary cigarette to put out in the non existent ashtray.

"Make sure it's out love," she'd keep insisting. When she'd first started to lose her sight she must have worried endlessly about whether she'd left her cigarette ends still burning in the ashtray. But not enough to give up smoking of course, at least not until those final weeks when she couldn't even breathe let alone smoke

I brought her fresh bilberry pies from the bakers on the market and fed them to her in tiny pieces. She opened her toothless mouth expectantly like a baby bird. Those pies were the only thing she'd eat; she turned her face away for everything else.

Both my sister and I stayed together with her throughout the day and we talked about our childhood days; our wonderful dad with his crazy sense of humour and how he had always made us laugh. That's the reason my mum had married him she always said, because of his daft sense of humour and how he had been able to make her smile even through those awful times when she'd had her nervous breakdown after the tragic loss of her two babies. We talked about my mum's sisters and the things they used to get up to as children; the stories she had told us about how they all used to sleep in the same bed and take turns at singing hymns and reciting poetry. We talked about our granddad, her dad, when he'd kept a vigil at her mother's bedside for three days after she'd died and wouldn't leave her until her funeral. Then he'd come home and written 'Annie' in nails on her tiny, now redundant, wooden clogs.

Sometimes my mum would sing to herself, her eyes bright with tears, romantic songs from those wartime days.

They'd given her a catheter so she wouldn't have to keep getting up to go on the commode and I remembered my dad, when he'd first been ill in Ibiza, before his brain tumour had been diagnosed and the nurse had given him a catheter and he'd thought she'd been really kind and thoughtful by giving him a hot water bottle.

My mum's restless hands were never still; they were constantly busy with doing things of the past for us: putting out dinners, knitting us jumpers, slicing the roast beef, combing our hair.

Although none of the medical staff said anything outright, both my sister and I knew our mum was never going to get out of that hospital bed. It was just a matter of time now, another week, a few more days maybe.

"You know, you are a remarkable family," the nurse commented to me about the way we'd been looking after our mum and the fact that we'd never left her side.

"Well, we've got a remarkable mother," I told her.

But unfortunately, we were not to have her for much longer. On the very last night, I'd stayed with her and my sister had gone home to get some rest. But as soon as it got light she was back with red-rimmed eyes and she'd obviously spent all night crying. I reluctantly let her take over and I drove into town to try to get some more bilberry pies and maybe a salmon sandwich from M&S. My mum had always enjoyed those and I was just putting the carrier bags in the boot of the car when my sister called me from the hospital on my mobile to break the news to me that our beloved mum had died.

I drove back to the hospital in a complete daze and found my mum lying there with her mouth open in a fixed round 'o' and her once busy and restless hands crossed over her chest, finally still.

The nurses gave us a plastic bag containing her pink and pale blue pyjamas and her bits and pieces, and we brought them home, but we couldn't open the bag. My sister kept assuring me that she had passed away very peacefully and it was better for her now, she was no longer in pain.

But somehow that pain had passed on to me and I felt an agony of loss, a loss that I cannot compare to any other I have known.

Not even Brian.

CHAPTER 37

Love is all I have to give

I lost my beloved mum on December the 30th 2005. And lost is the appropriate word, because as time and life goes on, as it somehow does, I find I am still looking for her - and even looking out for her, as if she was still here. Maybe she is and I will find her again in some form or another. I'd like to think so.

We'd given her a good 'Irish' send off however. Although my mum was deeply religious, she wasn't what you would call a regular church goer, so we had to find a local church to host the service and the Reverend came round to the house a few days before the funeral and my sister and I told him a few interesting snippets about her life. He was with us for two hours actually - so, quite a few snippets then! He was particularly captivated by the story of how my mum, during the war, when my dad had been flying off on his night time missions on the old Lancaster Bombers, had stayed in a Bed and Breakfast close to the airfield. She would count the planes as they took off, then lie awake all night waiting for them to come back, counting them one by one as they returned, praying that my dad had made it back. The Reverend, or Dave to his mates and parishioners, thought that very courageous of her and I'd never really thought of it in that way. But it was, wasn't it?

After the service, I read out a few of my mum's poems (she was always writing poetry, which we used to tease her about unmercifully, because her poems actually rhymed) and then we played some of her favourite music. She'd loved music and always had a song for everything and every occasion.

One of our friends from Ibiza had recorded some of her favourite songs on a CD, and I phoned her in Ibiza and asked if we could play one of them at the funeral. She said she'd be honoured, as she'd really loved my mum - as had many people, her two daughters most of all. This was followed by '*Stardust*' by Nat King Cole, my mum's favourite song of all, and then '*Ave Maria*' by the Dutch violinist, Andre Rieu, with his bevy of female violinists, who my mum had also loved and whom I'd taken her to see in Manchester. Needless to say, there wasn't a dry eye in the house. For her obituary, we chose an old photograph of her when she was young and beautiful to try to erase the traumatic memories of her tragic end.

Afterwards, we all went to the 'Clog and Billycock' for a buffet and a few drinks of course and it was strange to be there in what was once our old home, surrounded by spirits in all senses of the word. Talk about a trip down memory lane – I only wish my mum could have been with us. But on saying that, it felt like she was, as was my dad, and it goes without saying that Brian was looking down on the proceedings because after all, that's where this whole story began.

I'm sad my mum never got to see my book in print, she would have loved that more than anything, but perhaps her spirit will. It was my mum after all who gave me the spirit and the will to persist and never give up.

And I never will.

CHAPTER 38

The Graveyard shift

Today, I went to the clinic for my three monthly tests. I'd been so preoccupied with caring for my mum and then her tragic death that I hadn't even enquired about my last results. But my T cell count (that's the good guys) had risen from 410 to 600 and the deadly virus was still undetectable. I started crying when the doctor told me, because I couldn't rush home and tell my mum the good news. Then, because death and burials were at the forefront of my mind, I asked my doctor about the possibility of being buried in the same grave as my mum (as we'd bought two for the price of one apparently!) and he told me that yes I could - but only if I was buried in a plastic bag.

I'm quite fond of my mum's grave actually and I've taken to prowling around the graveyard and reading people's epitaphs and tidying their flowers up. My mum's plot is on the top of the hill and looks down over the park. On Sundays, in the field below, people fly remote control planes and I hope the familiar drone of the tiny plane's engines reminds her of my dad. A few new neighbours have moved in since my mum's been in residence, and we now have an Auntie Bessie and an Auntie Edna and someone's beloved granddad called Les. It's quite busy up there on a Sunday afternoon, with families coming to visit their lost ones with bunches of fresh flowers and trowels and watering cans to plant daffodils and snowdrops. We are forbidden by the cemetery rules and regulations to adorn the graves with statues or ornaments, as they are allegedly a health and safety hazard, but of course everyone does. Some of them are quite artistic and others are a bit like something you'd find on a caravan site. The graves of babies and small children are absolutely heartbreaking, with toys and teddies and special keepsakes and messages. Some graves have the most peculiar things written on the tombstones. I know, because I've been wandering around, trying to find inspiration for what to inscribe on my mum's, which is in the shape of a white marble book with the pages open.

I do wonder sometimes how long I've got and if I'll manage to reach that lofty goal of publishing this book before HIV wipes me out. But on the whole my health is pretty good these days, better probably than the health of people who haven't even got HIV as we are so closely monitored. Dr Gayed told me today, when I tentatively hedged around the delicate question of prognosis, that it's years since he lost a patient to AIDS, but he still couldn't offer me any false promises. But then, when it boils down to it, nobody really knows how much time they've got, do they? All I know is that someone must be watching over me because last night, after I'd taken my medication, the customary hallucinatory light show commenced, as it does every night, but the format had changed and instead of the usual mismatch of horrific images, I had thousands of tiny translucent butterfly wings fluttering behind my eyes. It was almost as though by fluttering their wings they were conjuring up the energy for me to heal myself, like tiny wind machines.

They say that if a butterfly lands on you it's a loved one's spirit reaching out to touch you, so I think they must have been sent by my mum. And typical of my mum, she wouldn't just send the one, she sent a whole brigade. They're probably all my ancestors from centuries past, banding together and fluttering their collective wings to give me the strength to carry on, which I surely will, if only for her sake.

CHAPTER 39

She's a Lumberjack and she's OK

I finally did it. I told my son Ben that I was HIV positive. It took me four years to find the necessary courage and in some ways, it was mainly down to a comment made by a counsellor. I'd been referred for counselling by my family doctor as I'd fallen into such a black pit of depression and grief after my mum died, I didn't think I would ever be able to clamber my way back out of it. My son was witnessing my steady decline as my depression was making me even more physically ill than I already was and the fact that I couldn't tell him why I was ill was making matters worse and was a huge weight on my shoulders, which seemed to get heavier by the day. One way or another, things had to come to a head; or it was only a matter of time before I exploded or went under with the pressure of it all. The counsellor worked with me through this dilemma of why I either couldn't or wouldn't tell Ben what was wrong with me and then one day he said that some would say that Ben actually had a right to know. That comment stayed with me and refused to go away. Maybe Ben did have a right to know, if only for his personal safety, if I should have an accident at home or if he ever had to look after me when I was sick.

Then something else happened. We were taking part in a drama therapy exercise at uni where first we had to pretend to be a tree and then we were handed a metaphorical axe to do with as we pleased. Some of my fellow students set about chopping each other down (which makes you wonder what their particular issues were all about) but I just stood there clutching my axe to my chest, feeling overwhelmed and frightened and unable to make a move. Then I suddenly realized what was rooting me to the spot, it was fear; fear of the huge tree that was towering over me – the HIV tree. I couldn't take my axe to it even though it was dwarfing the rest of the forest, taking the sun off me, cutting out the light and depriving me of oxygen. If I wanted to see the light again, or even be able to breathe, the answer was simple – I had to chop down the tree.

When I got home that night Ben and I started having a row about something, I can't remember what, we always seemed to be arguing about something these days, which was probably down to me, as my nerves were shattered and the slightest little thing could set me off. The argument got more and more heated until I was screaming my head off at him - and then I broke down and started crying.

"Stop it will you, just stop it," I sobbed, "This is making me ill."

"What actually is wrong with you mum," Ben suddenly asked me, looking me directly in the eyes. I looked straight back at him and we stood staring at each other while the question, should I, shouldn't I, battled away in my mind, as it has been doing for the last four years, driving me mad. Then something came over me, I was so fed up of the lies and pretence and of feeling ashamed. My terrible secret had to come out. The time had come.

"Do you really want to know what's wrong with me?" I looked at him defiantly.

He nodded his head nervously.

"Well, I'll tell you what's wrong with me. I am HIV positive," and before he could say anything I railed on, "And if you are going to be paranoid about sitting on the same loo seat as me or drinking out of the same cups you can fuck off and live somewhere else."

There, it was out. I'd actually said it and there was no going back. It felt good – like I'd got rid of something bad.

Ben looked at his ranting mother in total shock.

"But that doesn't mean I am going to die," I quickly pointed out, as ever wanting to protect him, "At least not in the near future. Well, I hope not."

I then set out to explain to him what it did actually mean. I told him everything I had learnt about HIV, how you could and couldn't be infected, about the medication, how I believed I had become infected - and then I became angry again, anticipating his rejection and possible paranoia. "So there you are, now you know and if you are going to be paranoid about me cooking your meals or serving your food you can cook for your bloody self – it's high time you learnt anyway."

"No mum," he looked puzzled, "I'll look after you," was all he said.

"Well, I'll get on with making dinner then," I reached for a pan, "What do you fancy eating?"

"I'll help you," he said.

And he did.

It hasn't been all plain sailing since then of course, we've had our ups and downs and there have been times when I could have mercifully strangled him. But on the whole, if it hadn't of been for his acceptance of me, and with his agreement of course, I wouldn't have been able to go on to do what I did, which was to go public about my HIV status in order to raise awareness in an attempt to reduce the stigma and prejudice associated with this terrible disease. My son's total and unconditional acceptance of me and everything that now went with me, enabled me to also accept him for what and who he was and not what I wanted him to be.

Unconditional love – something that HIV teaches you.

Once I'd chopped down the HIV tree, I attacked the whole bloody forest, the stigma tree, the tree of prejudice and most of all the tree of Shame. Down they all fell – one by one. Timber! I was a lumberjack and I was feeling OK! I was out of the forest – out of the HIV closet and it felt great. Terrifying but great. I was free at last to say what I wanted, to tell the truth – to help other positive people to dispel their fears and their false shame.

And once I'd started I couldn't stop; I spoke out on the radio, I talked to the newspapers. I made a speech on World AIDS day at Blackburn Cathedral – the first time I had 'come out' in my home town.

Then I was asked to speak on the Jeremy Vine Show for BBC Radio 2 about what it was like to live with HIV. The morning that I was due to go on air I woke up with the idea for 'hivine' in my head, a website and blog for positive people, especially women who were being forced to live 'invisible' lives through fear of being stigmatised and discriminated against.

While I was speaking to the great British public on the BBC my sister was busy setting up the website for me. That day it received 750 hits and it's gone on from there – the rest is history as they say. Since I started "hivine" it has received over 400.000 hits and is still going strong.

I love the idea that my, at times, humorous and slightly eccentric blogs are helping to raise awareness about HIV through surfers typing in unrelated search engine terms, such as knitting for example, and arriving at my site completely by accident. Hopefully they leave with a wider awareness and more acceptance of what it is like for we positive people who have to cope with the stigma of HIV on a day to day basis.

I finally got to use my hard-won counselling skills by working as a pre and post test counsellor on the Point of Care Rapid HIV testing team at Body Positive North West. This is a pilot project aimed at encouraging people to "GO4IT" and get tested, a scheme which will hopefully save lives and help control the spread of HIV. This is a project dear to my heart, because if I had not been tested for HIV and subsequently diagnosed, I would have surely died. I don't want that to happen to other people, especially women, who often, by the fact that they are in a monogamous relationship, do not think they are at risk. But they are: all women, as well as men, are very much in danger and HIV is not selective or restricted to gay men or drug users as was once believed. HIV can and does infect anyone, as I am here to prove. Over the last sixteen years the rate of HIV infection among women has rapidly increased and women now account for over 50% of global infections. There are 19.2 million women around the world who are now living with HIV/AIDS which is a shocking and little known fact.

Because of this and in order to try to raise awareness, I became an HIV activist and joined ICW, The International Community of Women Living with HIV/AIDS and also POZFEM-UK the only national network of women living with HIV in the UK, for which I am now a regional coordinator and through which I have met so many wonderful women – all positive and all truly amazing. When I am feeling down I only have to think of this incredible band of women and I feel instantly uplifted. They have all put their heads over the parapet in the fight against HIV and unstintingly continue to do so.

Closer to home I started a weekly HIV support group for positive women in Blackburn called, unsurprisingly, HIVINE and I was also elected Chair of the mixed support group in our area THRIVINE.

In 2008 I was very proud to act as a representative of Body Positive North West at the International AIDS conference in Mexico. It was an amazing experience to be with all those positive people from all over the world and I learnt so much and met so many inspiring men and women. Besides I'd always wanted to go to Mexico, it had been a long cherished dream of mine and to think that it only came about because of HIV.

Life works in very mysterious ways sometimes.